The Political Economy of China's Changing Relations with Southeast Asia

The Political Economy of China's Changing Relations with Southeast Asia

JOHN WONG

St. Martin's Press   New York

All rights reserved. For information, write:
St. Martin's Press, Inc., 175 Fifth Avenue, New York, NY 10010
Printed in Hong Kong
Published in the United Kingdom by The Macmillan Press Ltd
First published in the United States of America in 1984

ISBN 0-312-62258-9

Library of Congress Cataloging in Publication Data

Wong, John, 1939–
  The political economy of China's changing relations
with Southeast Asia.

  Includes bibliographical references and index.
  1. China—Foreign economic relations—Asia, Southeastern. 2. Asia, Southeastern—Foreign economic
relations—China. I. Title.
HF1604.Z4A7858 1984   337.51059   83–40198
ISBN 0-312-62258-9

To Aline, Tien Yin and Tien Hua

ASEAN: Indonesia, Malaysia, Philippines, Singapore, Thailand

Source: C. P. Fitzgerald, *China and Southeast Asia* (Longman, 1971).

Contents

Preface

I

President Nixon's visit to Beijing (Peking) ten years ago ushered in a new era of international politics for Southeast Asia, particularly in its overall relations with the People's Republic of China. Nixon's trip quickened the opening up of China, which in the aftermath of the Cultural Revolution also increasingly felt the need to coexist with countries in Southeast Asia on a non-ideological basis. But the impact has been more dramatic for countries in Southeast Asia. Following the 'Nixon shock', these countries had to be reconciled to the reality of the shift of the political balance brought about by the thawing of the Cold War and sought more realistic ways and means to live with China as a powerful neighbour to their north, operated under a different social and economic system. Hence the process of normalisation.

I started to modify my academic interest in China from the primary concern with its domestic economic problems to its external economic relations with Southeast Asia at the time when the détente was about to unfold itself in the region. I was able to watch and document the many exciting events which cropped up from the efforts of countries in Southeast Asia to normalise their relations with China. In retrospect, normalisation has not been a smooth process but one fraught with a lot of political twists and turns especially during the initial periods. Meanwhile, my own research focus has increasingly broadened to include Southeast Asian economic studies, which has thus enabled me to relate the 'China problem' for each of these Southeast Asian countries to its specific political and economic context. Consequently this study could perhaps claim one rather unique feature, which is the way it attempts to blend 'China scholarship' with 'Southeast Asia scholarship' and to offer a distinct and balanced perspective on Sino–Southeast Asian issues so as to be different from the view held by either a China expert working on primary source materials from China or a Southeast Asian specialist taking into consideration often narrowly based country-specific standpoints.

This study is primarily concerned with the economic aspects of China's relations with the five Southeast Asian countries – namely, Indonesia, Malaysia, the Philippines, Singapore and Thailand – which together constitute the Association of Southeast Asian Nations (ASEAN). Strictly speaking, the main focus is on their trade relations with China, as their economic interaction in other areas has not been significantly developed. In order to bring about a more comprehensive treatment of the subject, a political economy approach is adopted. Economic relations among states, even for those functioning on liberal market forces, are seldom confined to the simple exchange of goods and services. In particular, the primary role of politics cannot be ruled out from any discussion of economic relations between a socialist economy and a market economy. It would be a highly uninspiring as well as unrealistic and narrow exercise if this book were to take the easy way out by just analysing the structure and patterns of China's trade with the ASEAN countries on the basis of published trade statistics and then drawing its conclusions within a certain neo-classical economic framework such as the maximisation of economic welfare or other forms of trade-off from trade.

As Professor Peter Wiles has stressed, foreign economic relations of states are basically a political act and an economist should make no apology in trespassing beyond the borders of so-called 'pure economics', for 'such borders, like international ones, exist only to be trampled upon'.* I have therefore not hestitated to venture boldly into the discipline of international relations in order to capture the related elements at work. Except for Chapter 1, which is fully devoted

---

* See P. J. D. Wiles, *Communist International Economics* (Oxford: Basil Blackwell, 1968) Preface.

to the economic analysis of the overall pattern of China's economic relations with ASEAN in a more standard manner, the other five chapters, dealing with China's bilateral relations with the individual ASEAN countries, follow a distinct political economy approach. In these five chapters, I try first to depict a broad picture of China's overall relations with each of the five ASEAN countries through the past three decades and then analyse the trade pattern and trade behaviour against the underlying political events or whatever relevant institutional forces are at work. On certain issues I have gone into some lengths for their historical backgrounds. I believe that a proper historical perspective would render it less hazardous to assess the present status of some policy issues as well as provide a coherent framework to test their consistency. Many thorny problems that have persistently bedevilled the present Sino—ASEAN relationship are in fact rooted in their past. The Sino—Indonesian diplomatic impasse is a case in point. Neither economic logic nor political arguments, however cogent, can adequately explain the unwillingness on the part of the present Indonesian leadership to re-establish ties with Beijing. But historical factors can throw much light on this issue.

It will be noted that this book is based on source materials emanating essentially from the Southeast Asian region, with min-imum reliance on official data from China. I have also drawn from such regional publications as the *Far Eastern Economic Review*. Those with experience in area studies will readily appreciate that the great challenge for the groundwork research for this kind of scholarly pursuit lies not just in laboriously bringing together scattered information from often disparate local sources but also in the meticulous sifting and interpreting of the arrayed materials. It is well known that some local information of the 1950s and the 1960s, when the region was under the influence of the Cold War, is heavily biased and is replete with much political rhetoric. It is therefore imperative that such information be subjected to careful scrutiny and balanced interpretation.

II

Historically, China and Southeast Asia have been dealing with each other for centuries, and the past three turbulent decades covered in this book constitute but a brief interlude in their age-old relationship. Now the demise of the Cold War has finally restored their relationship to the level of normality, with both sides being willing to come to terms with each other. But the apparent stability in the overall relationship existing between China and the ASEAN countries should not be taken for granted. The shape of their future relations for the rest of the 1980s is still clouded by a great deal of uncertainty. A sharp deterioration of Sino–American relations or a rapid rapprochement between China and the Soviet Union could well estrange ASEAN from China. The Indochina situation would be another unstable parameter. As for China's bilateral relations with the individual ASEAN countries, the potential volatility is likely to stem from domestic developments in the ASEAN countries. For instance, a resurgence of the Communist movement in a specific ASEAN country or a mishandling of the ethnic Chinese issue by Beijing could easily rock China's existing relations with that ASEAN country. After all, China is still a Communist country, while all the ASEAN countries are not. This very basic difference would be enough to throw both sides back to the vortex of confrontational relations at the slightest provocation.

While Sino–ASEAN relations on the political level could easily succumb to unpredictable forces, their economic relationship seems to be facing better prospects for stability. The economic ties between China and ASEAN have been steadily strengthened in recent years. Furthermore, the economic intercourse has tended to detach from the past political and ideological entanglement and thus become more resilient to adverse political developments. Take Sino–ASEAN trade. It is in the process of getting into the upward spiral of trade and growth in the sense that as economic growth in China and in the ASEAN countries gets further underway, their two-way trade will also steadily expand. It is therefore not unrealistic to foresee the mildly optimistic scenario of a gradual broadening of Sino–ASEAN economic relationships throughout the 1980s even in the absence of a deepening of Sino–ASEAN political understanding. A substantial growth of economic interdependence will in the long run create the *realpolitik* condition for a more stable and durable political relationship.

III

I am grateful to the Stiftung Volkswagenwerk of West Germany for a generous research grant which enabled me to travel around the ASEAN countries and Hong Kong to collect and update materials for this book. Earlier, the Harvard–Yenching Institute of Harvard University had been kind enough to fund several of my research projects directly related to the topic of this book. To these two bodies I wish to express my gratitude.

Singapore   John Wong

List of Abbreviations

ADC	Advanced Developing Countries
APACL	Asian People's Anti-Communist League
ASEAN	Association of Southeast Asian Nations
CCP	Chinese Communist Party
EDB	Economic Development Board
FEER	*Far Eastern Economic Review*
GANEFO	Games of the New Emerging Forces
GDP	Gross Domestic Product
GNP	Gross National Product
HKS	*Hong Kong Standard*
MAAG	Military Advisory Assistance Group
MCP	Malayan Communist Party
MFA	Multi-Fiber Arrangement
MFN	Most Favoured Nation
MNC	Multi National Company
NASAKOM	Nationalism, Islam and Communism
NEC	National Executive Council
NIC	Newly Industrialised Country
ODA	Official Development Assistance
OECD	Organisation for Economic Co-operation and Development
PAP	People's Action Party
PKI	Partai Komunis Indonesia (Indonesian Communist Party)
SEATO	South East Asia Treaty Organisation

SMR   Standard Malaysian Rubber
SSR   Standard Singapore Rubber
ST   *Straits Times*
UMNO   United Malay National Organisation
UN   United Nations

A Note on Currency

	Unit	Exchange rate around mid-1983, per US dollar
China	Yuan or Renminbi (RMB)	1.98
Indonesia	Rupiah	965
Malaysia	Ringgit or Malaysian dollar (M$)	2.33
Philippines	Peso	11.02
Singapore	Singapore dollar (S$)	2.13
Thailand	Baht	23

1

China's Economic Relations with Southeast Asia: Changing Dimensions

Historical Backgrounds

China's relations with Southeast Asia, traditionally called *Nanyang* (or 'South Seas') by the Chinese, are extensive and deep-rooted on account of history, geography, and past migration in the region. China's early contact with the individual societies of Southeast Asia can be traced back to truly ancient times, even though 'China's intercourse overland with the countries on its southern border is of much greater order of antiquity than its contacts by sea.'[1] By the Sung dynasty (960–1280) Imperial China had established tributary relations with many states in Southeast Asia, and the tribute-bearing missions were, as noted by the eminent Harvard historian, John K. Fairbank, often a convenient 'cloak for trade'.[2] Fairbank has long stressed the importance of the Chinese maritime activities along the mainland coast and in *Nanyang* even prior to the famous expeditions by Admiral Zheng He (Cheng Ho) in the fifteenth century. Indeed, when European adventurers and traders eventually reached Southeast Asia in the sixteenth century, they found Chinese merchants already active in all the ports and on the main trade routes. Much of this commercial activity on the part of Chinese merchants stemmed directly or indirectly from the traditional tribute system, which was the principal means by which Imperial China conducted foreign relations with its neighbouring states.[3]

By virtue of its vast physical size, huge population and pre-eminent cultural system, China has over the ages cast a heavy shadow over its relatively small neighbours to its south. Though always uneasy and at times a little apprehensive, China's southern neighbours did not seriously view Imperial China as a real menace to their independent existence. This is particularly true of the five members of the existing Association of Southeast Asian Nations (ASEAN).–comprising Indonesia, Malaysia, the Philippines, Singapore and Thailand – which are not contiguous to China. Indeed, Imperial China was primarily an inward-looking continental power, with little serious territorial ambition overseas. Apart from several invasions and incursions into adjacent Annam (Vietnam) and Burma, Chinese imperial rulers never embarked on any broad territorial expansion southwards into *Nanyang*. The tribute system was merely a diplomatic device which was used by China to pursue inter-state relations with the non-Chinese societies under the concept of 'Chinese world order' based on the Confucianist framework.[4] It should not be viewed as a system of dependency in the modern sense of the term whereby China sought to impose its political and economic domination over its weaker southern neighbours. The tributary diplomacy, though outwardly inegalitarian, was not a system of international relations which operated invariably in favour of China or was inherently biased against the tributary states. It would thus be misleading to regard the tribute system as a simple expression of Chinese chauvinism in relation to the non-Chinese societies.[5]

It should be noted that historically none of the present five ASEAN states was ever under Chinese control. Traditionally, except for Singapore, these societies did not fall into the Chinese culture area in the sense of being influenced by mainstream Chinese civilisation, e.g. the Chinese ideographic written language and the Confucian system of government, as in the case of Korea or Vietnam.

Economically it is quite simple to explain why Imperial China had little or no colonising initiative towards its southern neighbours. The traditional Chinese economy was agrarian in nature, self-sufficient and basically secluded from international economic activities. This economy was often not sufficiently productive to sustain a large-scale colonising enterprise overseas, and whatever surplus the economy could produce was usually drained away to shore up defensive efforts in Northwest China to keep off the nomadic hordes. The Chinese Imperial Court, preoccupied through the ages with the problem of security in the north, had no extra energy – nor had the Chinese economy the extra capacity – for any costly overseas ambition. The economic incentive for embarking on such a colonising undertaking was just not there. With a pre-industrial economic structure, the Chinese empire was then under no compelling need to expand into *Nanyang*, either for the purpose of controlling raw material supplies or for securing a market outlet for its products, as were the later European colonial powers. In fact, the Chinese Imperial Court, with all its Confucian prejudice, was often anti-commercial in its orientation.

Thus, China's early contact with the states of *Nanyang* did not lead to outright Chinese domination of the region. Further, Chinese early commercial involvements with *Nanyang*, though brisk at times, remained basically small in scale and represented largely unorganised individual efforts, nothing comparable to the level of activities later mounted by, say, the British East India Company. After the nineteenth century, Chinese trade with *Nanyang* began to rise more rapidly, along with the steady inflow of Chinese migrants into the region. Since then, the overseas Chinese have played a crucial role not only in the economic development and social progress of their host countries in Southeast Asia, but also in affecting the economic and political relations between these countries and China.

After the formation of the People's Republic in 1949, China's relations with the neighbouring countries to its south assumed a new dimension, with complex ideological and geo-political elements entering into the picture. China soon began to adopt a general posture which was perceived by some ASEAN countries as a threat, real or imagined, to their own security. Although these countries might have understood that Imperial China had no political designs towards the region in the past, they reacted differently towards the New China, which was marked by a strong revolutionary impulse and armed with a proselytising Marxist ideology. Hence their apprehension of Communist China.

ASEAN's unfavourable image of China was formed partly by the distortions of international Cold War politics and partly by the misleading revolutionary rhetoric of China's own creation. Under the urge of 'proletarian internationalism', especially in the 1960s, Beijing (Peking) started to preach revolution in the region. This naturally gave rise to hostility and suspicion on the part of the ASEAN governments, which were particularly disturbed at Beijing's vocal support of the local Communist movements. Consequently the ASEAN countries either allied themselves with the United States for the 'containment' of China or shunned contact with China altogether. Economically and socially, China and ASEAN also drifted apart. China's centrally planned economy and its highly socialistic structure seemed completely alien to the post-colonial economic and social organisations operating in the ASEAN countries. Such economic and social differences further widened their political distance and sharpened their ideological differences.

Economic relations between states cannot be divorced from the reality of their overall political relationship. This is particularly true of trade relations between a market economy and a socialist economy, as both sides tend to mix politics with trade. Thus during the Cold War decades of the 1950s and the 1960s China's bilateral economic relations with the individual ASEAN countries followed a tortuous course in parallel with the ups and downs of its political relations with each of them. Table 1.1 sketches out the major political and economic events in China and the corresponding events related to the ASEAN countries during the past three decades.

In the early 1950s, China's trade with countries in ASEAN entered the doldrums, partly because of the unfavourable political climate and partly due to China's efforts in redirecting trade towards its socialist partners. From the outset, the Philippine government shunned all forms of contact with any Communist country and imposed an outright ban on trade with China. In Thailand, direct trade with China in the early 1950s, though not illegal, was officially discouraged. In Indonesia, trade with China prior to 1953 had hardly started as Sino-Indonesian diplomatic relations were still inhibited. Even in Malaysia and Singapore, where trade was normally free from ideological considerations, the China trade was hampered by the UN embargo (see Chapter 3).

After the Bandung Conference in 1955, China's relations with the ASEAN region improved considerably, providing a more conducive political base for China to expand its economic contact with the region. But the real economic impetus for the growth of China's trade with the region towards the later part of the 1950s stemmed from two sources. First, China felt the need to reduce its excessive trade dependency on the Soviet bloc – which at its peak took up as much as 74 per cent of China's total trade – by returning to traditional markets. Secondly, China's socialist industrialisation under the First Five-Year Plan, 1953–7, began to bear fruits, with the Chinese economy turning out a wide variety of labour-intensive manufactured

TABLE 1.1 *Chronology of Major Political and Economic Events in China and the Development of Relationships with ASEAN*

Period	Year		Relationships with the ASEAN countries
Economic rehabilitation period	1949	The establishment of the People's Republic	
	1950		To follow UN Embargo Malaya/Singapore banned rubber exports to China.
	1951	The Korea War	
	1952	Land reform	
First Five-year Plan – good growth performance	1953		Exchange of ambassors between China and Indonesia.
	1954	Cooperativization	
	1955		Zhou En-lai attended the Bandung Conference; signed the Dual Nationality Treaty with Indonesia.
	1956	Collectivization: "Let Hundred Flowers Bloom"	Indonesian President Sukaro's State visit to Beijing.
	1957		
Second Five-year Plan (short-lived)	1958	Formation of People's Communes	China's "trade offensive" in Southeast Asia, Thailand banned all trade with China by Decree No. 53.
	1959	The Great Leep Forward	
	1960	Sino-Soviet Disputes and the Russian pull-out	Malayan Government restricted imports of Chinese textiles.
Third Five-year Plan (unpublished)	1961	Natural calamities (1959–61)	
	1962		Chinese Foreign Minister Chen Yi visited Jakarta.
	1963	Economic recovery period	Chinese President Liu Shao-qi's visit to Indonesia. The 'Beijing–Jakarta Axis'.
	1964		
	1965		Indonesian Communist Party (PKI) ousted by the October coup
	1966	The Cultural Revolution	
	1967		Suspension of Sino-Indonesian diplomatic relations

TABLE 1.1 (contd)

		Relationships with the ASEAN countries
	1968	Downfall of Liu Shao-qi and Deng Xiao-ping	Beijing advocated "revolutionary movement" in Southeast Asia
	1969		
	1970	The Lin Bian Incident	Malaysia's call for the neutralization of Southeast Asia and other early signs of detente.
Fourth Five-year Plan- (unpublished)	1971	China's admission into UN	Afro-Asian Table Tennis Game in Beijing – the "Ping Pong Diplomacy"
	1972	Nixon's visit to Beijing	The first official Philippine Trade Mission to China
	1973	Large complete-plant imports	Thailand legalized China trade. Malaysia recognized China.
	1974		
	1975	The Four Modernisations	The Philippines and Thailand recognized China.
Fifth Five-year Plan – as part of the Ten-Year Plan	1976	Downfall of the "Gang of Four"	Chinese petroleum supplied to the Philippines and Thailand at 'friendship prices'.
	1977	Economic readjustment period	
	1978		Deng Xiao-ping's official visit to Thailand, Malaysia and Singapore
	1979	De-maoisation	China's punitive military action against Vietnam.
	1980	Emerging of new pragmatic leadership under Deng Xiao-ping	Agreement to exchange trade representatives with Singapore.
Sixth Five-year Plan	1981	Further economic readjustment	Premier Zhao Ziyang's state visit to the Philippines, Malaysia, Singapore and Thailand.
	1982	12th Congress of Chinese Communist Party further boost to post-Mao leadership for economic growth.	

products which found ready markets in many Southeast Asian countries that had yet to initiate their own industrialisation programme. As Beijing relentlessly pushed its exports into Southeast Asia in the late 1950s, a move then widely publicised as China's 'trade offensive', some Asian governments grew alarmed. In particular, the sudden influx of Chinese textile goods into the markets of Malaysia/Singapore prompted the Malayan Federal government to impose restriction on the import of some Chinese-made goods, sparking off a trade dispute that was to mar Sino-Malaysian relations for many years. In Thailand, a military coup by the right-wing Field Marshal Sarit Thanarat in 1958 led to a total ban on trade with China by the proclamation of the revolutionary Decree No. 53. Although Sino-Indonesian trade remained thriving throughout the early part of the 1960s, it too eventually succumbed to political interference. After the abortive coup in 1965, Jakarta suspended all forms of contact with Beijing in 1967. In the late 1960s, only Malaysia and Singapore in the region maintained direct trade with China, and that trade was carried out in the absence of a formal diplomatic framework.

In the early 1970s the spread of international détente to Southeast Asia resulted in the removal of Cold War restraints from Sino-ASEAN relations. Favourable political preconditions were thus created for the ASEAN countries to start normalising relations with China. Malaysia, the Philippines and Thailand established diplomatic relations with China one after another in the middle of the 1970s; Singapore is virtually on a *de facto* relationship with China following their exchange of trade representatives in 1981.[6] Of the five ASEAN countries, only Indonesia has yet to resume full diplomatic links with China, broken in 1967.

Apart from the thawing of the Cold War, new geo-political forces which emerged in the late 1970s have also tended to boost the Sino-ASEAN relationship to a higher level. The deterioration of the political situation in Indochina following the Vietnamese invasion of Kampuchea and the resultant exodus of Vietnamese refugees have greatly alarmed the ASEAN countries, which are concerned over the possible spillovers of political instability from Indochina. On the other hand, the subsequent Chinese punitive military attack on Vietnam, coupled with China's major global diplomatic realignment towards closer co-operation with the United States and the other industrial democracies, has clearly demonstrated to ASEAN that

China could be an important stabilising force in the region. This is particularly seen by Thailand, the frontline state in the Indochina conflict, and by the Philippines, the one ASEAN country geographically most proximate to China. In fact, China has consistently and openly pledged support to the ASEAN organisation, and there are also issues for discussion (for example, the Kampuchea issue) over which the interests of China and ASEAN tend to converge.

Meanwhile domestic developments in China in the later part of the 1970s, following the fall of the 'Gang of Four', were also conducive to China's efforts in developing better understanding with the ASEAN countries. Along with the launching of the Four-Modernisation programme, Beijing stepped up its internal liberalisation of policies, culminating in open de-maoification and the complete official repudiation of the Cultural Revolution at the Twelfth National Congress of the Communist Party of China in September 1982. Likewise, the Chinese economy has been progressively opened up to greater foreign trade and foreign capital inflow and allowed to respond to greater free play of market forces. Indeed, the General Secretary, Hu Yaobang, at the Twelfth National Congress, emphasised the need for the Chinese economy to move away from the past pattern of overcentralised control by 'mandatory planning' to a more flexible system which allows considerable scope for 'guidance planning' and 'market regulation', to be implemented by means of 'economic levers'.[7] These pragmatic changes would not only have far-reaching effects on China's economic modernisation, but would also affect China's conduct of foreign relations. Increased political and economic flexibility would make it easier for China to engage in constructive political dialogue, or enter into genuine development co-operation, with ASEAN on a truly non-ideological basis.

The new trends generated by the changing international environment and domestic conditions in China are likely to intensify, in a general sense, the historical ties between China and ASEAN with profound geo-political implications. The emerging pattern of Sino–ASEAN relations will be more pragmatic in its orientation, in sharp contrast to the confrontational approach of the past. However, this does not preclude variation and fluctuation, within the overall regional geo-political framework, in China's bilateral relations with the individual ASEAN countries according to the latter's domestic political conditions and their own perception of China. The Philippines and Thailand have been able to develop a relatively close relationship with China because much past tension stemmed from the Cold War; the advent of international détente has simply removed the main basis of their mutual suspicion. In the case of Indonesia and Malaysia (and to some extent also Singapore, which does not normally operate its China policy independently of its Indonesian and Malaysian neighbours), their legacies of tension with China were not entirely linked to the externally generated Cold War, but have been complicated by such domestic issues as China's party-to-party links with their local communist movements and the presence of ethnic Chinese. These are issues which the present Chinese leadership has often referred to as problems 'left over from history', but which, if they remain unresolved, could potentially destabilise China's relations with these countries, or at the very least make it difficult to upgrade them to the more friendly level which currently characterises China's relations with the Philippines and Thailand.

There is also the Chinese side of the coin. The stability of China's relations with ASEAN, as with other countries, hinges crucially on its continuing internal stability. This essentially depends upon whether the present leadership in Beijing could survive a peaceful and smooth transition of power once Mr Deng Xiaoping (Teng Hsiao-ping) and other aging leaders pass from the scene. A few scenarios could be drawn for the next few years, the worst of which would envisage China as being ruled again by xenophobic and Maoist-oriented leaders, which would certainly impair China's relations with ASEAN.

In the long run, for Sino—ASEAN relationship to endure, political détente is a necessary but insufficient condition. Growing relationship must also be forged on some viable economic foundation such as mutually beneficial trade relations. Thus ASEAN is watching China intently as it emerges from the long period of internal political and ideological strifes and turns its full attention to economic development. Politically, a stable and secure China, fully absorbed in orderly economic development, would contribute to the region's stability, so vital for ASEAN's own economic growth and development. But the ASEAN countries themselves are also strongly committed to the pursuit of economic development and they clearly want to avoid any negative spillovers from the growing Chinese economy. It is obvious that the evolving Sino—ASEAN economic relationship is going to be a dynamic one, with both competitive and complementary interactions. Although in some ways, an economically resurgent China could be a disruptive force, Chinese economic growth could also offer rising opportunities to some ASEAN countries and eventually produce beneficial impacts on the ASEAN region as a whole.

China and ASEAN in Comparative Perspective

The Chinese economy used to present a sharp contrast to the economies of ASEAN. China is a continental-sized country with a vast population. The Chinese economy is inward-looking in its orientation, a feature partly due to its physical size and partly to its socialist economic system. A big economy is inherently less dependent on external economic operations and tends to have a higher degree of self-sufficiency. But central planning, with its penchant for autarchy (or what the Chinese called 'self reliance') plus its basic aversion to active participation in international economic affairs, has certainly exacerbated the inwardly directed nature of the Chinese economy. Consequently, China has never been a great trading nation despite its apparently huge market potentials. In 1980, China's world share of exports was only 0.9 per cent, its trade–GDP ratio 15 per cent, and its trade turnovers per capita US$39, which were among the lowest in the Third World and certainly well below those of ASEAN's.

In contrast the ASEAN countries, with the exception of Indonesia, are generally small- to medium-sized economies, primarily operated on the free enterprise basis. The ASEAN economies are by nature very open and outward-looking, having derived a large proportion of their GNP from external activities, through the export of goods and services. Foreign investment also plays a crucial role in the growth of the ASEAN economies by making available to them not only capital but also technology and access to foreign export markets. The ASEAN economies, with the exception of the industrialised city-state Singapore, also have a large natural resource base and depend heavily on primary product exports for their economic growth. The ASEAN region as a whole annually exports a high proportion of the world's natural rubber, tin, and palm oil, and a significant amount of petroleum, rice, and other geographic-specific products. The bulk of these exports is destined for the industrial countries of the West and Japan, which in return supply capital and technology to the region.[8]

In recent years, the share of manufactured goods in ASEAN's total exports has been rising rapidly as a new source of ASEAN's economic growth; but most of ASEAN's manufactured exports are also absorbed by the industrial countries. Suffice it to say that the ASEAN economies, in distinct contrast to the largely self-sufficient nature of the Chinese economy, are heavily dependent on the capitalist countries.

By forging a close linkage with the advanced capitalist economies, ASEAN has been able to harness the forces of international capitalism to speed its own economic growth. On the other hand, China has apparently paid a price for upholding its relative economic independence. Table 1.2 shows the comparative economic performance of China and ASEAN. It can be seen that China's per capita income of US$290 in 1980 was by far lower than that of all the ASEAN countries. However, there is obviously a large downward bias in arriving at China's GNP because its socialist economic structure contains many non-market economic activities as well as an undervalued service sector. Similarly there is some upward bias for Singapore's GNP because of its urban-based economic structure. It may also be noted that China is actually doing quite well in terms of employment, income distribution, reduction of poverty and rural development, thanks to the trade-off created by the equity-oriented Maoist development strategies adopted in the past.[9] In particular, 'China's reputation for meeting the basic needs of its people is, on the whole, deserved.'[10] Table 1.3 attempts to list some available socio-economic indicators for China and ASEAN, and clearly points to the fact that the levels of social development in China are comparable with and in some cases even higher than the average standards of ASEAN.

Despite its relatively good 'equity performance', China's overall economic growth performance, in terms of both long-term growth trends of the past two decades and immediate growth potentials, clearly lags behind that of ASEAN. The Chinese leaders have in fact so admitted. Together with the East Asian NICs (Newly Industrialising Countries) such as Hong Kong and South Korea, ASEAN forms one of the world's most dynamic growth regions on the western rims of the Pacific basin. It is partly the recognition of this fact that has spurred the Chinese leaders to pursue an open-door economic policy in order to capture the international economic mechanisms to revitalise the rather stagnant Chinese economy.

Pattern of Sino–ASEAN Trade

Trade is the most direct form of economic interaction between states. While foreign trade is the means of ASEAN's economic growth, Chinese economy, as previously noted, is essentially not trade-oriented. This does not imply that foreign trade is not important to the economic planning of China. On the contrary, as one China expert has pointed out, foreign trade has played a 'very significant role both in maintaining stability and in contributing to growth' in China even at the time when trade was quantitatively small.[11]

During the past three decades, China's foreign trade policy has undergone fundamental changes, from the strict observation of the Stalinist model of autarchy in the 1950s to the recent open-door strategy, with increasing recognition of the market principle of comparative advantage. Both the volume of trade turnover and the pattern of trade have fluctuated wildly, particularly in the 1950s and 1960s, influenced by the erratic swings of the internal economy caused by periodic political movements such as the Great Leap Forward and the Cultural Revolution. In the first few years after the formation of the People's Republic, the government drastically re-oriented trade towards the Soviet bloc, culminating in 1955 when 74 per cent of trade was carried out with the socialist partners. Since then the reverse trend towards the traditional pattern has set in, accelerated in the late 1950s by the worsening of Sino–Soviet relations. China's trade with the market economies has currently been stabilised at over 80 per cent. In particular, China's trade with the industrial countries of the West and Japan has grown rapidly as China has had to import wheat as well as machinery and capital equipment from these countries. Today China's trade dependency on the advanced capitalist countries has reached 50 per cent, a level probably larger than any other socialist country and almost comparable to the 60 per cent level of ASEAN.

As China redirected trade towards the Soviet bloc in the early 1950s, the share of the whole of Southeast Asia (which includes Burma and the Indochinese states, as well as the ASEAN countries) in China's trade was drastically reduced to a mere 1.7 per cent in 1953. The UN embargo on China had also contributed to this low level. However, China's trade with the Southeast Asian region began to pick up rapidly during the later part of the 1950s as its trade dependency on the Soviet bloc was successfully reduced. Indeed, China mounted its first 'trade offensive' towards the region around 1958, with Chinese-made light industrial products flooding into the Southeast Asian markets in large quantities so that the proportion of Southeast Asia in China's overall trade rose to the peak of 5.4 per cent in 1959. Throughout the 1960s the share stayed around 5–6 per cent. The bulk of China's trade with the region centred in Singapore and Malaysia, as the Philippines and Thailand at that time imposed a trade ban on China. In the 1970s, with the ASEAN countries normalising relations with China under the general spread of international détente, Sino–ASEAN trade had inched up to 7–8 per cent of China's total turnover. In recent years, 7 per cent seems to be the norm.

Over the years, two outstanding features have been built into the Sino–ASEAN trade structure. First, as is obvious from the commodity composition of China's exports shown in Table 1.4, the ASEAN markets have been a highly significant outlet for such goods as agricultural products and light manufactures, which China has been exporting overseas. Much of this merchandise, from traditional foodstuffs to various kinds of wares and tools or low-priced garments and textile piece-goods, has a strong demand in the region, particularly in the cities and small towns with a large concentration of ethnic Chinese.

Secondly, as can be seen from Table 1.5, China developed a viable trade pattern (up to the middle of the 1970s at least) by which it sought to trade in surplus with developing countries by pushing the export of rice, foodstuffs, traditional products and a wide variety of labour-intensive manufactured goods, while in deficit with its imports of cheap food (wheat), capital equipment and technology from the industrial countries. In the past, China made a great effort to keep its trade in balance, and the surplus derived from trading with the developing world was usually adequate to cover the deficits incurred with the advanced countries. And ASEAN had been China's very important source of trade surplus, next to Hong Kong and Macau. This trade pattern has been changing in recent years as China is opening up its economy. On the one hand, China finds it increasingly difficult to keep its trade in balance due to its massive imports of expensive plants and equipment from the industrial countries to meet the requirement of its economic modernisation. On the other hand, as it has developed bilateral relations with individual

ASEAN countries, China is under constant political pressure, particularly from Malaysia and the Philippines, to increase purchases from the region so as to reduce its trade surplus with them. On the whole, China still enjoys a favourable balance of trade with ASEAN, even though the region has ceased to be an important source of export earnings for China.

The benefits of trade are, of course, mutual. From the standpoint of ASEAN, an increase in trade with China (or for that matter, with other socialist countries as well[12]) is seen as one of the most effective means of diversifying the region's high geographical concentration of trade. In the 1960s, almost 70 per cent of ASEAN's trade was conducted with the industrial countries of the West and Japan. In recent years, the proportion still stands at the high level of over 60 per cent, despite ASEAN's efforts to diversify its trade base. ASEAN's close commercial integration with the industrial economies is due not only to former colonial links but also to the fact that these industrial economies happen to be the major market outlet for the region's manufactured exports as well as the main consumers of the region's primary commodities. Nevertheless, the existing trade pattern of ASEAN, with its excessive economic dependency on the industrial countries, is quite undesirable in that it renders ASEAN's open economics too vulnerable to adverse developments in these countries. Clearly, one way for ASEAN to achieve a more successful market diversification lies in the promotion of both greater intra-regional trade and closer trade ties with other country groups, such as the socialist countries or the Middle East. (See Table 1.6.)

Viewed from this angle, the role of socialist countries in ASEAN's total trade structure is clearly not something with only marginal significance. The share of socialist countries in ASEAN's trade is at present about 3 per cent, and China is responsible for more than three-quarters of it. The small share represents unexploited potential markets or alternatively indicates room for future expansion. Thus, Sino–ASEAN trade can grow rapidly in future without fear of disrupting the existing trade pattern of ASEAN. Furthermore, the growth of Sino–ASEAN trade is broadly in line with the long-term strategy of market diversification to which the ASEAN governments have committed themselves. In an overall sense, viewed from the perspective of ASEAN, Sino–ASEAN trade is based on a significant economic rationale.

Although it is desirable for ASEAN to increase its trade with China (in the same way as it increases intra–ASEAN trade) as a means of reducing its trade dependency on the industrial countries, it is not easy to achieve this task in the short run owing to many institutional and structural factors. It can be seen from Table 1.6 that China's share in ASEAN's overall trade has not grown over the last decade – indeed, it has marginally declined. So has the share for intra – ASEAN trade, despite intensive efforts undertaken in recent years towards regional economic cooperation. Present day Sino–ASEAN trade (and intra–ASEAN trade) is still largely composed of 'traditional' commodity items which would not offer a dynamic source of trade growth. The same point is illuminated in Table 1.5, which shows that ASEAN's share in China's overall trade turnover has picked up slowly in absolute terms since 1975, when China started to open its economy to world trade; but has plummeted sharply in relative terms. In other words, as China has pursued an open-door economic policy since the mid-1970s, it has also intensified its economic ties more with the advanced capitalist economies than with Third World countries. China looks to the industrial countries for the supply of high-value capital goods; at the same time these industrial countries provide market access for the export of Chinese low-cost labour-intensive products. The pattern is sufficiently clear. Sino–ASEAN trade is not going to experience a dramatic expansion without drastically changing its traditional trade structure. The prospects for the future growth of Sino–ASEAN trade depend crucially on the success of China's ongoing economic modernisation efforts.

China's Drive to Economic Modernisation

The past pattern of Sino–ASEAN trade, as discussed in the preceding section, offers a useful perspective for analysing the prospects of China's increasing trade with the ASEAN region. But the dynamics of China's broadening economic ties with the region are likely to be influenced primarily by its own internal economic forces. In other words, the future shape of China's economic relations with ASEAN or, broadly, the ways in which the Chinese economy is integrated with other parts of the Asia–Pacific economic region, depend very much on the process of China's economic growth and development for the rest of this decade.

After years of internecine political struggle and unfruitful experiment with the ideologically motivated Maoist development strategies, China has finally come to realise that old-fashioned economic growth is still the most effective means by which to transform China into a modern state and to improve the standard of living of its people. Mao's egalitarian ideals might be appealing and socially justifiable, but the necessary material basis has to be created. Thus, China sharply reversed its main economic development strategy in the mid-1970s by making a strong commitment to economic growth before it had settled the problem of political succession.

In January 1975, at the Fourth National People's Congress, Premier Zhou Enlai (Chou En-lai) called for a return to the essentially pragmatic and growth-oriented development strategy based on the 'comprehensive modernisation of agriculture, industry, national defence, and science and technology before the end of the century.'[13] Such is the genesis of the much-publicised Four-Modernisation Programme. Meanwhile, Zhou also envisaged an equally ambitious ten-year development plan for the transitional period aimed at building up a 'relatively comprehensive industrial and economic system', which would in turn serve as the foundation for achieving even more far-reaching goals by the year 2000. The details of the plan as contained in the '*Outline of the Ten-Year Plan for the Development of the National Economy, 1976–85*' were finally presented in February 1978 to China's Fifth National People's Congress by Zhou's successor Hua Guofeng.[14] According to the Plan, by 1985, China aimed at:

● doubling steel output from 30 million tons in 1977 to 60 million tons
● doubling coal output from 450 million tons in 1977 to 900 million tons
● increasing grain output from 285 million tons in 1977 to 400 million tons
● maintaining an overall industrial growth rate of 10 per cent per annum.

In order to fulfil these ambitious targets, Chinese planners envisaged mobilising US$600 billion worth of capital investment to be spread over more than 120 major construction projects and numerous smaller supporting ones. Admittedly, the implementation of all these vast projects would require financial resources of such a magnitude as to exceed China's domestic capability. Hence the need for external financing. This at once created a great stir in early 1979 in the world's major financial centres, and revived the old myth of the China market in the West. Not surprisingly, many ASEAN governments were growing concerned over the long-term consequences of the possible massive diversion of western resources to development in China at the expense of other needy developing countries, including ASEAN.[15]

No sooner had the Ten-Year Plan been unveiled than the Chinese government found it necessary to revise the targets and readjust the priorities. Economically and politically, China was in no position then to carry out such a large development programme. The economy seemed to be losing its growth momentum even during the period when the Ten-Year Plan was being mapped out: industrial growth fell sharply during 1974–6 and agricultural output stagnated during 1975–7.[16] Post-Mao political differences and the resultant uncertainty aggravated the economic situation. After Deng Xiaoping was returned to power in the middle of 1978, the leadership succession struggle became intensified. Political control of China eventually passed from Hua to Deng and Deng's protegés, Hu Yaobang and Zhao Ziyang. More pragmatic, the Deng group soon discovered to their dismay that the Chinese economy was afflicted with numerous structural problems – widening fiscal deficits, chronic resource shortage, weak infrastructure, major production bottlenecks, management chaos and bureaucratic inertia, which all gave rise to what the government called 'serious imbalances' in the economy. But these structural problems had to be tackled before the modernisation programme could proceed.

In mid-1979, Beijing announced publicly that the original targets in the Ten-Year Plan were being drastically modified and China would have to undergo a three-year period of vigorous economic readjustment starting from 1979. Strong measures were therefore undertaken to slow down capital investment, to reduce budget deficits, to control inflation, and to shake out inefficient enterprises. In the external sector, the economic retrenchment resulted in the massive cancellation of foreign purchase orders and postponement of joint development programmes, culminating in the suspension of the controversial big Baoshan Steel Complex near Shanghai.

As a result of extensive readjustments and retrenchments, China's economic growth began to slow down. In 1980 the economy grew at 5 per cent and in 1981, at only 3 per cent. The major source of the economic slow-down had been cutbacks in industrial production, with the gross value of industrial output in the first quarter of 1981 actually declining by 0.2 per cent, though picking up in the subsequent quarters.[17] The main cause for the decline in industrial growth was the substantial curtailment of capital spending on heavy industries as required by the economic readjustment policy. Heavy industry, once self-serving under the Stalinist type of development strategy, was revamped during 1979–81 so as to provide more growth potentials for agriculture and light industries. Accordingly, the number of state-supported big and medium-sized construction projects was cut back from 1624 in 1978 to 663 in 1981. At the same time, investment priorities for capital construction were also re-set, with the share for heavy industries being reduced from 51 per cent in 1978 to 40 per cent in 1981.[18]

In effect, the vigorous implementation of the official policy of 'readjustment, restructuring, consolidation and improvement' during 1979–81, in drastically retrenching heavy industries and diverting resources to agriculture and light industries, had practically killed the original 'Four Modernisations' as contained in the Ten-Year Development Plan. Originally, the Plan called for a big push development strategy based on the dynamic growth of some key heavy industries, but the readjustment programme removed virtually all the growth momentum of the heavy industrial sector by shelving or slowing down the development of the major capital construction projects.

The actual output in 1980 in the key sectors clearly served to indicate that even if the Ten-Year Plan were not to be shelved, its targets were not likely to be realised:[19]

	1980	1981
Steel output (million tons)	37	36
Coal output (million tons)	620	620
Grain output (million tons)	320	325

On 1 December 1981, the Ten-Year Development Plan was officially superseded by the announcement of the Sixth Five-Year Plan when Premier Zhao Ziyang presented his report *The Present Economic Situation and the Principles for Future Economic Construction* to the Fifth National People's Congress.[20] Zhao confirmed that the tasks of readjustment and restructuring would be extended for another five years or more so that China could properly sort out the 'relationship between the different sectors of the national economy and within the individual sectors' and could rationalise the

'setup of production, the product mix, the technological make-up, the line-up of enterprises, and the organisational structure.' In the meantime, the Sixth Five-Year Plan (1981–85) details of which have yet to be unveiled, would be introduced but the economy would be expected to grow only at a 'steady and realistic rate' during this transitional period.

The period of reform and readjustment had to be extended, apparently because the Chinese economic planners and technocrats had now found the problems facing China were far worse than they had originally expected. The constraints were not just confined to the structural defects of the economy but also operated in a wide political and social context. For over two decades China had developed under the radical Maoist strategy, with politics and ideology taking precedence over economics and with revolutionary fervour and mass movements dominating every aspect of economic life. The idea that orderly economic progress, based on careful planning and rational management, and appropriately moderated by market incentives and international economic forces, is still alien to many cadres and bureaucrats at the medium and the grassroots levels, and in fact to the whole generation of somewhat confused Chinese youths who had been brought up under totally different life experiences. Thus the problems of China's modernisation would not be just those of amassing the required capital and technology or building up an adequate physical infrastructure, but would include the more delicate task of developing a proper institutional structure that would match the Chinese style of mixed socialist economic system. The whole exercise would go beyond the pure economic strategy of working out the proper patterns of resource allocation or resource utilisation. It had to include fundamental changes in the social structure, the social ethos, and even the attitude and behaviour of the population. Hence Premier Zhao Ziyang called for concerted efforts to 'blaze a new trial' in order to meet the new challenge.[21]

Having dropped the all-out growth-dominating development strategy for a more balanced and realistic progress, it appeared that China was not going to splash into the world economy with a disruptive impact on the existing international economic order as it could have under the original 'Four Modernisation Programme'. Instead, China would go through a difficult period of transition before it could resume dynamic higher growth.

At the twelfth National Congress of the Chinese Communist Party in September 1982, General Secretary Hu Yaobang, apparently encouraged by good progress in the recent economic readjustment, set forth the general targets of quadrupling the gross annual value of industrial and agricultural production to 2800 billion yuan by the year 2000. This has sparked off debate among Chinese economists as to whether the objective could be realised, given the existence of a number of serious constraints such as the slugguish increase in agricultural productivity and the low degree of energy utilisation. The noted Chinese economist Mr Xue Muqiao took the optimistic view that Hu's targets could be achieved. But it would mean that the Chinese economy under the Sixth Five-Year Plan (1981–85) had to grow at the average rate of 5 per cent and under the Seventh Five-Year Plan (1986–90), at 6 per cent; or at an average annual increase of 7.2 per cent for the two decades.[22] This projected high economic growth, impressive as it might seem for China, is not all that an impressive feat in the context of ASEAN's past growth records. Furthermore, as China fulfils the targets by producing its material GNP to 2800 billion yuan by the end of the century, the amount will work out to around only US$ 1200 on a per capita basis, which will still not be sufficient for China to close its expected average income gaps with ASEAN.

It should, however, be noted that from the standpoint of dynamic international economic relations, even a slowly growing Chinese economy in its transitional stage could still exert a powerful influence over or interact closely with the ASEAN economies. By its sheer physical size and potential the Chinese economy, at whatever tempo of progress, can be expected to produce significant spillovers on its ASEAN neighbours to the south.

Complementary Demands vs Competitive Supplies*

A growing Chinese economy will inevitably create both positive and negative feed-backs on the ASEAN economies. As the Chinese

* This section is largely based on my paper 'The Impact of China's Economic Modernisation on ASEAN', presented at the 'International Symposium on Two Decades of Asian Development and Outlook for the 1980s', organised by the Institute of Developing Economies, Tokyo, 8–11 March 1982.

economy grows, its markets will expand and exports increase, creating potentially favourable opportunities for ASEAN. At the same time, the Chinese economy will also create keen competition with the ASEAN economies, which are expected to be growing even more rapidly. In a static context, one can perhaps question crudely whether the opening of China is for the good of ASEAN. But realistic evaluation should be based on some dynamic considerations. In a dynamic situation – since both the Chinese and the ASEAN economies are growing – it would be more difficult to sort out the balance of net benefits and costs for ASEAN from the slowly modernising Chinese economy. In this section we shall further analyse the Sino– ASEAN trade structure in order to generate some observations on the possible scenarios.

THE PRIMARY-COMMODITY BALANCE IN CHINA'S TRADE

The importance of primary exports as the mainspring for the economic growth of the ASEAN countries hardly needs emphasis. Suffice it to add that the historically strong economic inter-relationship between ASEAN and the advanced capitalist economies largely arises from the fact that the latter has been complementing the former by absorbing a high volume of the former's exports of raw materials and natural resources. To be economically more closely integrated with the ASEAN region, China needs to meet the trade requirements of ASEAN by importing more of its primary products. Therefore, what raw materials and how much of them China can buy from or sell to ASEAN will be a crucial factor in determining the actual levels of complementarity in the Sino–ASEAN economic relationship.

As can be seen from Table 1.7, there is a heavy concentration of primary products in the Sino–ASEAN trade. In fact, a few specific commodity items dominate the trade flow between China and individual ASEAN countries. Thus, rice figures prominently in Indonesian and Malaysian imports from China, while petroleum virtually dominates those of the Philippines and Thailand. For years, Malaysia's exports to China have consisted of virtually nothing but rubber; and rubber is still predominant in Singapore's China-bound exports. Sugar constitutes on overwhelming share in the Philippines' exports to China. Such a commodity pattern points to the existence of significant resource complementarity between China and the individual ASEAN countries.

The exact role of China in the primary-product economy of ASEAN, however, seems to be more complicated. On the one hand, China is seen as a large and regular buyer in the Kuala Lumpur and Singapore rubber markets, and is becoming important in the Philippine copper market, while Chinese demands for the region's sugar, spices and other tropical products are rapidly expanding. On the other hand, China seems to compete with the region in the export of several important commodities. China is the world's foremost rice exporter, even more important than Thailand. At one time, China's exports of petroleum and tin had unsettled these two markets.

The overall picture of Chinese demand for and supply of primary commodities is nevertheless quite clear, particularly in respect of the recent trends. An UNCTAD study several years ago showed that China had a substantial deficit in its world trade in primary commodities.[23] As can be seen from Table 1.8, China is basically deficient in the 'ten core commodities' for which UNCTAD has called for special trading arrangements under the proposed Integrated Commodity Agreements. China also lacks other geographic-specific commodities and forest products, as might be expected. In 1975, at the peak of the first world energy and food crises (which had spared China on account of its economic isolation) China moved into the world commodity markets by pushing its exports of petroleum and rice. As a result of the export of these two high-priced commodity items, China was able to chalk up a surplus in its primary-commodity world trade balance for that year, creating a false impression of China as a significant natural-resource exporting country. In actual fact, since 1976 China has reverted to a deficit position in its world trade in primary commodities; this position has been worsening, as the two balancing items, petroleum and rice, have failed to make up for the deficits (Table 1.8). These deficits will no doubt continue to grow in the 1980s, partly because China has abandoned the Maoist grain self-sufficiency policy and therefore needs to increase the import of wheat for urban consumption,[24] and partly as a result of the expected decline in the export of petroleum products.

From the standpoint of ASEAN, whether or not China will constitute a real threat to its primary-product economy crucially hinges on the export behaviour of three Chinese products: petroleum, rice and tin. With great political fanfare, Chinese petroleum was first shipped to the Philippines and Thailand at the peak of the oil crisis in the mid-1970s.[25] In reality, the Chinese supplies, though important as a source of emergency supply during the crisis years, represented only a small fraction of the total demand in the Philippines and Thailand. The Chinese crude did not compete directly with Indonesia's petroleum exports to the ASEAN markets, which basically depended on sources from the Middle East. Even in the Japanese market, which took up a great deal of Indonesian petroleum, Chinese crude posed no direct threat to Indonesia simply because of China's small market share.

According to the recent World Bank Report, the outlook for Chinese petroleum exports in the 1980s does not look good, with the growth of China's primary energy production expected to slow down. With rising domestic demand due to industrial growth and inefficient energy utilisation, China may well cease to be a net energy exporter of any significance in future.[26]

Similarly, Chinese rice exports to ASEAN have not imposed competitive pressures on Thailand. This is because the governments of the rice-deficient countries in ASEAN often intervene in their domestic rice markets by working out market-share arrangements for different suppliers. On account of its geographical and political advantages (as a member of ASEAN) Thailand has maintained a dominant share in the ASEAN markets for its rice exports, with Chinese rice playing only a supplementary role. Under such a dualistic market pattern, there is really not much direct competition between Thai rice and Chinese rice which, after all, often appear as 'differentiated' commodities in the eyes of the habitual Asian rice eaters. Finally, the co-operative spirit of Beijing towards Thailand is fully reflected in the somewhat bizarre event of the rice trade in recent years: in 1976 China, as rice exporter, bought rice from Thailand when that country had the problem of disposing of its rice surplus![27]

Even less of a problem is created by Chinese tin. Over 70 per cent of world's tin exports annually come from ASEAN. China is not a member of the International Tin Council. China made a splash in the world tin market in 1975 by exporting a large quantity of tin metal, amounting to 8.5 per cent of the world total, mainly to the United States.[28] Ever since, the volume has been on the decline. Chinese tin output is now mainly absorbed by domestic demand, with the Chinese share of the world tin market being reduced to a trickle of 1.1 per cent for 1979.

On balance, the existing pattern of Chinese demand and supply for primary products works to the benefit of ASEAN. This conforms to the common notion of complementarity between the relatively resource-poor China and the resource-rich ASEAN. Table 1.9, laboriously compiled, serves to show that whereas the exports of the ASEAN countries minus Singapore are predominantly made up of resource-based commodities, the natural-resource contents of Chinese exports are just at the world average level, considerably below those of the four ASEAN countries. As the Chinese economy grows more rapidly in future, it will reduce the proportion of resource-based commodities in its total exports and at the same time generate more import demands for ASEAN's own primary commodities.

Some economists have recently pointed out that the centrally planned economies of Eastern Europe have absorbed an excessive amount of natural-resource product in their growth due to various biases arising from technology, demand patterns and price structures.[29] Whether this is true or not for China, its steady progress in industrialisation will in future certainly increase its overall demand for ASEAN's raw materials.

COMPETITIVE PRESSURES ON MANUFACTURED EXPORTS

It is not in the natural resource area, in which ASEAN has in so many ways clear comparative advantage over China, that ASEAN is apt to be apprehensive of rising competitive pressures from China. Rather, it is in the area of trade in manufactured products that such pressures are seen to be building up from the rapidly industrialising China. Increasingly, manufacturing growth constitutes a dynamic source of overall economic growth of the ASEAN countries, and competition involving trade in manufactured products is therefore likely to be a sensitive issue in the future Sino-ASEAN economic relations.

The question of the potential rise of Chinese manufactured exports has two dimensions, each with equally serious implications for ASEAN. First, there is concern over the successfully industrialised China flooding its low-priced manufactured products, be they labour-intensive consumer goods or medium-technology producer goods, into the ASEAN markets. This would present serious direct competition to the many local industries in the region, some of which are still quite fragile having just emerged from the so-called import substitution phase of industrialisation. Secondly, China could appear as an even more serious threat to ASEAN by competing indirectly in a third country market, be it a developing country or an industrial one. In recent years, ASEAN's industrialisation process has become more export-oriented, with manufactured exports constituting an increasing proportion of the ASEAN total. As latecomers, both China and ASEAN (excepting Singapore) tend to specialise in the simple, labour-intensive manufactures for exports, and hence compete with each other in the slowly expanding or, in some cases, even contracting export markets.

As can be seen from Table 1.10, about 70 per cent of China's manufactured exports are destined for the markets of the developing countries, in exact contrast to the Asian NICs like Hong Kong and South Korea, which send 70 per cent of their exports to the industrial countries, with the ASEAN countries roughly in between. This does seem to convey the general impression that the Third World rather than advanced countries is a natural 'dumping' ground for the cheap Chinese manufactures.

'Dumping' always assumes a political overtone and tends to make things look worse than they really are. Careful reading of Table 1.10 does not actually support the 'dumping' argument. Chinese exports of all categories of goods have no unduly large shares in the individual ASEAN markets. Chinese market shares of around 2 per cent are generally comparable with those of Hong Kong and South Korea – although the exports of Hong Kong and South Korea, unlike those of China, are made up primarily of manufactured goods – but often smaller than those held by other ASEAN countries. For instance, China's share in the Indonesian market in 1979 amounted to only 1.8 per cent, considerably below 7.4 per cent for Singapore and 3 per cent for Thailand (Table 1.11).

In future, as China's new industrialisation efforts bear fruit, China could, of course, make use of its large pool of cheap labour to mass produce a wide range of consumer goods such as electronics, textiles, shoes, plastics, toys, and the like for the ASEAN markets. If China could produce these goods cheaply and efficiently and supply them to ASEAN at low prices, this would enhance the welfare of the ASEAN consumers and help the ASEAN economies to reduce their inflationary pressures. There are no cogent economic reasons for the ASEAN manufacturers to fear open competition from China, or for that matter from India or Bangladesh, especially since most ASEAN economies have all phased out import substitution policy in favour of the more outward-looking export-oriented strategy. Further, cheap labour does not mean efficient labour. Two decades ago when Chinese manufacturers made their debút in the Southeast Asian markets, China seemed to possess many clear advantages in the region which had hardly started its own industrialisation. Over the years, industrial stagnation in China due to frequent political interventions has eroded a great deal of Chinese industrial competitiveness *vis-à-vis* ASEAN. As the former Philippine Minister of Industry, Vicente Paterno, once remarked: 'China has low-cost labour, yes, but I think they have to compete in the same way as anybody else.'[30] In an aggregate sense, the existing market shares of Chinese exports to the ASEAN markets are still too small, so that Chinese exports will have to grow many times before they can threaten serious disruption.

By comparison, ASEAN is more worried over the increased competitive pressures created by China's attempt to enlarge its market shares for manufactured exports in the industrial countries. As shown in Table 1.12, the present volume of Chinese exports to the industrial countries is conspicuously small, particularly in the US market. As China's modernisation proceeds, Chinese demand for capital equipment and technology from the industrial countries will grow and this eventually may lead to a larger market share for Chinese products in these advanced countries. This appears to be the case for Chinese exports to Japan. Furthermore, as China is opening up to more foreign investment under various schemes of joint venture arrangements, it may eventually improve the access of Chinese products to the markets of the industrial countries. With imported technology and foreign marketing skills, China may quickly move to upgrade the quality of its manufactured exports and divert them more towards the advanced countries. According to the World Bank, this could soon happen.[31] The volume of China's manufactured exports is forecast to grow at 10 per cent a year throughout the 1980s, even possibly 15 per cent, depending on whether it can successfully break into the markets of the richer countries, especially in the OECD, and increase its currently very small market shares. Then the question for ASEAN would be – will the thrust of Chinese manufactured products into the advanced countries produce displacement effects on ASEAN's own manufactured exports in those markets? This applies particularly to the labour-intensive manufactures like textiles and clothing.

At present, the markets in advanced countries for manufactured products from the developing world are mainly captured by a few dynamic NICs, which in Asia include South Korea, Taiwan, Hong Kong and Singapore. Except for Singapore, textiles and clothing constitute a very high proportion of the exports of these NICs: for example., 46 per cent for Hong Kong and 32 per cent for South Korea in 1979; and the bulk of the textiles and clothing exports are for the industrial countries.[32]

In 1979, textiles and clothing constituted 24 per cent of China's total exports, and 27 per cent of China's manufactured exports went to the industrial countries.[33] Thus, the amount of Chinese textile goods exported to the industrial countries in 1979 works out at around US $900 million as compared with US$ 340 million for Singapore, $330 million for Thailand, $215 million for the Philippines, $120 million for Malaysia and an insignificant amount for Indonesia. But the Chinese volume, though much larger than that of ASEAN, bore no comparison with $5 billion for Hong Kong or $3.6 billion for South Korea. Nevertheless, from the standpoint of ASEAN, the problem of competition would appear to be more from China than from the Asian NICs. To begin with, ASEAN products are likely to meet head-on competition from Chinese products rather than from the higher grade Hong Kong-made equivalents. Not just in textiles but also in many other lines of manufacturing, the Asian NICs, driven by shifting comparative advantage, are moving towards higher value-added and more skill-intensive activities, thus posing less of a direct menace to the latecomers in ASEAN. The pattern is clearly borne out in Table 1.13, which shows that China over the past two decades still clings to a high level of labour-intensive products in its total manufactured exports (around 44 per cent), whereas Japan has clearly given up on labour-intensive exports during the same period (a reduction of share from 13 per cent in 1964 to 1 per cent in 1979) and other Asian NICs, namely, Hong Kong, South Korea and Singapore, are in the process of shedding their comparative advantage in labour-intensive exports in favour of more high value-added activities, as manifested in the declining shares of labour-intensive products in their total exports. At the same time, such ASEAN countries as the Philippines and Thailand are pushing for more and more labour-intensive manufactured exports.

This implies that while the Asian NICs seem to fit in nicely with the overall pattern of export specialisation in the Western Pacific region,

China's persistent adherence to a high level of labour-intensive exports could well create difficulties for its eventual integration with the region's economy. At least, there is 'certainly a possibility that the opening up of China could retard the growth and reduce the benefits of Southeast Asian Exports of labour-intensive manufactures, especially if the OECD countries maintain slow import growth in these commodities.'[34] Obviously, 'labour-intensive' manufactures are a broad categorisation comprising a wide variety of goods so that there is room for individual centres to specialise. Further, even the textile and clothing industry is not restrictively labour-intensive, as has often been commonly thought. The industry is quite capable of progress in terms of product differentiation and product sophistication, as the technical change in the textile industry in Hong Kong and Japan in recent years has demonstrated.[35] None the less, in the short run, the ASEAN countries would still view China as a direct competitor in the export markets until China starts harmonising its exports by either moving up to higher capital- or skill-intensity or speeding up technological change in its 'labour-intensive' activities.

It is clear that China is actively seeking to expand its world market share in labour-intensive manufactures and it could well succeed through bilateral negotiation or sheer political pressure on the individual industrial countries. Were it to do so, some ASEAN exporters might well be crowded out.

Competition is a norm only in a normal world, but obviously not in the situation of the present industrial countries, which are persistently plagued by chronic economic recession with high levels of unemployment. With rising protectionism, the markets of the advanced countries are really like a 'zero-sum game' in which expansion of Chinese exports would easily be viewed by ASEAN as having been achieved at the expense of its own exports. The recently concluded negotiation on the new Multi-Fiber Arrangement (MFA) fully underscores such a sentiment. In attempting to reduce the existing market shares for the established textiles exporters like Hong Kong, Taiwan and South Korea, the renewed MFA has made no effort to create new market opportunity for the newcomers.[36] Thus the impact on ASEAN (and on other developing countries) by the Chinese penetration into markets of the advanced countries depends much on the economic outlook of the latter.

Proper evaluation of the balance of benefits and cost on ASEAN arising from China's economic modernisation has to be made in the perspective of individual ASEAN countries. The distribution of the beneficial spillovers among ASEAN countries from a rise in the Chinese demand for the region's products is quite uneven, and so is the distribution of cost. Thus an increase in Chinese demand for natural rubber will obviously benefit Malaysia and not the Philippines, while an influx of labour-intensive Chinese manufactures into the world market will hurt Thailand and the Philippines but not Singapore, which is currently phasing out labour-intensive industries through vigorous economic restructuring.

A balanced picture should also take into account some of the more positive aspects. In the long run, as its economic development gets underway China, as a market of one billion consumers, need not be exclusively monopolised by the industrial countries. Even now China, as a market outlet for ASEAN, is mainly captured by Singapore with its exports of television sets and oil rigs, produced by the MNCs based in Singapore. The prospects of China as an alternative outlet for resource-based manufactures from other ASEAN countries, though currently remote, should not be entirely ruled out for the future.

The factors of history and geography have always exerted a powerful influence on a nation's perception of its neighbours, which in turn affect their overall economic relations. In the case of ASEAN, its perception of China is likely to remain unbalanced for some time, partly owing to the historical legacies of the Cold War, and partly because of ASEAN's fear of being overshadowed by a close neighbour of one billion people. On account of the geo-political forces, China has always maintained a strong political presence in the ASEAN region, albeit indirectly or psychologically. It is thus easy to understand ASEAN's instinctive reluctance to see a rapid increase in the scale of the Chinese economic influence in the region as well. Accordingly, ASEAN was initially quite apprehensive of China's economic modernisation efforts, although the line of economic reasoning that we have set out would indicate that a resurgent Chinese economy might well interact positively with the ASEAN economies.

With the Chinese modernisation programme recently shifting into low gear, it now appears that the Chinese economy will go through a rather drawn-out process of transition and readjustment before it can take off into dynamic economic growth. As far as the countries in the Asia-Pacific region are concerned, this may prove to be a blessing in disguise, because a gradually emerging China would smooth out the process of integrating the Chinese economy with the region's economic system and could therefore minimise any short-term disruptive impact on the ASEAN economies.

Unlike Sino–Japanese economic relations, which are based on strong and clear-cut complementarity, capable of developing into a viable 'economic symbiosis' in future, Sino–ASEAN economic relations are fraught with competitive elements, at least at the present stage of their economic development. Obviously, it would be difficult for China and ASEAN to evolve a relationship of the same depth and breadth. Still, their future course of economic relations could be developed more productively if both sides would maximise their interaction in sectors of mutual benefit and avoid areas of economic friction. So long as political détente continues to prevail in the region, both sides could eventually adjust their economic relations to mutual advantage.

2

Indonesia's Relations with China

Introduction

Indonesia was the first ASEAN country to establish diplomatic relations with the People's Republic of China soon after it was proclaimed on 1 October 1949.[1] However, after periods of swinging to the extremes, Sino–Indonesian relations were abruptly suspended in the wake of *Gestapu*, the Indonesian *coup* in September 1965. Today, three of the five ASEAN countries – Malaysia, Thailand and the Philippines – have established diplomatic relations with China dating from the mid-1970s and the fourth one, Singapore, has informally established official links with Beijing by setting up a trade office there. This leaves Indonesia, ironically, the only country in the ASEAN region – in fact one of a handful in the world – which has no direct official dialogues with China.

It has been a full decade since President Nixon's visit to Beijing, which ushered in an era of détente for Asia. Successive Asian countries, including those like the Philippines which were once staunch supporters of the Cold War strategy, have in the meantime established diplomatic ties with China. Indonesia's persistent refusal to resume official links with Beijing does seem to be one of the rare diplomatic exceptions in modern times. In the long run, Indonesia's adamant stand on China could have far-reaching consequences for itself and for the region. As the biggest country in Southeast Asia, Indonesia could play a potentially leading role both in intra–regional

31

politics and in dealing with powers from outside the region, but the diplomatic inflexibility manifested in its inward-looking foreign policy and the rigidity of its attitude towards China could well diminish its effectiveness in playing out such a role. In the perception of the present Indonesian power elites, who have lived through the upheaval of the turbulent Sukarno period, the existing policy of deliberately avoiding China appears to be better than the alternative which could, in their view, only lead to another confrontation. Of course, this is not positive diplomacy, and could well be a short-sighted approach. By normalising relations Indonesia could actually work together with China to harmonise their conflicting interests. This could in turn lead to an overall enhancement of regional peace and stability.

Continuing Sino—Indonesian diplomatic impasse has equally serious consequences for China. In fact, China's diplomatic failure in Indonesia has continued to hurt Beijing, and the loss cannot be offset by diplomatic gains resulting from opening up new relations with the other ASEAN states. Without untying the Indonesian knot, China is severely constrained in its efforts to develop a more positive relationship with ASEAN as a whole or to increase its political and economic involvement in the region's development. With unmended fences over Jakarta, China would find it extremely hard to improve bilateral relationships with Malaysia and Singapore. Furthermore, without patching up with Indonesia, China would continue to operate an incomplete foreign policy towards Southeast Asia, thereby reducing the effectiveness and manoeuverability of its efforts to check the growth of the 'hegemonic' influence of the Soviet Union over the region, or to contain the expansive Vietnam. The post-Mao leadership in Beijing is thus paying heavily for the diplomatic misadventures of the less pragmatic leaders of the previous generation, who unrealistically extended Mao's 'United Front' strategy to international relations by forging an anti-imperialist coalition with the unstable Sukarno regime.

China seemed to have come close to achieving its foreign policy goals in 1965 with the formation of the Beijing—Jakarta axis, which represented the most sensational diplomatic breakthrough in a decade for Beijing in terms of *realpolitik* gains as well as in fulfilling the ideological premises of China's foreign policy at that time. In striking a close political alignment with Indonesia, Beijing had demonstrated its success in breaking out from the encirclement imposed on China by both 'US imperialism' and the 'Socialist imperialism' of the Soviet Union. The alliance with Indonesia served not only as a base for China to outflank hostile international forces, such as the US-initiated Southeast Asia Treaty Organisation (SEATO), but also as a platform for rallying the independent Afro–Asian regimes to form the 'newly emerging forces' to engage in a common revolutionary struggle against the 'Imperialist' powers. To this end, Beijing directed all its institutional and material resources to sustain the alliance and supported it with trade and aid. Thus Chinese share in Indonesia's total trade in 1965 reached the record level of 11 per cent, and China became Indonesia's second largest supplier of goods. At the same time, China also extended a substantial amount of aid to Jakarta.

As China's political and economic relations with Indonesia reached their zenith in the middle of 1965, Beijing little realised that its apparent solidarity with the Sukarno regime was actually built upon a soft foundation, which was further weakened by the continuing rivalry between the PKI, (*Partai Komunis Indonesia* – Indonesian Communist Party) and the Indonesian army. Nor were the Chinese leaders aware that their over-inflated foreign policy ambitions, far outstretched the limited material resources then available with which to achieve them: China simply played power politics with rhetoric, but with no real power. Thus the much-publicized 'Beijing-Jakarta Axis' collapsed like a house of cards when an abortive coup sparked off a strong *putsch* from a right-wing military junta led by General Suharto, who eventually brought down the Sukarno regime. Hence a violent end to the Beijing-Jakarta alliance, turning what might have been China's most spectacular diplomatic achievement into a disaster, with a lingering legacy of mutual mistrust. After the fall of Sukarno, Sino–Indonesian relations were broken off and Sino–Indonesian trade dwindled to a trickle – to only 0.5 per cent of Indonesia's total trade by 1980.

China's diplomatic misadventure in Indonesia not only holds lessons for the future course of Sino–Indonesian relations but also significant implications for China's overall approach to Southeast Asia. The serious setbacks in Indonesia were not only a vicissitude of the type which China had often experienced in its past dealing with other countries in Southeast Asia, but were also a direct outcome of China's misguided foreign policy in pursuit of unrealistic objectives. As will be seen later in this chapter and in subsequent chapters,

China's approach to relations with other ASEAN countries had been fundamentally pragmatic and cautious, aiming at modest goals and as far as possible avoiding confrontation and direct entanglement in domestic matters. In contrast, Chinese policy towards Indonesia as it culminated in the formation of the 'Beijing-Jakarta axis' in 1965 represented a clear break from Beijing's traditional approach, following instead an offensive type of strategy with a high posture and a strong interventionist orientation. Such an ambitious policy, shaped by both revolutionary ideology and *realpolitik* objectives, was designed to force a change in the region's geo-political balance. Naturally this kind of 'high-powered' foreign policy entails high risks, even for a true superpower like the United States or the Soviet Union.

The collapse of a country's major foreign policy is often caused by a combination of unforeseen exogenous forces and unfavourable 'structural' factors. Specifically in terms of 'structural' problems, Chinese failure in Indonesia brought to the fore the issues and problems which had bedevilled Beijing's relations with Indonesia from the very outset: their political and social incompatibilities, Indonesia's historical fear of China, strong anti-Chinese undercurrents in Indonesian society, and China's support for the local Communist movement. In many ways China's bilateral relations with other ASEAN countries were beset with the same sort of problems. Faced with so many sensitive and potentially explosive issues, China would have been better off in its relations with Indonesia had it followed a gingerly approach with a low profile.

The absence of official Chinese representation in Jakarta, capital of the largest nation in Southeast Asia and the headquarters of the ASEAN organisation, is a constant reminder to the Chinese leadership of their past diplomatic failure. But it also serves the useful purpose of keeping the experience alive and helping future policymakers in Beijing to devise a more productive political and economic relationship with individual ASEAN countries.

Early Relations

China's contact with the Indonesian archipelago, as with other parts of *Nanyang*, can be traced back to the early centuries. In fact, early

Sino–Indonesian trade was reported to be 'well under way in the fifth century'.[2] From the ninth century on, Chinese traders were definitely known to have frequented Java and Borneo. When the Dutch landed in Java in 1596, they found 'a scattered population of Chinese working in every province of the island'.[3] But the early Chinese settlements in Indonesia were only the product of unorganised individual activities on the part of enterprising traders from the South China coast, certainly not the direct outcome of any systematic colonisation efforts on the part of the successive Chinese governments, which seldom had imperialist ambitions over the Indonesian archipelago. Historically, Indonesia had never come under Chinese domination.

The nineteenth century saw the rapid influx of a large number of Chinese immigrant labourers to the Netherlands East Indies to work in the mines and plantations, a departure from their traditional commercial activities. The Chinese had played key economic roles in this Dutch colony as 'middlemen collecting agricultural produce for export; as retail merchants; and as licensed operators of salt, opium, and other revenue-producing monopolies'.[4] But their economic position, though important, did not prevent them from becoming 'expendable', as it actually happened in 1740 when a large number of Chinese in Java were massacred by the Dutch colonialists.[5]

In order to maximise their exploitation of Indonesia, the Dutch pursued a colonial policy embodied in the so-called 'Culture System'. Essentially, the Chinese were put in the intermediate position under the overall 'colonial caste structure', being segregated from both the ruling elites and the indigenous population. While the Chinese were barred from penetrating into the modern sector activities such as plantation agriculture, mines, finance and export trade, which were dominated by the Dutch, they were also prohibited from owning and cultivating land. The openings left for the Chinese were in retail trade, money-lending and other pursuits, which did not endear them later to the Indonesian nationalists. In this way, economic and social alienation from the local population rendered the Chinese politically vulnerable and made them appear in the eyes of the natives as alien exploiters or handmaidens of the Dutch. In other words, long before Indonesia's independence, Dutch colonial policy had sown the seeds of conflict between the Chinese and the local population.[6]

On the other hand, the social and political segregation of the Chinese in Indonesia, as in other parts of Southeast Asia, had been caused as much by their own traditional attitudes in sticking to a largely self-imposed policy of non-involvement in local political movements and striving to maintain their strong cultural identity. There were of course many exceptions to this generalisation, and a distinction should be made between the local-born *peranakan* Chinese and the foreign-born *totok* (or 'pure blood') Chinese.[7] It is nevertheless true that by the twentieth century, 'the socioeconomic situation had made inevitable the isolation of the Chinese from the mainstream of the Indonesian movement for national independence'.[8] If the Chinese minority did not contribute much to Indonesia's anti-colonial movement, they did not stand to gain politically either from the independence movement or from the successive post-independence governments. In fact, many Indonesian national leaders were deeply resentful of the 'neutrality' of the Chinese and their failure to provide positive support to the independence movement during the critical phase of its struggle. This accounts for a period of anti-Chinese violence which occurred during the immediate aftermath of the war, when Indonesia waged its independence struggle, until complete sovereignty was achieved with the Roundtable Conference in the Hague in November 1949.[9]

With the restoration of order after independence, violence against the Chinese community on a large scale subsided for a while. However, anti-Chinese sentiments persisted and soon developed into a recurrent problem of Indonesian society, much influenced by political, economic, social and religious issues. In entering into diplomatic relations with Indonesia, Beijing was thus landed with the task of having to take care of 2 million or so ethnic Chinese against whom their host country had developed deep-rooted antagonism. The task became even more delicate as not all of the 'overseas Chinese' were ideologically acceptable to Beijing, with many of them being petty bourgeoisie and some even members of the 'compradore class'. At the same time, Indonesia, unlike other Southeast Asian colonies, had fought for its own independence and therefore appeared to Beijing to be a country with a strong revolutionary potential as well as a distinct Third World identity. It was one country in Southeast Asia with which China could possibly cultivate a strong political relationship. Right from the start, Beijing inherited a complicated and yet challenging diplomatic situation.

In the economic spheres, it would be amiss not to record the brisk trade between China and Indonesia before the war. In 1933, for instance, Chinese exports to Indonesia amounted to 9 per cent of China's total exports, making Indonesia China's most important market outlet in Southeast Asia, although the same volume represented only 2 per cent of Indonesia's total imports. Chinese exports comprised mainly foodstuffs, with soya beans being most important. But there were also cotton yarn and cotton piece-goods. In return, Indonesia exported raw materials to China, particularly kerosene and sugar. Though China's imports from Indonesia constituted only 4 per cent of China's total imports, this share was again higher than that of the other Southeast Asian countries.

In the 1930s, as it is today, Sino–Indonesian trade was characterised by its special commodity structure. Before the war, Indonesia imported almost all its soya beans from China while China obtained a third of its imported kerosene (an extremely important source of fuel and energy in the pre-war rural China) and half of its sugar from Indonesia.[10]

Relations during 'Constitutional Democracy'

Although Indonesia was among the first few countries, along with the Soviet Union and Britain, to extend diplomatic recognition to the People's Republic of China, its relations with China did not begin smoothly, especially between September 1950 and April 1952. During this period Indonesia was ruled by governments dominated by anti-Communist Islamic factions, particularly the Cabinet headed by Dr Sukiman (April 1951–April 1952), who was openly pro-Western and strongly suspicious of Beijing for its support of the PKI. It was not until the middle of 1953, upon the ascension to power of the left-of-centre Ali Sastroamidjojo government which depended on the PKI support for its majority, that Sino–Indonesian relations were brought up to an amicable level.

In July 1950, Beijing's first ambassador, Mr Wang Ren-shu, an Indonesia old-hand, took up his appointment in Jakarta, and he lost no time in getting rid of the former Kuomintang influence on the Chinese community in Indonesia. As his first major success, the Bank of China in Jakarta shifted allegiance to Beijing. However, Wang's zealous activities in the Chinese community soon aroused suspicion from the Indonesian government, which was still cautious and cool in its relations with Beijing, – this being reflected in the appointment of only a *Chargé d'Affaires ad Interim* to Beijing. Further, in 1951, Jakarta had a diplomatic row with Beijing by obstructing the entry of Chinese embassy personnel into Indonesia.[11]

After the fall of Sukiman in March 1952, the new government, headed by the moderate Wilopo, started to improve relations with Beijing. But the real turning-point for Sino–Indonesian relations in the 1950s came in June 1953 with the formation of the government by Ali Sastroamidjojo. Ali steered Indonesia's foreign policy into a sharp turn by actively pursuing a foreign policy of anti-colonialism and non-alignment, like that being championed in Burma and India. He demonstrated his commitments to the new policy by normalising relations with all the Communist countries, as well as by his decision to upgrade Indonesia's relations with China with the appointment in October 1953 of a prominent member of the Indonesian establishment, Arnold Mononutu, as Indonesia's first ammbassador to Beijing.

A month later, Indonesia's first economic mission went to Beijing and concluded a trade agreement with China, declaring that Indonesia would no longer abide by the American-initiated UN embargo on China, especially with regard to rubber exports. China naturally responded to Indonesia's new foreign policy initiative with great enthusiasm. In June 1954, the Chinese trade delegation returned a visit to Indonesia and promised to make a big purchase of Indonesian rubber. In November, Beijing dispatched a more experienced career diplomat, Mr Huang Zhen, to replace Ambassador Wang, thus laying a sounder basis for closer relations.

Meanwhile Ali's government proceeded to deal with the controversial and sensitive issue of the civil status of the Chinese in Indonesia in a sensible and rational manner. The lessening of Sino–Indonesian tension had now provided a much more conducive climate for both sides to tackle this problem with minimum political fuss. Thus Ambassador Mononutu's first task was to approach the Chinese government with a view to settling the issue of Chinese citizenship. Beijing was receptive to the Indonesian move because China too wanted to clear the old obstacle in the way of further improving relations with Indonesia. The Chinese government had also come to realise the political costs and diplomatic ramifications of sticking to the archaic Chinese nationality law based on the principle of *jus sanguinis*. In December 1954, a Sino–Indonesian joint communiqué was issued on the preliminary discussion of the Chinese citizenship status. In April 1955, as thé highlight of the Afro–Asian Conference in Bandung, the Sino–Indonesian Dual Nationality Treaty was signed. The treaty stipulated that the overseas Chinese in Indonesia would have to choose the nationality of one country within two years and, failing that, their citizenship would be determined by the nationality of their father. Needless to say, the Treaty was of great historic significance because for the first time China formally abandoned its traditional claim that *all* Chinese were its nationals, thus marking an important step towards the ultimate settlement of the Chinese citizenship problem not only in Indonesia, but also in the rest of Southeast Asia.[12]

The main purpose of Chinese Premier Zhou Enlai's attendance at the Bandung Conference was of course not just to conclude the Dual Nationality Treaty or even to consolidate Sino–Indonesian relations, but to achieve broader foreign policy objectives within the framework of the non-alignment movement in the Third World. The Bandung Conference represented China's first major diplomatic breakthrough in a decade. Prior to Bandung, China's overall foreign policy had become remarkably moderate and conciliatory, a tactic characterised by the Western media as China's 'smile diplomacy' or 'peace offensive'. In Bandung, Premier Zhou, through its personal charm and persuasive arguments, not only won over such Asian neutrals as India and Burma, but also managed to make a strong impression on the rightist regimes such as the Philippines and Thailand. At the conference, Zhou pledged that China had 'no intention whatsoever to subvert the governments of its neighbouring countries'.[13] The new Chinese policy towards the 'overseas Chinese', as reflected in the Sino–Indonesian treaty on dual nationality, was a timely demonstration of Beijing's renunciation of any attempt to use the ethnic Chinese in Southeast Asia for ulterior political purposes. 'Most of the delegates attending the historic meeting were convinced by Zhou Enlai's presentation of China's desire to see the principle of peaceful coexistence become the basis of relations among all the non-Western states'.[14]

In the context of Sino–Indonesian relations, the Bandung Conference provided a great impetus for mutual understanding. In part as a result of Zhou's impressive diplomatic performance, many Indonesian elites, like those in India, became increasingly well-disposed towards socialism. Most of them also tended to view the Chinese revolution in a non-ideological and more sympathetic context, while being critical of the Dullesian policy of isolating China. Domestic politics in Indonesia were also conducive to Sino–Indonesian relations. At the first Parliamentary election held in 1955, the PKI emerged as the fourth largest party, and the PKI of course endorsed Indonesia's close relations with China as well as the Indonesian government's non-alignment foreign policy in general. Over the Indonesian political spectrum, the right-wing groups (such as the Muslim group or the *Masjumi*[15]) tended to be anti-Chinese (and, as was often the case, anti–China as well), whereas the left-wing groups, particularly the PKI, were inherently more tolerant towards the Chinese minority in Indonesia. The principal reason for the conspicuous absence of strong anti-Chinese sentiments among the leftists was their generally internationalist outlook as well as the anti-racial character of Marxist ideology.[16]

After the Bandung breakthrough, Sino–Indonesian relations developed by leaps and bounds, as evidenced by the shuttling of visiting dignitaries and the exchange of cultural and good-will groups between the two countries, culminating in President Sukarno's first state visit to Beijing on 30 September 1956. Chinese leaders spared no efforts in entertaining Sukarno, who was immensely impressed by China's economic progress, national unity and social discipline, seemingly possible only under an effective socialist government. Indeed, the year 1956 marked the high point of China's economic and social development in the 1950's and even of relative political freedom (under the so-called 'Hundred Flowers' period). China really had much to display to its flamboyant guest from a country which was still characterised by enormous economic backwardness as well as lack of national integration. It has been argued that the impression Sukarno gained from his China trip inspired, or at least greatly reinforced, his concept of 'Guided Democracy', which he duly announced upon his return to Jakarta.

Crises Under 'Guided Democracy'

In 1956 Mohd Hatta, a pro-Western moderate, hastened the decline of the constitutional experiment with his resignation from the vice-presidency following his disagreement with Sukarno, who in any case 'had never been enthusiastic about the parliamentary system' on the ground that it was not suitable for conditions in Indonesia. Sukarno believed instead in the building of a 'just and prosperous society' for Indonesia under a new form of democracy, *demokrasi terpimpin* (democracy with leadership, hence popularly called 'guided democracy'), which would function harmoniously within the Indonesian social system, emphasising such traditional Indonesian social features as mutual help (*gotong-rojong*), consensus (*mufakat*), and collective deliberation (*musjawarat*).[17]

Meanwhile, Indonesian politics fell back into disunity and dissension as a result of the widening ethnic and regional conflicts which eventually led Sukarno to dissolve the cabinet and declare martial law. In the circumstances, Sukarno came to rely heavily on the PKI to counterbalance the right-wing elements, including the military and the Muslims, as well as to support his programme for the 'guided democracy'. The close alignment between Sukarno and the PKI added a new dimension to Sino–Indonesian relations.

While the PKI's sympathy for the Indonesian Chinese was well-known, Sukarno's attitude was more ambiguous. But it is clear that he was not fundamentally antipathetic towards the Chinese minority.[18] He might have made anti–Communist or anti-Chinese outbursts earlier on, but he was 'never afflicted with the racist attitudes towards the local Chinese commonly shared by nearly all segments of the Indonesian elite'.[19] Whatever his past inclinations, Sukarno had clearly become more well-disposed towards the Chinese minority in Indonesia after his China trip.

It might easily be assumed that with Sukarno and the PKI (both being the prime sources for friendly policies towards China) becoming increasingly interdependent for mutual political survival, a strong and lasting political base had once and for all been created for the growth of a stable Sino–Indonesian relationship. But such an over-simplified assumption ignored strong anti-Chinese sentiments embedded in Indonesian society. To begin with, the Sino–Indonesian Treaty of Dual Nationality, though a considerable land-mark towards solving the touchy 'Chinese issue', had not really succeeded in alleviating the deep-rooted anti-Chinese feelings – the right-wing groups, including the *Masjumi and Partai Katholik*, were opposed to it from the start.[20] Even after the treaty was ratified by the Indonesian Parliament in 1957, there were considerable variations in its interpretation and the resultant controversy persisted. To implement the Treaty, the Citizenship Act was proposed in 1958 and passed in June 1979.

In May 1958, a rebellion broke out against Sukarno; this was primarily separatist and anti-Communist in nature, receiving material support from the United States and Taiwan. Beijing naturally threw its whole weight behind Sukarno in what it viewed as a common cause of anti-imperialist struggle. The rebellion led to a public outcry, fanned by the leftist and ultra-nationalist groups, against the pro-Taiwan Indonesian Chinese. But the campaign against the Nationalist Chinese soon ran out of hand and degenerated into an indiscriminate outbreak against the entire Chinese community in Indonesia, regardless of whether they were *peranakans* or *totoks*, pro-Beijing or pro-Taiwan.

In 1959, the Indonesian government promulgated measures banning aliens from operating retail trade in rural areas, and this provides yet another revealing example of how latent anti-Chinese sentiments, once given release, could easily develop into an upheaval against Chinese. At first, the Indonesian Chinese, particularly the *peranakans*, did not think that the ban would have much effect on them and went on with business as usual. But the ban soon developed legal and political muscle following its endorsement by Sukarno with the promulgation of a presidential decree (PP-10/1959). In some regions, such as West Java, the over-zealous local military authorities took it upon themselves to issue additional orders aiming to evict all Chinese from the rural areas. The ban was originally motivated by economic nationalism but it soon erupted into a widespread anti-Chinese fervour.[21] In many areas, the focus of the upheaval was no longer against 'aliens' in control of small shops, but also against all 'foreign' schools and 'foreign' newspapers, and even against the display of 'foreign' characters in their shops or houses. Hence one correspondent noted :[22]

> The Westerners in this Afro-Asian country do not appear to be worried by this wave of xenophobia for – *une fois n'est pas coutume* – it is not directed against them. The Americans as a matter of fact are not at all displeased by it since the 'foreigners' in question are the Chinese and the country most concerned is Communist China.

The retail trade ban thus plunged Sino–Indonesian relations into a major crisis. The intensity of anti-Chinese feelings generated by the ban had caught both Sukarno and Beijing by surprise and presented each with a great dilemma. Ideologically, Sukarno shared the anti-capitalist and anti-middleman feeling, which was the basic rationale in the original policy of banning the Chinese from operating retail trade in rural areas. Furthermore, the ban was crucial in restructuring the Indonesian economy for the transition towards the 'Guided Economy'. Thus, 'Sukarno and other defenders of the Chinese, most notably the PKI, were in the awkward position of having to justify the continued existence of the most conspicuous group of 'capitalists' in Indonesian society at a time when socialism and national identity were potent slogans under 'Guided Democracy'.[23] On the other hand, the disruption caused by the ban would severely dislocate the rural economy because of the economic weaknesses of the indigenous Indonesians, who had yet to develop the capability to assume the indispensable economic functions hitherto performed by the ethnic Chinese. Furthermore, the rampant anti-Chinese upheaval would inevitably draw Beijing into the conflict and thus jeopardise the budding anti-Imperialist alliance with China.

Much more was at stake on Beijing's side. Violent protests against the Chinese community in Jakarta and in other places brought the Chinese Embassy in direct confrontation with the Indonesian authorities, resulting in a series of mutual recriminations and accusations, at one time even threatening to break up diplomatic ties. Like Sukarno, the Chinese leaders in Beijing found it hard to defend the interests of the Chinese as petty capitalists and middlemen on ideological grounds; but at the same time Beijing had to protect the rights and interests of the Chinese nationals, especially those who had opted to retain Chinese citizenship under the recent Treaty for Dual Nationality. In particular, Beijing found the supplementary 'residence ban' (which would eventually drive all ethnic Chinese out of the rural areas in West Java) most unacceptable. In short, China was faced with such a formidable dilemma that it was left with no course of action which did not sacrifice one or more of its broader policy objectives.[24] In simple terms, Beijing ran the risk of rupturing its official relations with Jakarta if the Chinese government were to put up a spirited defence of the rights and interests of Chinese nationals in Indonesia against the full brunt of Indonesian nationalism. Alternatively, Beijing had to face the consequence of losing face to Taiwan and to all the other overseas Chinese communities if the Chinese government were to stand idly by.

Initially, Beijing concentrated its diplomatic efforts into putting pressure on the Indonesian government to abandon the anti-Chinese measures, and invited Indonesia's Foreign Minister, Dr Subandrio, to visit Beijing in October 1959 for talks. But Subandrio's meeting with his Chinese counterpart, Marshal Chen Yi did not result in any agreement. Meanwhile, the ban developed into a large-scale anti-Chinese movement, involving Sukarno himself as the President. The right-wing groups further exploited the situation by tangling it up with latent anti-Communist sentiments. Subsequently, the personnel of the Chinese Embassy were involved in direct confrontation with the Indonesian army as the latter attempted to remove Chinese traders by force. There were violent clashes in Jakarta and in some areas in West Java. For a time there appeared to be no restraining force available in Indonesia to check the rampant anti-Chinese tide. Beijing soon ran out of political and economic leverages.

In the circumstances, China had to make a diplomatic retreat by taking more 'passive measures' in order to salvage whatever official relations with Indonesia still remained. In December 1959, China put into action its plans to evacuate the ethnic Chinese – not just the *totoks*, but also the *peranakans* who wished to leave Indonesia for China. Eventually over 100 000 Chinese from Indonesia were repatriated to China, and it had been a costly operation for Beijing. But it helped to defuse the situation. In the end, the anti-Chinese issue was finally settled by firm intervention from Sukarno, who began to see the imminent danger of letting the right-wing elements run out of hand.

Although China did not so much win the struggle for Sukarno's support as the anti-Communist forces lost it through their extremist action, the shift of Chinese policy from confrontation to accommodation had obviously made it easier for Sukarno to intervene and hence prevented the rift from becoming a disastrous diplomatic rupture. The conciliatory efforts culminated in the visit to Jakarta in March 1961 of Marshal Chen Yi who, with recriminations still fresh in his mind, had to reassert his new faith in the Bandung spirit, 'with his pride securely swallowed'.[25]

The anti-Chinese issue was settled for a moment, but not buried. In May 1963, anti-Chinese riots broke out again over a small incident in Bandung, coming in the wake of the visit of the Chinese Head of State, Liu Shaoqi, to Jakarta in April 1963. Fortunately, by this time, Sino–Indonesian relations had started to warm up to a cordial level.

The Dual Nationality Treaty had already been implemented, which resulted in de-naturalising many Indonesian Chinese their Chinese citizenship status and thus provided Beijing an excuse to refrain from getting itself directly involved in the conflict. Above all, the personal power and prestige of Sukarno had in the meantime increased as a result of his success in curbing the various right-wing political groups. Consequently, Sukarno was able to suppress the anti-Chinese movement promptly this time, accusing the movement of being instigated by 'counter-revolutionary elements' and 'foreign subversive agents'.[26]

The 'Beijing–Jakarta Axis'

The Chinese effort to reconcile with Indonesia eventually bore fruit, with Sukarno accepting Marshal Chen Yi's invitation to pay another visit to China in June 1961. Dramatically, Sino–Indonesian relations began to improve, reaching another high watermark in April 1963 with China's Chairman Liu Shaoqi's first state visit to Indonesia. Sukarno demonstrated his personal commitment to the growing Sino–Indonesian relations with his firm intervention to put an end to the 1963 anti-Chinese riots.

The subsequent momentum in the strengthening of their relations was generated by a common strategy to de-emphasise domestic issues in Indonesia, which could easily arouse enmity on both sides, while turning attention to external issues on which both sides could find a great deal of common ground. In this way, Beijing and Jakarta could easily and expediently gloss over their underlying differences, particularly with regard to the explosive overseas Chinese issue, so that they could proceed to work out diplomatic co-operation over a wide range of international issues, from the ones like Taiwan and West Irian, which were of immediate relevance to their respective national interests, to those, like problems in the Congo, which only remotely concerned them in the area of ideology.

From Beijing's standpoint, its close alignment with Indonesia not only met the ideological premises of its foreign policy but also fulfilled its *realpolitik* needs. As a vast underdeveloped country with a large Communist party – the PKI boasting of being the third largest in the world at the time – and with a highly nationalistic leadership bent on continuing its anti-colonial and anti-imperial policy, Indonesia indeed appeared to be a country with full revolutionary potentials and one with which China could build a coalition as a 'third force' to rival the American and the Soviet blocs. In the early 1960s China's international position was extremely isolated on account of incessant hostility from the United States, the political and ideological break with the Soviet Union, and the border conflict with India. China was badly in need of the Indonesian alliance in order to forge the New Emerging Forces (NEFO) as a 'united front' to counter the influence of the United States and the Soviet Union.

Sukarno, as already noted, was also in need of Chinese support to carry through the romantic economic and social revolutions under 'Guided Democracy'. But the more decisive impetus that had driven Sukarno towards Beijing was the formation of Malaysia, which was viewed as a 'neo-colonial' creation and the ploy of imperialist powers to block Indonesia's traditional hegemony over the Malay states in the region. In launching the campaign of *Konfrontasi* to *ganjang* (crush) Malaysia, Sukarno also badly needed the diplomatic and material support of China.[27] And China incurred virtually no political costs in throwing its full support behind Sukarno's confrontation with Malaysia, which in any case had no political relations with China and had greatly irritated Beijing in the late 1950s by mounting a trade ban against certain Chinese products.

After Liu's visit to Jakarta both countries worked out a number of joint diplomatic ventures, designed to bring Sino–Indonesian relations into high gear, culminating in the convocation of the Games of the New Emerging Forces (GANEFO). Lavishly financed by Beijing, the GANEFO was held in Jakarta in November 1963 with a great fanfare, attended by some 51 countries. It was an occasion fully exploited by both Indonesia and China for their own political purposes.[28]

Meanwhile, the increase in the level of Sino–Indonesian co-operation was duly matched by the increase in affiliation between the Chinese Communist Party (CCP) and the PKI. After the middle of 1963, PKI's General Secretary, Aidit, decided to side with the CCP over the Sino–Soviet ideological dispute. Aidit's decision was influenced as much by the softening of the revolutionary ardour on the part of the Soviet Communist Party due to revisionism, as by the failure of the Soviet government to provide clear-cut support to

Indonesia over its confrontation with Malaysia. The winning over of the PKI to the Chinese side was of course considered by Beijing a crowning victory in its ideological struggle with the Soviet Union, particularly in the context of the 1960s, when ideological motives took precedence over every other consideration in almost all policy areas.

PKI's ambitious bid for more power and greater influence in Sukarno's government actually complicated matters for Beijing. In August 1964 Sukarno asserted that the goal of the Indonesian revolution was socialism and that the best means of achieving this goal under the Guided Democracy was to combine nationalism, Islam and Communism, a fusion called NASAKOM. Immediately, the PKI pressed for the formation of a NASAKOM cabinet and even a NASAKOM system in the armed forces, thus heightening the suspicion of the anti-Communist groups. The growing ambition of the PKI in domestic politics had the effect of uniting Sukarno's opponents, who were not just anti-Communist but also resentful of Indonesia's increasing diplomatic dependency on China.[29]

In the third quarter of 1965, Beijing seemed to have come close to achieving great-power politics in Southeast Asia by forming a long-sought anti-imperialist alliance with Indonesia and by winning over to the Chinese side the world's third largest Communist party, the PKI. However, all these 'achievements' were no more than self-delusion, and they were shattered almost overnight by the *Gestapu*, or the 30th September Coup.

Despite early allegations of China's involvement with the coup, mostly advanced by the Western media within the Cold War framework, China was obviously as much caught by surprise by the coup as any other country. After the détente, there was virtually no serious suggestion implicating China's role in the coup. In recent years, even the PKI's true role in the coup was seriously disputed.[30] The true nature of the coup and the real plotters behind the scene may continue to be an enigma for a long time to come. But as far as China's involvement is concerned, it is clear that if there were a single shred of concrete evidence which might incriminate Beijing, the post-coup Indonesian government, strongly anti-Chinese and vengefully anti-Communist, would have no qualms whatsoever in exposing it.

The coup brought the Beijing-Sukarno-PKI alliance to a violent end. It provided the army with the excellent chance to seize power and liquidate the PKI by force. It also sparked off another anti-Chinese avalanche, which in the past could have been restrained by Sukarno had he still been in power but was now more or less condoned by the military junta headed by General Suharto, who was swept into power after having suppressed the dissident officers who originally started the coup.[31] Having been closely allied with the PKI, China was obliged to provide political asylum to some leading PKI exiles. Accordingly, Sino–Indonesian relations sharply deteriorated. Later, as the Indonesian generals intensified their campaign against the Chinese minority in Indonesia and allowed mobs to attack the Chinese Embassy in Jakarta, Beijing also took a radical line by encouraging the PKI remnants to take up armed struggle to overthrow the military government. After a series of ugly confrontations, formal Sino–Indonesian relations were finally suspended in October 1967.[32]

The Growth and Structure of Sino–Indonesian Trade

With Sino–Indonesian relations so riven with political vicissitudes during this period, what has been the role of trade in the relationship? How have economic relations intertwined with political relations?

Sino–Indonesian trade started off from a very low level, not because of direct political intervention but because of the severe dislocations both economies had suffered as a result of their respective revolutions. Between 1950 and 1952, Chinese imports of raw materials from Indonesia virtually came to a halt while Indonesian imports of even traditional items from China were reduced to a trickle. It was not until the signing of the 1953 Trade Agreement that Sino–Indonesian trade was finally revived, and by this time the Chinese economy had been fully rehabilitated.

Once Sino–Indonesian relations were normalised after Ali came to power, the two-way trade moved ahead quite fast. In 1954, China exported US$ 3.5 million worth of goods to Indonesia in exchange for US$2.8 million of Indonesian imports. In the following year, riding high on the Bandung spirit, Chinese exports to Indonesia trebled and then doubled again in 1956. In the same period, Indonesia's exports to China increased by $2\frac{1}{2}$ times in 1955 and by another 80 per cent for 1965. (See Table 2.1.)

The favourable political environment after the Bandung Conference in 1955 was a great boost to the development of Sino–Indonesian economic relations, with the trade having grown by another great leap, reaching a peak in 1959. As shown in Table 2.1, Indonesia's imports from China in 1959 had increased by six times over 1955 and exports to China by eight times. Unlike other countries in Southeast Asia, Indonesia had managed to keep its trade deficits with China to a minimum, because trade between China and Indonesia was mainly conducted on a government-to-government basis with both sides agreeing to maintain the trade in balance as a matter of principle (Article III of the 1953 Trade Agreement).

In 1955 as Chinese goods reached Indonesia in large quantities, they captured 1.6 per cent of Indonesia's market. By 1959, the Chinese share jumped to 13.4 per cent, far surpassing the 3.7 per cent of the Netherlands. As for Indonesia's exports to China, the share increased from 0.6 per cent in 1955 to 5.9 per cent in 1959, ranking Indonesia as China's most important source of imports from Southeast Asia. (See Table 2.2.)

The sharp rise of Sino–Indonesian trade between 1955 and 1959 was not just the result of increased Sino–Indonesian understanding during this period but also part of China's overall trade drive to Southeast Asia. In the later part of the 1950s, successful implementation of the First Five-Year Plan had enabled China to produce a wide variety of light industrial products which found ready markets in countries in Southeast Asia, which had yet to start their industrialisation. Apart from rice, foodstuffs, and other traditional items, China began to export to Indonesia for the first time a wide range of manufactured goods such as sewing machines, paper products, household goods, cement and building materials, as well as cheap cotton piece goods. Chinese goods competed fiercely with similar goods from Japan and virtually drove the high-priced Indian products out of the Indonesian market.[33] Apart from selling at genuinely low prices, China also adopted various aggressive sales techniques to undercut its rivals. The same phenomenon was seen in the markets of Malaysia and Singapore. In fact, the rapid advance of Chinese imports in Malaysia and Singapore so alarmed the Malayan Federal government that anti-dumping measures were instituted to curb Chinese textile imports. However, the Indonesian government did not choose to intervene against Chinese imports, partly because the trade was regarded as mutually beneficial. The Malayan trade ban against China, as will be discussed in the next chapter, was primarily motivated by hostile political factors which were not present in the Indonesian scene at that time.

Indonesia's imports from China started to decline in 1960, coinciding with the decline in Sino–Indonesian political relations due to the anti-Chinese crisis, sparked off by the retail trade ban. In reality, the fall of the two-way trade after 1959 was due more to China's domestic economic setback caused by the collapse of the Great Leap Forward movement, for similar decline was also experienced in Pan-Malaya's trade with China.

Sino–Indonesian trade started its recovery in 1963. After 1964, the trade began to shoot up in conjunction with the buoyant state of Sino–Indonesian relations as both countries headed towards closer diplomatic alignment. By 1965, with the formation of the Beijing-Jakarta axis, Sino–Indonesian trade reached a new peak with a total turnover of US$ 139 million. In 1959 China, taking up 13.4 per cent share of the market, was Indonesia's third largest supplier of goods, after Japan and the United States. By 1965, China's relative share in Indonesian market increased to the record level of 16.5 per cent and climbed up to the second position. This brief episode of brisk trade between China and Indonesia was a typical example of how trade could interact with political relations, with the two mutually reinforcing each other.

The commodity composition of Sino–Indonesian trade was relatively simple. In 1955, when the trade started to grow rapidly, Indonesia's imports from China consisted predominantly of textile goods to the extent of 70 per cent. Since then, textiles continued to grow in absolute terms but their relative share tended to fluctuate in accordance with the amount of Indonesia's rice purchases each year. Thus in 1959, when Indonesia imported a huge quantity of rice from China (amounting to 44 per cent of its total rice imports), the proportion of textiles fell to 25 per cent. In 1963, when the Chinese rice exports were cut down, the textiles share went up. Rice has since been a dominant item in Indonesia's imports from China until very recently. (See Table 2.3.)

For almost three decades until 1979, Indonesia has persistently suffered from rice deficits, so that it became the world's largest rice importing country. In the early 1960s, Indonesia's rice imports rapidly increased, both in absolute quantity and in terms of the world share. Alarmed by the drain on the country's scarce foreign exchange,

Sukarno attempted to ban rice imports in August 1964 except from countries with unexpired rice agreements, which included Burma, Thailand and China. After the 1965 coup, Indonesia reappeared as a major rice importer.[34] With the single exception of 1959, Indonesia was not over-dependent upon China for rice supply. Before 1965, Burma used to be Indonesia's largest source of rice imports, with Thailand coming next and with China occasionally supplying a substantial volume. After Indonesia's suspension of its diplomatic relations with China, the rice supply from China, mainly via Hong Kong as re-exports, at times dwindled to a minimal level. But during the world food crisis of 1973–4, China suddenly emerged to become Indonesia's top supplier when supplies from other regular sources plummeted.[35] In 1974, Chinese rice accounted for 55 per cent of Indonesia's total foreign rice, and in 1975 it jumped to 75 per cent. With a 75 per cent share, rice thus became the single most important item in China's exports to Indonesia in 1975.[36]

The prevailing position of Chinese textiles in the Indonesian market also merits attention. Since the middle of the 1950s, Chinese textiles steadily expanded their shares in the Indonesian market. As shown in Table 2.4, during the peak year of 1965 Indonesia imported 76 per cent of its cotton weaving yarns and 35 per cent of its cotton fabrics from China. The proportions would be higher still if the sizeable amounts of Hong Kong's exports (of China origins) to Indonesia were also taken into account.

As for Indonesia's exports to China, the commodity structure was exceedingly simple: it was almost entirely made up of rubber. At times, China did try to diversify a little by importing some amounts of sugar, spices and quinine salts. But even for rubber, from Indonesia's standpoint, the Chinese demand was not all that important. In the best year, 1964, when China shifted some of its rubber purchases from the Singapore rubber market to Indonesia in support of Sukarno's confrontation against Malaysia, China only bought 19 per cent of Indonesia's total rubber exports. There were two reasons for this low import demand. First, the Chinese economy was obviously too underdeveloped to generate a higher consumption for natural rubber. Second, Indonesian rubber was not sufficiently competitive against Malaysian rubber in terms of quality and standardisation.[37] The upshot none the less underscores one basic structural weakness in China's trade relations not just with Indonesia, but with the rest of Southeast Asia: namely, the relatively limited absorptive capacity of the Chinese economy for the raw materials from Southeast Asia.

To strengthen its alignment with Jakarta, Beijing also employed an active economic assistance programme as part of its economic diplomacy. In trading with the non-aligned Afro–Asian countries, China in the 1960s always stressed its policy of 'equality and mutual benefit'. To uphold such a principle, China must not allow excessive trade imbalances to be built up in its bilateral trade relations with friendly countries. In the case of Indonesia, the principle of balance of trade was also provided in the Sino–Indonesian Trade Agreement of 1953, as one of the cornerstones of mutual benefit. Since the re-opening of regular trade in 1955, Indonesia's imports from China tended to outstrip the growth of its exports to China, leaving the trade balance increasingly in China's favour. To allow Indonesia to import rice and to reduce Indonesia's overall trade deficits with China, Beijing had to grant a loan of US$ 11.5 million to Indonesia in April 1958 at a nominal interest charge of 2.5 per cent. Soon another loan of US$ 13 million was extended on the same terms in October 1958.[38]

In October 1961, following the abatement of the anti-Chinese movement in Jakarta, China signed an economic co-operation agreement with Indonesia, offering another low-interest loan of US$ 30 million for developmental purposes. The agreement was later revised in August 1963 in order to cover Chinese assistance in the construction of eight spinning mills in Indonesia. As Sino–Indonesian relations moved into high gear in 1965, China's aid programme also expanded considerably. In January 1965 China offered an interest-free loan of US$ 50 million to Indonesia to bolster the 'Beijing-Jakarta axis', and on the very eve of the *Gestapu*, 30 September 1965, China further committed two more such loans totalling US$ 150 million.

In retrospect, no amount of economic benefit from China's trade and aid packages, however favourable to Indonesia, could have stemmed the tide of political change sparked off by the *Gestapu*, and the subsequent spread of anti-Chinese violence. When Beijing was finally forced by hostile political climate to abandon its economic aid programme to Indonesia in 1966, the total economic aid effort extended between 1956 and 1966 in net terms amounted to US$ 105 million.[39] The aid projects completed included a paper mill and two textile mills, plus others (such as a conference hall) which were started but had not been fully completed owing to the sudden freezing of Sino–Indonesian relations after 1966.

It was recognised by such international organisations as the OECD that China had made the 'most important aid effort among the countries with a centrally-planned economy'.[40] Between 1956 and 1972, China had extended a total of US$ 2699 million of economic credits and grants to Third World countries, 49 per cent of which had gone to Africa.[41] Between 1969 and 1972, the net flow of bilateral ODA (Official Development Assistance) from the OECD countries and from multilateral agencies to Indonesia amounted to US$ 1879 million, or equivalent to 70 per cent of China's total aid efforts for two decades. In other words, Beijing would have to concentrate its entire aid effort upon Indonesia to keep it within the Chinese orbit. Indonesia is a big, underdeveloped country with an appetite for economic assistance well beyond any single source, and certainly beyond the limited capacity of the almost equally underdeveloped China. This simple extrapolation is sufficient to show that it could have been a disastrous economic liability for China to sustain the Beijing-Jakarta axis, had it not been broken up by the coup.

Sluggish Return to Normality

Whether or not the PKI was really the main culprit behind the coup, the plotters failed to gain control of power and thus allowed the army to take counter-measures by staging its own *putsch*. In one stroke, the army led by General Suharto succeeded in virtually wiping out the PKI and other opponents after a violent purge. In the process the pent-up anti-Chinese feelings were also unleashed, interacting with and mutually reinforcing the anti-Communist movement instigated by the army. China soon fell victim to this relentless anti-Communist movement. Seized by its own political upheaval arising from the Cultural Revolution, Beijing also took a tough line against Indonesia. In the event, Beijing's clumsy diplomatic tactics, manifested in its violent attack on the Indonesian government in the post-coup period, actually played into the hands of Suharto who, after stripping Sukarno of all his power and influence through a series of shrewd manoeuvres, finally moved to deliver his *coup de grâce* to the

Beijing-Jakarta axis on 24 April 1967 by expelling the Chinese envoy from Jakarta.[42] The demise of the Sino–Indonesian alliance left behind scars of bitterness and personal antipathy that were to render subsequent normalisation of relations extremely difficult.

As China emerged from the Cultural Revolution to embark upon a conciliatory foreign policy, it again stressed peaceful coexistence with its neighbouring countries to the south, and moved quietly out of polemic areas with Indonesia. After 1969, Chinese media coverage of Indonesian affairs dropped off sharply and Chinese declarations of support for the PKI became more perfunctory.[43] As the general détente swept through the region, following President Nixon's Beijing trip, China made it known that it was ready to start new relations with countries in Southeast Asia free from the past Cold War assumptions. China proved this by starting rapprochement with countries like the Philippines and Thailand, which had been staunchly anti-Communist. In this way, the ball was in the court of Jakarta, and the onus was on Indonesia for any delay in the resumption of Sino–Indonesian relations.

On the Indonesian side, the hard-line policy towards China seemed to be showing signs of softening up around 1970, partly in response to the pressure of international détente and partly because Suharto had by now securely consolidated his political position against any potential threat from the ill-fated PKI. Thus, in 1969, Foreign Minister Adam Malik declared that Indonesia would welcome restoration of relations with China provided China stopped what he called 'subversive activities in Indonesia and anti-Indonesian propaganda'. In 1971, following the first signs of Sino–American rapprochement, Malik announced that Indonesia was also taking certain unspecified initiatives in an effort to re-open diplomatic relations with China. He was particularly in favour of resuming direct trade links with China for the simple reason that Chinese goods were already plentiful in Jakarta, having got in through indirect channels. He also encouraged Indonesian businessmen to take the initiative in establishing direct trade deals with China without having to wait for the government. Above all, Malik was chairing the historic UN General Assembly session which voted China into the United Nations. He could not have failed to observe the wind of change towards détente in world politics, and that may explain why he has ever since become one of the leading advocates among the Indonesian power elite for the normalisation of relations with China.

In practice, however, the Indonesian government's approach to China throughout the early part of the 1970s was extremely cautious. While other countries in the region pressed on with the détente process, Indonesia even tried to 'dampen the China mood' by prohibiting Indonesian participation in the Afro–Asian Table Tennis Tournament held in Beijing in November 1971. Jakarta sought to rationalise its policy of avoiding China by resorting to Cold War rhetoric, such as accusing China of continuing support for the outlawed PKI.[44]

After the Philippines and Thailand had recognised China in response to the new geo-political balance brought about by the fall of Indochina, Jakarta seemed to be running out of credible rationale for further procrastination. In November 1975 Malik began to unveil the real obstacles for Sino–Indonesian relations by attributing them to 'strong anti-Chinese feelings within the country', so that 'the decision to normalise relations with Peking could not be taken without considering the repercussion in the next hundred years in Indonesia'.[45] As President Ford was on his way to Beijing to renew. Sino–American détente, Malik, in his most candid moment, frankly admitted that it was only Indonesia's domestic problems, not the external behaviour of China, that had so far kept his country from re-establishing diplomatic ties:[46]

There are no obstacles between the two governments . . . The difficulty, frankly speaking, is not between Indonesia and China but between ourselves. Here there is not only anti-Communist feeling but also anti-Chinese. That's what makes us afraid. . . . We need time to educate both the Indonesians and the Chinese (in Indonesia).

Malik's disclosure came as no surprise to any serious student of Indonesian affairs. In a nutshell, the real impediment to normalisation, shorn of its political rhetoric, boils down to: (1) the latent anti-Sinicism in Indonesian society and (2) the opposition from the Indonesian military and the ultra-rightist groups. Modern Indonesian history is replete with incidents of outbursts against the ethnic Chinese. Even during its comparatively short spell of relationship with China, there were still several anti-Chinese outbreaks, as discussed above. Suffice it to say that traditional anti-Sinicism in Indonesia has deep economic and social roots, quite transcending politics and ideology. But this sentiment has been often used by some politicians to deploy the ethnic Chinese in what has been known as 'scapegoat politics'.[47]

Opposition from the right-wing groups against the resumption of diplomatic links with China is easily understandable. China was the main external backer of the PKI, which was threatening the army and was ideologically antipathetic towards the Muslims. Furthermore, the PKI was widely perceived to be the real plotter of the coup and China was thus implicated. Many opponents of the normalisation policy still retained, even well into the 1970s, bitter memories of the bloody coup, while others still believed in the 'bogey of international communist conspiracy'.

As an example of the latter kind of political mentality among some members of the right-wing groups, Lieut-Gen Yoga Sugama on 25 November 1975, accused China of 'undermining Indonesia's growing industry by smuggling in Chinese-made goods worth US$40 million a year'.[48] The statement was promptly corrected the following day by Malik, who explained the smuggling activities could not be attributed to Beijing and that a great deal of Chinese-made goods were in fact legally brought into Indonesia as re-exports from Singapore and Hong Kong.

The event also provides a glimpse of the long-standing policy debate on China among the Indonesian power elites. By and large, progressive and forward-looking elements in Indonesia's foreign affairs establishment and some relatively more liberal politicians, such as Vice-President Malik, might have recognised the advantages of normalising relations with China in line with the predominant world trends. However, the conservative forces in the Indonesian power structure, mainly represented by the anti-Communist military but with strong backing from the ultra-nationalist and religious elements, were obviously not fully reconciled to the idea of rapprochement with China, which they regarded as the primary source of the coup. As they controlled the power apparatus in the country, their adamant refusal to accept normalisation with Beijing naturally resulted in an absence of headway in Sino–Indonesian détente, leaving the liberals to play 'shadow diplomacy'. Thus for over a decade since the Indonesian government, under the international pressure of détente, started re-examining its China policy, the official views on the question of resuming diplomatic ties with Beijing have often been reduced to a chronicle of inconsistent statements and self-justifying rhetoric.

In January 1977 Adam Malik (then still Foreign Minister) announced that normalisation of relations with China would be carried out after the general election in May 1977, as all obstacles to re-establishing relations had been eliminated. He further noted that Beijing had already stopped its hostile propaganda against Indonesia and no longer supported the PKI exiles.[49] In fact, at the 25th Congress of the Soviet Communist Party in early 1976, the PKI, along with the Philippine Communist Party, dramatically switched its allegiance from Beijing to Moscow.

Earlier, the powerful Lt-General Ali Murtopo, Deputy Chief of the State Intelligence, also said that the Indonesian government had 'solved the status of about two million of the four million Chinese living in Indonesia'.[50] In March 1977 there were clear signs that the Indonesian government was finally preparing to resume diplomatic ties with China, as Malik in a television interview confirmed that 'China had prepared the former embassy in Peking, and a new Chinese embassy in Jakarta was being arranged'.[51]

Hardly had these optimistic remarks been uttered than other members of the Indonesian government were preparing to backtrack. On 21 May 1977, after China's official Xin-hua news agency reported that Chairman Hua Guofeng in Beijing had 'received cordially' Jusuf Adjitorop, a prominent leader of the PKI, Indonesia's Defence Minister Gen Maraden Panggabean, in his capacity as interim Foreign Minister, quickly accused Hua of 'committing an act that would not help immediate normalisation of relations between the two countries'.[52] When Chinese Senior Vice-Premier Deng Xiaoping refused to declare during his three-nation ASEAN tour China's readiness to abandon party-to-party relations with the local Communist movements in ASEAN, Indonesia's new Foreign Minister, Professor Mochtar Kusumaatmadja, immediately responded by stating that Deng's failure to dissociate China from local insurgents had caused a 'setback' in Indonesia's normalisation process with China.[53] About three years later, in August 1981, Chinese Premier Zhao Ziyang during his ASEAN trip explained to the Malaysian leadership that China's connection with the regional Communist Parties was a 'question left over from history' and that China needed time to resolve that problem. Zhao also emphasised that China's support of the local Communists had not got beyond the political and moral aspects. The Malaysian government, now under the new leadership of Mahathir, was not happy with Zhao's clarification. Mochtar was the first outside Malaysia to respond by pointing out that Zhao's explanation was not 'convincing'.[54]

Was Mochtar looking for a new *raison d'être* for his government's failure to come up with some positive action to end the deadlock with China? Back in October 1978 Mochtar declared that Indonesia had already finalised preparations for normalising relations with China, though he could not provide an exact time.[55] Less than three months later, speaking to Indonesian newspaper editors, he had quietly altered his position, stating that Indonesia 'still has no intention' of normalising relations with China.[56] Towards the end of 1979, he was once again more optimistic. He told the press at the Singapore airport that 'Indonesia had long had the intention of normalising relations with China; but the question was putting it into effect'. He further reported that the position had 'improved politically and technically', with Indonesia 'now far more down the road towards normalisation'.[57]

In fact, at the beginning of 1980, Mochtar provided so many clear hints of his government's intensified efforts at normalisation that rumours started to circulate in Jakarta that exchange of ambassadors was imminent. But the let-down came a few weeks later, when President Suharto made no reference whatever to relations with China in his long, wide-ranging budget speech in Parliament. Hence noted one journalist:[58]

> It is not the first time the civilian-led Foreign Ministry appears to be out of step with some other probably more powerful departments of Indonesia's military-backed government.

Having squashed the rumours started by Mochtar, Suharto himself rekindled speculation by telling the departing West German Ambassador, Gunther Schoedel (leaving for his new assignment in Beijing) that diplomatic relations with China would be restored in the 'near future'.[59] By now few observers would remain seriously interested in the Indonesian 'time table' except that this was the first time Mr Suharto was reported to have issued such a clear overture. All along, Suharto had been extremely reticent over the China policy, allowing his ministers to issue numerous ambiguous statements, which were denied or re-interpretated later.

As it happened, optimism did not last. In less than a month Mochtar reduced expectation for a quick breakthrough when he was reported as saying that he saw no reason for an early resumption of diplomatic ties with China.[60] With so much confusion already in the air Malik, now Vice-President, found it necessary to do some explaining in regard to Indonesia's interpretation of the word 'soon', which government officials had used so often in their China policy announcements. Jokingly, Malik explained: 'Soon in the Javanese language might mean quite a long time – a day, a month or a year.'[61] But a year had *soon* passed by! Surprisingly, Malik attempted yet another normalisation forecast in July 1981 when he stated that Indonesia would 'consider normalising diplomatic relations with China after next year's general election.'[62] The general election was duly carried out in May 1982 (without resulting in any major reshuffle of the Indonesian power structure), but the normalisation was not. Twice Malik's normalisation predictions did not come true, and Malik was the Vice-President of Indonesia. Has the Sino–Indonesian rapprochement process in recent years run into new problems?

It should be noted that Sino–Indonesian relations at the unofficial level have experienced considerable improvement since 1977. In September 1978 a Chinese delegation visited Indonesia to attend an international forestry conference, and its chief delegate Mr Wang Pin was warmly received by President Suharto. In April 1980 China also sent a small delegation to participate in the 25th commemoration of the Bandung Conference. On that occasion, the official Chinese Xinhua news agency featured a dispatch praising Indonesia for upholding the non-alignment spirit of Bandung and making an 'indirect but firm appeal' to Indonesia for the early resumption of relations.[63] Above all, beginning with February 1980, Indonesia opened its door to direct trade with China, initially confined to certain commodities determined on a case-by-case basis.[64]

In the meantime Sino–Indonesian relations at the political level were complicated by the development of the Indochina situation, particularly over the Kampuchea issue. Since China's military intervention in Vietnam, the convergence of interests between China and ASEAN as a whole began to shift. At the same time, ASEAN's formerly unified stand on Vietnam was also showing strains, with Thailand and to some extent, Singapore, clearly identifying Vietnam as the main threat to ASEAN's security, whereas Indonesia, along with Malaysia, favoured a more conciliatory approach towards Vietnam. In Jakarta, there was a growing feeling that China was trying to exploit ASEAN's opposition to Vietnam's action in Kampuchea for political support in the conflict between Beijing and

Hanoi.[65] This was opposite to the view held in Bangkok, the capital of the frontline state of ASEAN.[66] Worse still, Indonesia took the view that in the long run China was in effect more dangerous than Vietnam in this region.[67]

In this way, Indonesian opponents to the normalisation policy could now employ the new geo-political rationale to reinforce existing domestic inflexibility. On the occasion of the 6th Asian Table-Tennis Tournament held in Jakarta in May 1982, in which the Chinese teams also took part, Mochtar fell back on rhetoric by repeating that Sino–Indonesian relations were improving but breakthrough could only be made when Beijing changed its attitude towards the PKI.[68] Clearly, Indonesia's détente with China could be a long drawn-out process. Significantly, China's well-tried 'Ping-Pong Diplomacy', which had successfully spearheaded China's détente process with all the other ASEAN countries, has failed this time to complete its task in the remaining one, the largest in ASEAN!

The Logic of Diplomatic Impasse

From the outset, Indonesia was clearly holding the initiative in its own hands over the resumption of Sino–Indonesian relations, and many Indonesian leaders were perceptibly proud of this. Back in 1973 Malik had this to announce: 'They [the Chinese] are awaiting from us. We shall inform them if and when the preparations have been completed'.[69] In 1980 Mochtar, with a touch of arrogance, was also quoted as saying that 'Indonesian influence, individually and through ASEAN, was stronger than that of China'. For this reason, he did not 'understand why some people in Indonesia wanted an early resumption of relations.'[70] The proud Javanese seemed to be twisting the tail of the dragon. From the standpoint of Beijing, there appeared to be no better alternative than taking a passive approach, for in so doing the responsibility for the diplomatic impasse would be squarely on Indonesia.

As for the sources of impasse, the main themes have been brought out for discussion in the previous section. But they merit recapitulation in this concluding section. Basically, the major obstacles as perceived by the Indonesian leadership boiled down to: (1) Beijing's past and continuing connection with the now decimated PKI and (2) the question of ethnic Chinese in Indonesia.

Many Indonesian military leaders, as pointed out earlier, not only viewed the attempted coup as the entire work of the PKI but also felt that Beijing somehow must have a role in it. Psychologically they linked their personal trauma of violence during and after the coup to the China issue. Subsequently, China's refusal to discontinue party-to-party relations with the PKI had, in their view, further reduced China's credibility and therefore reinforced their view that the 'Chinese tiger has not changed its stripes'.[71] Above all, some ultra-conservative elements of this group still have the Cold War mentality, fearing that potential subversive activities could be conducted by a Chinese embassy in Jakarta, even though the Indonesian government 'is said to be satisfied that the Chinese diplomatic missions in Kuala Lumpur, Bangkok and Manila have behaved correctly, with no suggestion of interference in the internal affairs of their host countries'.[72] The military quarters are naturally concerned with the security aspects of the China issue. But it is ironic that of all the ASEAN states Indonesia, being the strongest and physically most remote from China, should choose to be most apprehensive of China's threat in terms of territorial designs. Suffice it to say that the perception of China by the Indonesian military is as much affected by their personal prejudices and emotions as their ideological differences with China. None the less their views on China, however unrealistic, have reinforced those held by some elements of the Indonesian press.[73]

The Indonesian ruling elites have every right to stamp out the PKI in their country and to keep out the influence of Communism, be it the Russian form, the Chinese or the Vietnamese. The Indonesian economy has performed better under the existing political and social system and should continue to prosper without socialism. But it is becoming increasingly untenable to link domestic anti-Communist policy to the diplomatic question of re-establishing relations with one single Communist country (China) which ironically happens to be also the Communist country domestically engaged in the rapid process of de-maoisation (in a way, actual de-socialisation) and externally leaning towards the West. Furthermore, one fundamental ground rule in diplomacy is that recognition of a foreign government does not imply endorsement of its political and ideological systems.

Of greater concern should be the domestic anti-Chinese issue, which still poses a real problem in Indonesia today; the Indonesian government is perfectly sensible in taking various preventive measures before setting up ties with Beijing. As recently as 1980 there have been two outbreaks of anti-Chinese riots, one in Ujungpandang in April and the other in Semarang and Solo in Central Java in December. In both cases violence flared up over small incidents, which clearly reflects the social-pathological nature of the problem.[74] In both cases, the violence was localised and order restored after the security forces took stern action against the rioters.[75] These recent incidents are sufficient to show that anti-Chinese feelings are still widespread and deep-seated in Indonesian society. At the same time, they also serve to show that anti-Chinese sentiments have complex domestic, social and economic origins, entirely unrelated to any action or consequences of behaviour on the part of China.[76] Above all, the riots would not spread if there were no politically-motivated instigators. In short, the Indonesian government should find the problem of the residual anti-Chinese feelings manageable if they would refrain from playing 'scapegoat politics'.

It should be emphasised that the Indonesian government in recent years has indeed taken major steps towards a quick solution of its 'Chinese problem' in order to clear the way for the eventual re-opening of diplomatic ties with Beijing. Of three million or so ethnic Chinese in Indonesia, just over two-thirds have taken up Indonesian citizenship since the implementation of the Dual Nationality Act in 1960, leaving about 800 000 of them still stateless. In February 1980 President Suharto issued decrees to simplify procedures for granting citizenship to the alien Chinese.[77] Given the poor state of the Indonesian bureaucracy, it would take many more years to complete the registration process.[78] Prior to this the Chairman of the Parliamentary Commission on Foreign Affairs, Chalid Mawardi, had criticised the government for linking normalisation with the problem of overseas Chinese in Indonesia, because 'the problem would never be settled as the Chinese live in Indonesia forever'.[79]

Equally significant has been Beijing's efforts towards defusing the overseas Chinese issue in general. In setting up diplomatic relations with the individual ASEAN countries, China has always made a point of stressing that those ethnic Chinese taking up citizenship of their host countries would no longer be considered as Chinese nationals. In a further move the Chinese National People's Congress passed a new citizenship law in September 1980, to the effect that 'no dual nationality will be recognized for any Chinese national'.[80] So in legally preventing overseas Chinese from retaining Chinese citizenship, Beijing has done what it can in an effort to lay to rest the 'overseas Chinese bogey', which has concerned the Indonesian diehards for years.

What would Indonesia really get out of its renewed diplomatic relations with China? This is the question some realists in Jakarta used to pose in their policy debate on China.[81] To begin with, there are always competitive and complementary areas in economic relations among states, and it is up to individual governments to work out co-operative programmes to enhance their complementary relationship. In static terms, there is probably not much benefit for the Indonesian economy in the short run from interacting with the Chinese economy after the restoration of diplomatic relations. Actually, Indonesia would have immediately to repay China its past debt, totalling US$54 million, incurred by the Sukarno regime. Sino-Indonesian trade at its current level is still small in absolute and relative terms, and should remain quantitatively insignificant for some time, until the Chinese economy has become more extensively industrialised and can generate greater import demand for Indonesia's natural-resource-based exports. The resumption of Sino-Indonesian diplomatic relations could of course result in more direct trade, thus cutting out Singapore and Hong Kong. Indonesia could also diversify its export markets by sending some rubber and timber to China. In return, China could be relied upon as a supplementary source of supply for rice if domestic harvests in Indonesia fall short. Other than these, there are in fact not many *tangible* benefits in the economic balance sheet of a renewed Sino-Indonesian relationship. But the real point at issue is – should state-to-state relations be subjected to rigorous cost-benefit analysis? How many foreign embassies in Jakarta would have passed such a test? More specifically, how could the long-term spillover effects of the restoration of relations be included in the calculus, such as Indonesia's greater diplomatic leverage and better image as a truly non-aligned nation?

The futility of providing a complete rational explanation of government policies in Southeast Asia, as attempted above, becomes more apparent if considerations are taken of the political reality of these countries, which generally follow an authoritarian style of government. This means that the outcome of Sino-Indonesian relations, in the final analysis, depends very much on the personal decision of President Suharto, who alone has the real power to galvanise diverse opinions into a kind of consensus for such a difficult decision. Unfortunately Suharto, a leading member of the coup generation himself, is still very much haunted by the past. From Nixon to Marcos and Razak, leaders who have demonstrated considerable statesmanship in untying their Gordian knot on China have precisely the courage and the determination to declare a break with the past.*

* It has almost become a ritual that the final stage of détente with China is always marked by the foreign head of state making a well-publicised trip to Beijing, culminating in a grand tour of the Great Wall. This must have bothered Suharto, a very proud Javanese, who also does not seem to enjoy foreign travels. Hence the impasse?

3

Malaysia/Singapore's Relations with China – I

Introduction

'Malaysia' in this study refers to 'Peninsular Malaysia', which was known as the Federation of Malaya before 1963. From 1963 until its separation in 1965, Singapore was part of Malaysia. Throughout this chapter, the term 'Malaya' and 'Malaysia' are often used interchangeably, with 'Malaya' being used for the historical period. To reduce confusion, the term 'Pan-Malaya' is also introduced in order to include Singapore.

Pan-Malayan relations with China over the past three decades are characterised by two distinct features. Malaysia was the first nation in the ASEAN region to begin thawing its Cold War relationship with China, a process started soon after the perceptive Malaysian Prime Minister Tun Abdul Razak put forth in 1970 the celebrated concept of neutralising Southeast Asia. As the international détente in the region began in the early 1970s, Malaysia also became the first ASEAN country in the détente era to establish full diplomatic relations with China, thus pioneering the way for the Philippines and Thailand to follow suit. Malaysia's diplomatic breakthrough with China became even more significant if the event were put in the context of their past mutual suspicion, antagonism and fear. For years, both before and after Malaysia's independence, the Malaysian government had been the direct target of the armed Communist insurgency. Worse still, the Malaysian insurgent movement (like

Singapore's local Communist movement) was basically led and controlled by the ethnic Chinese, and Beijing at one time openly provided them with moral and perhaps even material support. Malaysia's relations with China were thus linked Malaysia's international security and racial problems, which remain the most explosive political and social issues in Malaysia to this day.

Indeed, the question of ethnic Chinese has been and will still be a critical problem in Malaysia's, and even Singapore's, official relations with China. Pan-Malaya houses the largest conglomerate of immigrant Chinese in the world. The population of ethnic Chinese in these two countries is the largest outside of mainland China and Taiwan. With Chinese constituting more than 75 per cent of its total population, Singapore is basically a Chinese city and has been at times labelled as a 'Third China'. In the case of Malaysia, ethnic Chinese make up almost 40 per cent of its population and they wield disproportionately powerful economic influence. At the time when Malaysia's relations with China were very tense, the Malaysian Chinese were feared as a potential Trojan horse. In actual fact, most Chinese in Malaysia and Singapore have started to integrate themselves politically and socially with the local communities since the Communist revolution on the Chinese mainland. But the majority still retain their dominant traditional values, which inevitably link them culturally and even emotionally to China. Such links, however ambiguous and symbolic, have affected Malaysia's and Singapore's official relations with China.

Against the groundswell of international Cold War politics and domestic social and racial tensions, Prime Minister Razak's move to normalise relations with China at such an early stage actually equalled the efforts of President Nixon's in courage, far-sightedness and statesmanship. That is all the more remarkable for a country like Malaysia which used to follow an inward-looking foreign policy, maintaining a low profile in international and regional politics.

Pan-Malayan economic relations with China present an even sharper contrast to those of other ASEAN countries. For years, Malaysia and Singapore have been very much at the hub of China's overall economic relationship with the ASEAN region. China's trade with Malaysia and Singapore is by far the most important in terms of size, structure and durability, forming the mainstay of its overall trade with the whole region. There were times in the past when China's trade with Southeast Asia was virtually confined to Pan-

Malaya as direct trade with other ASEAN countries was either banned or reduced to a trickle owing to political intervention. Even in 1980, after China had resumed direct trade with all the ASEAN countries, the combined share of Malaysia and Singapore still accounted for 60 per cent of China's trade with ASEAN as a whole.

Furthermore, the Sino–Pan-Malayan trade has been the most durable in the sense that it has survived the most stormy period of the late 1950s, when a kind of 'trade war' was fought between the two sides in the market place of Malaysia. Indeed, Malaysia and Singapore are rare examples of countries, including the socialist states, which have successfully maintained continuous trade relations with China without having succumbed to the interferences of the Cold War, which in the case of Indonesia and Thailand had brought their trade with China to a complete halt. More significantly, for the greater part of the past three decades, China's trade activities with Malaysia and Singapore have been conducted in the absence of a formal diplomatic framework, each side being content with informal but practical arrangements that none the less proved quite effective in overcoming their political differences and even their mutual ideo-logical antipathy. Apart from the obvious economic considerations, some overriding historical forces or 'structural factors' must have operated to sustain this trade.

Historically speaking, trade between China and Pan-Malaya dates back to the early centuries. A 'fair amount' of trade was recorded as early as the Tang Dynasty (618–907). The early trade activities were, as usual, mixed with the tribute-bearing missions, a peculiarly Chinese way of conducting diplomacy with the smaller states in *Nanyang*. Regular and steady growth in trade started only after the second part of the nineteenth century, with the increased influx of Chinese immigrant labour into British Malaya.[1]

The Chinese had frequented the Malay lands long before the Portuguese conquered Malacca in 1511. In 1349, a Chinese trader gave an account of life in Tumasik, the name for old Singapore.[2] At this time the emperors of Ming Dynasty (1368–1644) sent a series of missions to *Nanyang* with a view to re-establishing the declining Chinese influence, and one of the envoys came to Malacca in 1403. Above all, the famous Admiral Cheng Ho led one expedition to Malacca in 1409 and subsequently made Malacca one of China's tributary states. However it was not until 1786, when Captain Francis Light of the English East India Company took possession of Penang, and Sir T. S. Raffles, also of the English East India Company, acquired a settlement in Singapore in 1819, that sizeable Chinese communities in Malaya began to grow.[3] In 1826 Penang, Malacca and Singapore were administratively brought together to form the Straits Settlements, subject to the British government of Bengal.

The economies of the Straits Settlements grew rapidly, partly because of peace and stability and partly due to the free trade policy of the British rulers. Singapore's free port status had been instrumental in its development into a major centre of trade for the whole Southeast Asian region. After 1842, when Hong Kong became a British colony, Singapore linked up with it to become an entrepôt centre for the rapidly growing trade between China and Southeast Asia.

Meanwhile, the population of the Straits Settlements grew along with the expansion of trade and other economic opportunities. In particular, Chinese immigrants began to flock to the Straits Settlements. In 1860, ethnic Chinese constituted 60 per cent of Singapore's total population of 82 000, 15 per cent of Malacca's 67 000, and nearly 30 per cent of Penang's 67 000.[4] The Chinese migrated into Malaya largely under the contract-labour system. They not only worked as traders and craftsmen, but also cultivated the land, and they soon dominated the economic life of the Straits Settlements.[5]

China's trade with British Malaya between 1868 and 1933 showed brisk growth, with Malaya's share in China's total trade fluctuating between 1 and 2 per cent.[6] The pre-war peak of Sino–Malayan trade was reached in 1926 with a turnover of about US $50 million, which level was never surpassed until after the Communists came into power in China. Throughout the 1930s the volume of this trade was reduced to around US $10 million, partly on account of the slow-down in the flow of Chinese immigrants to Malaya resulting from official restriction and partly as a result of the world depression.[7]

Before the Second World War Sino–Malayan trade appeared to be more important to Malaya than to China; it was around 8 per cent of Malaya's total imports but less than 2 per cent of China's. Chinese exports to Malaya were principally foodstuffs, traditional products and some sundry manufactures, including cotton piece-goods. In return Malaya supplied China with wood, bamboo and rattan as well as rubber and tin. The balance of trade, however, was consistently in China's favour, and such tendency has persisted to the present day.[8]

The trade was disrupted by the Japanese invasion of China, which also stirred up nationalism among the Chinese in Malaya, and their hostility towards Japan. Subsequently, as Japan conquered Malaya and Singapore in 1942, the Japanese militarists took revenge against the Chinese elites in Malaya and Singapore with wholesale massacres. The Japanese persecution drove many Chinese to join the Malayan People's Anti-Japanese Union, which was controlled by the Malayan Communist Party. The MCP, which was a predominantly Chinese organisation, actually received support from the Allies during the war. After the Japanese surrender the British returned to restore their authority and began to suppress the Communist movement – then the only credible challenge to British recolonialisation efforts. In the event the MCP took to the jungles and started armed guerilla warfare. This brought about the emergency in Malaya. Ever since, the question of MCP has been a thorny problem in Malaysia's and, to some extent also Singapore's, relations with China.

Development of Pan-Malaya's Trade with China, 1950–66

In 1947 China shipped M$122 million worth of goods to Pan-Malaya, representing 9 per cent of Pan-Malaya's total imports. It appeared that China was on the way to restoring its trade to the pre-war peak. However the civil war soon ravaged the Chinese economy and adversely affected China's overall foreign trade. In 1949 China's exports to Pan-Malaya were down to only M$76 million or just 4 per cent of Pan-Malaya's total imports.[9]

In contrast to some Southeast Asian countries, Sino–Pan-Malayan trade had not been terminated by the Communist revolution in China. In fact, the first year of the People's Republic seemed to mark an auspicious beginning for the new trade, with substantial increases in both China's exports to and imports from Pan-Malaya. China was particularly active in the Malayan rubber market in 1950, with a large purchase amounting to 39 000 tons, (or some 4 per cent of Malaya's total rubber exports in that year) as compared with China's average annual import of only 8000 tons between 1947 and 1949.[10] With this first shot China established its early credential as a potentially important buyer of Malayan rubber, the single most important commodity in Malaya's exports.

Chinese exports to Pan-Malaya started to decrease after 1952–53, as China set out to re-orient its overall foreign trade pattern towards socialist countries. Meanwhile, Pan-Malaya's exports to China also started their sharp decline, as the United Nations strategic embargo on China brought about a complete halt of rubber exports to China, thus reducing Pan-Malaya's exports, made up almost entirely of rubber, to a trickle between 1953 and 1955. (See Table 3.1.)

The turnabout came in 1956 when conditions favourable for the restoration of Sino–Pan-Malayan trade began to emerge. After success in industrialisation under the First Five-Year Plan (1953–57), the Chinese economy began to produce a wide range of labour-intensive manufactures for exports to the industrially less sophisticated markets. Countries in Southeast Asia, which had not yet started their industrialisation, became the natural target for China's first major trade drive, which was facilitated by the overall improvement of China's relations with the region following its participation in the Bandung Conference in 1955. In Bandung, Premier Zhou Enlai suggested positive measures whereby governments in Southeast Asia might resolve the citizenship status of the overseas Chinese. Pan-Malaya, not being a fully independent country at that time, did not take part in the Bandung Conference; but this did not prevent the political spillovers of the conference from reaching the Peninsula. Lee Kuan Yew, then only a budding politician, suggested that Malaya should sign a treaty with China similar to that concluded by Indonesia regarding the citizenship of overseas Chinese.[11]

In Pan-Malaya, the collapse of the Korea war boom touched off a recession, and economic hardship lent support to agitation against the UN embargo on rubber exports to China. Increasingly, the embargo came to be viewed as an unreasonable and ineffective Cold War policy pursued by the United States for its own political interest.[12] The clearest evidence of the self-defeating nature of the embargo could be seen in its many loopholes and its resultant lack of effectiveness in either undermining the Chinese economy or denying it supplies of strategic goods. To obtain rubber, China simply shifted its purchases from its traditional sources to Ceylon (now Sri Lanka). When Indonesia removed the rubber export restriction in early 1956, the Malayan government was under mounting pressure to follow suit.

Finally, on 4 June 1956, following Sir Anthony Eden's firm representation to the United States, the Malayan government announced the relaxation of the ban on shipments of Malayan rubber to China.[13] The lifting of the embargo coincided with the upturn of the Pan-Malayan economy. The renewed economic prosperity, coupled with the defeat of the Malayan Communist insurgents, made it possible for the Malayan authorities to be more relaxed and open-minded towards commercial contacts with China. On 17 July 1956 a 'China Products Exhibition' was staged in Kuala Lumpur; this drew huge crowds of people from different walks of life, especially the ethnic Chinese. The glittering display of a wide range of industrial artifacts, many of which were manufactured in China for the first time, made a deep impression on many ethnic Chinese in Malaya who took great pride in the industrial success of the 'New China'.

The exhibition was a great commercial success for China. It was a good sales promotion exercise, aimed at helping Chinese products to break into the local markets and promoting the long-term image of Chinese products as low-priced and reliable.[14] Indeed, this image, in part nurtured by an inherent sense of nationalism on the part of the ethnic Chinese, has lasted until recent years–when economic affluence has bred a generation of more sophisticated consumers who are less influenced by the cultural origins of the goods they purchase.

A month after the exhibition the first Malayan Trade Delegation, consisting mainly of influential Chinese business leaders, was invited to visit China. Although the mission was to have no official capacity, it had full government blessing and support. The delegation, apart from contracting on-the-spot deals with China's various export corporations, held talks with Chinese trade officials on means of improving the two-way trade between China and Pan-Malaya. China agreed to resume its purchase of Malayan rubber and undertook to supply Pan-Malaya with rice, soya beans, canned food, fruits and vegetables, sugar, cotton piece-goods, and a wide variety of light industrial products.[15]

In retrospect, the trade delegation appears to have paved the way for the rapid increase in Sino–Pan-Malayan trade for the following few years. In 1955 the total trade turnover was worth only M $27 million, but the volume rose to M $97 million in 1958, a threefold increase during that short period (Table 3.1). For the first time shops in Pan-Malaya were stuffed with Chinese merchandise: torches, toilet soap, fountain pens, sewing machines, bicycles, clocks, household hardware and a wide range of textile goods, in addition to the usual traditional items. All these products were very attractively priced.[16]

The climax of Sino–Pan-Malayan trade during the 1950s was reached in August 1958, when China became Pan-Malaya's best customer of rubber for the month with Chinese purchases totalling 15 000 tons.[17] In the same month, China offered to export to Malaya and Singapore first-grade rice at prices almost 25 per cent below those of Thailand, the traditional main source of supply for Pan-Malaya.[18] Meanwhile, China stepped up its export activity in Pan-Malaya in the manner that was widely dubbed as a 'trade offensive'. Individual Chinese firms often received letters from their former trade contacts in China, broken off by the Communist revolution. These offered attractive terms and conditions for trade. The Bank of China in Singapore and in Penang also actively promoted the China trade through easy credit and financing terms.[19]

The Malayan government soon came to realise that China's trade advance had gone too far and too fast, fearing that Malaya might become a convenient dumping ground for Chinese goods, which seemed to be undercutting all other foreign competitors as well as underselling local products. Kuala Lumpur was particularly concerned over the influx of cheap Chinese textiles and cement. Between 1955 and 1958, China's textile exports to Pan-Malayan markets increased by 140 per cent. In 1955 no Chinese-made cement had yet entered Malaya, but a year later it arrived in enormous quantities, at once capturing 15 per cent of the market.[20]

On 1 October 1958 the Malayan government took the textile merchants by surprise with the announcement that special permits would henceforth be required for importing cotton textiles of Chinese origin. On October 17 it was further specified that certain types of Chinese textiles, such as white and dyed cotton shirting and sheeting, white and dyed jeans, were banned from import. At the same time, restriction was also to be imposed on the import of cement from China. Pressure was put on the Singapore government to take similar action but Singapore, always more liberal towards trade and industry, only agreed to introduce the ban for a period of three months as a political gesture of support for the Federal government in Kuala Lumpur.[21] Towards the end of October the Malayan government further passed new banking legislation which prohibited the operation of 'banks under the effective control of a foreign government in the Federation', and stating that 'the only bank in the

Federation today which comes within the current policy is the Bank of China'.[22]

The immediate reaction'from China, apart from a loud protest, was surprisingly moderate. Chinese counter-measures took the form of sending open letters to ten big importers in Kuala Lumpur in the name of the China Council for the Promotion of Foreign Trade, a semi-government organisation, which charged the Malayan government with being unfriendly towards China by taking overtly discriminatory measures against Chinese goods.[23] Beijing also threatened to stop its purchase of Malayan rubber and suspend credit consignments of merchandise to Singapore and Malayan businessmen.

In reality the only concrete counter-action taken by China was the suspension, in November 1958, of the shipment of certain goods to Pan-Malaya. At the same time, Beijing left the door wide open for importers from Pan-Malaya, who could easily place orders for Chinese products through agents in Hong Kong.[24] Admittedly, this was a mild retaliatory action; but it was enough to stir up some uncertainty in the business communities in Kuala Lumpur and Singapore. In Singapore, the Chinese counter-measures touched off some panic buying and stockpiling of Chinese products.[25]

In retrospect the trade ban, which was never intended to be a total embargo but only a partial restriction on selective commodity items, did not produce much effect on the growth of Pan-Malaya's trade with China, as only about 15 per cent of China's annual exports to Pan-Malaya came under the restriction. This perhaps explains why the Chinese government remained calm in its initial response to Malayan government's 'anti-dumping' action. Beijing was wise in its half-hearted retaliation, which ensured that friction did not develop into a full-scale trade embargo, as had happened in Thailand after the 1958 military coup. In any case, the ban was introduced too late to have any impact on the trade for 1958, which still registered 21 per cent increase over 1957. But Sino–Pan-Malayan trade did hit the doldrums in 1959, falling by 17 per cent from 1958 (Table 3.1). The decline, however, was not just confined to textiles, which came under the ban, but also affected other products. Clearly, the tapering off of the trade after 1958 was due to additional factors. It later came to light that the Chinese economy experienced a serious setback between 1959 and 1961 as a result of the collapse of the Great Leap Forward movement. With drastic cutbacks of industrial and agricultural production in China the much-publicised Chinese 'trade offensive' in Southeast Asia, which at one time even 'hit the world's headlines'[26], fizzled out by itself by 1959, providing also a timely and convenient line of retreat for both China and Malaya.[27]

The downward slide in trade was arrested by 1960, and Chinese exports to Malaya began to pick up again in 1961. In spite of its economic difficulties, China managed to keep up substantial supplies of rice and sugar to the Pan-Malayan markets even though it had itself to import a large quantity of food from Australia and Canada. By 1963, the Chinese domestic economy had fully recovered, and so had its trade with Pan-Malaya. Despite the 'anti-dumping' legislation, China's total textile exports to Pan-Malaya in 1963 again soared to a high level of M $21 million, which was quite an increase from the low of M $16 million in 1959.

The formation of Malaysia in 1963 led to confrontation with Indonesia, which happened to be a close ally of China and a recipient of Chinese aid. This gave rise to a certain amount of trade diversion, especially with respect to the Chinese demand for Malayan rubber. In 1964, with a small purchase of only 114 tons, China virtually deserted the Malayan rubber market.[28] While causing a sharp decline in Malayan rubber exports to China, 'confrontation' did not check the steady growth of Chinese exports to Pan-Malaya. Consequently the trade balance grew even more unfavourable for Malaysia, providing Kuala Lumpur with new grounds for attempting another round of trade curbs on Chinese imports, which now included some relatively more capital-intensive items such as iron and steel products. Meanwhile, pressure was also put on the Singapore government to close down the Bank of China in Singapore.

As it turned out, political intervention this time was no more effective in checking the trade than it had been previously. The closure order on the Bank of China in Singapore was never implemented, as Singapore repealed it immediately after separation from Malaysia in August 1965. Similarly, the import restriction on certain Chinese goods did not prevent the increase of other items not covered by the ban. In fact, the trade of both Malaysia and Singapore with China continued to rise until 1967 when internal chaos in China caused by the Cultural Revolution started to restrict its growth.

The strained political relations between China and Malaysia were not immediately eased by the ending of confrontation. The Malaysian government continued to frown upon its China trade for some years more. At one point, the Malaysian government even contemplated to play the game of 'two-China' policy by strengthening trade links with Taiwan as a move to counteract Beijing's increasing commercial influence.[29] In any case, the tarnished external image of China during the Cultural Revolution only served to deepen the antagonism of the Malaysian government towards Beijing.

For Singapore, the shock of separation from Malaysia was politically and economically more important than the ending of 'Confrontation' with Indonesia. Both events, however, had an important bearing on Singapore's economic relations with China. In general, the conclusion of political hostility with Indonesia would provide Singapore the opportunity of resuming its former entrepôt role in the handling and transhipping of China's trade with Indonesia. In the short run, the separation actually had a mixed effect on Sino–Singapore economic relations. From the outset Singapore, as a free port, had been more liberal towards foreign trade than the relatively more inward-looking hinterlands of Malaysia. It had suffered no political or economic loss from Chinese 'dumping'. On the contrary, it stood to gain substantially from China's export drive, as 'Communist China is using the free port of Singapore as a focal point for its cut-rate drive to capture the important Southeast Asian textile market from Japan and India'.[30] The independent Singapore could now adopt a more open trade policy free from ideological hangovers. At the same time, it had to exercise great political sensitivity in conducting trade with China so as not to arouse fear from other Southeast Asian countries that Singapore might develop into a third China or gang up with China.[31]

Politics and Economics of Trade*

International trade has never been entirely free of political considerations even for countries with the best free trade traditions. The recent trade frictions between Japan and other developed countries are the latest examples of political intervention in the conduct of

* Part of this section is based on John Wong, *The Political Economy of Malaysia's Trade Relations with China* (Singapore, Institute of Southeast Asian Studies, Occasional Paper No. 20; February 1974).

foreign trade even in countries which usually depend on the working of the market forces for economic decision-making. When market economies deal with each other, political interventions in trade, such as tariffs, tax and subsidy policies, are considered legitimate because they are normally operated through 'means that preserve the appearance of free private competition'.[32] However, political interference becomes less acceptable to each party when a market economy is confronted with a socialist economy – because of their inherent structural as well as ideological differences. To the extent that economic activities in socialist countries are centrally-planned and foreign trade is a state monopoly, political influence on trade is an ever present possibility, and market economies are sometimes rightly wary of various consequences in trading freely with socialist countries. Thus East-West trade in the past, especially in the heyday of the Cold War, was frequently characterised by political recriminations, and slight issues could develop into 'intolerant diatribes leading to no solution'.[33] Such had actually been the case with Sino–Malayan trade until its normalisation in the 1970s.

The course of Sino–Malayan trade during the late 1950s and the early 1960s was indeed deeply coloured by politics. Until its extensive liberalisation in recent years, China had always insisted that, in theory, trade and politics could not be separated, even though more often than not China had approached trade with a great deal of hard-headed pragmatism. Ironically Malaya, a country known for its relatively liberal trading traditions, at least by average Third World standards, chose to play politics in its trading with China. It is to be remembered that a great deal of fuss during that period actually stemmed from the Malayan government's efforts to control and restrict its trade with China. Against the tense international political climate prevailing at that time and the rather weak institutional basis on which Sino–Malayan trade was conducted, even a small incident could easily be escalated into a 'trade war' with wide political ramifications. The moment Kuala Lumpur decided to regulate the import of certain Chinese products the event caught the world's headlines as the outbreak of a 'trade war' between Pan-Malaya and China. The Chinese export drive was sensationally described by Western media as a 'trade offensive', bent on 'dumping' cheap products to ruin the underdeveloped Southeast Asian economies. A typical example is found in the editorial of the *Far Eastern Economic Review* in November 1958, which declared that China had launched an 'economic war' against 'free countries' in Asia and called for an international crusade among the non-Communist countries to check it:[34]

> because the antagonists in this newest economic war are the Communist and the non-Communist nations of Asia. In so far as this is a part of the world-wide competition between the economic and ideological systems, a struggle between different valuations placed on human freedom and on the extent to which the present generation can be mortgaged for a future one, the advanced nations of the West have just as much at stake as their friends in this continent who are the direct victims of the new Peking's [economic] offensive.

EMBARGO

The United Nations trade embargo on China had been one of the factors aggravating, if not directly contributing to, the collapse of Malaya's short-lived export boom started by the Korea War. After the Chinese entered the war, the UN General Assembly recommended a strategic embargo against China. The United States government then extended it into restrictive trade embargo legislations against China, which spanned two full decades, starting with President Truman's Export Control Act of 1949 and ending with President Nixon's relaxation in July 1969.[35] Initially most non-Communist countries, under strong US pressure, complied with the UN embargo. With the ceasefire in Korea, however, ideologically motivated trade restrictions became increasingly difficult to justify. The first crack in the embargo came in 1952 with Ceylon's accepting a barter trade with China (Ceylonese rubber in exchange for Chinese rice) in the teeth of strong US opposition.

After 1954, pressure for reform and relaxation began to mount, particularly from member countries of the British Commonwealth and from Japan, which usually followed a less ideological trading policy. In that year, the prohibition list against the Eastern Soviet Bloc (the so-called COCOM list) was reduced whereas restrictions on trade with China (the so-called CHINCOM list) remained unchanged. During the first part of the 1950s, China maintained a very close political and economic relationship with the Soviet Union and countries in East Europe on account of China's 'Leaning to one side' policy, and depended on the Soviet Union for capital equipment and technology. The irrationality of the US-backed embargo in maintaining two separate lists against countries essentially in one bloc was obvious, because China could easily obtain goods denied to it in the CHINCOM list via the Soviet Union and its Eastern European allies. Once the banned goods could reach China, albeit indirectly, the whole cause of the embargo was lost. It only made China economically more dependent on the Soviet Union. The crack widened even more when countries in Western Europe decided to ignore the 'China differential' after 1954. And rubber was one of the 'marginal goods' that came under the 'China differential'. Hence high passion and strong feeling in Malaya over the embargo.

At the time of the imposition of the embargo, Malaya was still a British colony with a strong commitment to *laissez-faire* commercial policy, as in other British colonies. Malaya was naturally opposed to acts and policies which involve physical restriction on trade. Malayan resentment was heightened by the post-Korea War depression of the world rubber market. Hence the rubber merchants and plantation owners strongly disapproved of the China trade embargo.[36] In 1955 rubber and tin together accounted for 85 per cent of Malaya's total export earnings.[37] Thus a slump in primary product prices would also affect small holders, small traders and a diverse group indirectly.

It might be true that the China embargo incurred little direct cost to the United States on account of the limited trade potential between them at that time. As one China expert later rationalised:[38]

> At the time, the United States so dominated the world economy, and our economy depended so little on imports from China, that the restrictions on trade with China appeared to be a small price to pay for so important a goal in our foreign policy.

The same cannot be said of a small and open economy such as Malaya's, where export proceeds accounted for as much as 48 per cent of its GDP. The Malayan predicament caused by the trade embargo on China is best reflected in the misgivings voiced by the eminent Chicago economist, Harry Johnson:[39]

> attempts to restrict trade for political reasons, on either side, do far more damage to the country imposing the restrictions than to the intended victims of the restrictions, and especially so – for well-known theoretical reasons – when the restriction imposing countries are small and would normally be heavily engaged in trade.

Strictly speaking, the economic sanction was not without its cost even to the United States, which had to incur the burden of maintaining and policing the embargo, not to mention other, higher, costs in the form of negative political spillovers.[40] The cost-benefit calculus would appear even more unfavourable for the United States if the ineffectiveness of the embargo resulting from loopholes and non-compliance was taken into account. But it was the Dulles' era when Cold War rhetoric easily took precedence over rational economic issues. Thus Malaya's attempt to export rubber direct to China, instead of via ports in East Europe, met with strong criticism from the United States. The editorial of the *Far Eastern Economic Review* on 14 June 1956 thus noted:[41]

> Some congressmen of the more obscure type call the decision to ship Malayan and other rubber direct to China instead of through the Soviet Union or other devious routes as a 'tragic mistake'. What Britain is doing, said Senator Mundt, is making it easier for Red Communism to expand in Asia. 'Communism will dig its fangs into British interests in Asia as rapidly as it develops strength enough to do so' . . . One sympathises with the passion but not with the reasoning.

With opposition to the embargo steadily building up over the years, it is not surprising that as soon as the ban was lifted, in the middle of 1956, the Malayan Trade Delegation immediately took off for Beijing. One aspect of the delegation's activities in China was the negotiation of a rubber deal.[42]

DUMPING

The removal of the trade embargo coincided with China's move to expand its exports to the non-socialist countries and the resultant rapid export expansion was at first described as a 'well-calculated bid' to capture the Southeast Asian market in order to fulfil China's more grandiose plans for the 'flag to follow the trade'. Hence an eminent regional journalist warned in 1958:[43]

> From Tokyo to New Delhi, communist China's offensive in Asia is causing the greatest concern. Chinese goods in astonishing array and of high quality have already penetrated every market. Given the opportunity, they will capture the lot.

Japan, which had its own ambitious plans of economic expansion into Southeast Asia, was the first country to be deeply worried by the intrusion of Chinese exports into the South-east Asian market;[44] then India, being economically less efficient, became the first casualty of the so-called Chinese 'trade offensive' as Indian textiles were virtually squeezed out of some Southeast Asian markets, as in Indonesia.[45] The Chinese export expansion, launched with such momentum as to double its volume within two years, apparently became too much for the Malayan government – particularly since the drive was not mounted by individual traders from the private sector but was organised by a few state trading corporations, apparently with complete disregard for profits or costs. Thus China was accused of 'dumping' cheap textiles which, alleged Malayan Minister of Commerce and Industry, Mr Tan Siew Sin, 'were produced at the expense of the cost of living of the Chinese people'.[46] Accordingly, Mr Tan sought legislative measures to ban the import of Chinese textiles.

The 'anti-dumping' measures were introduced in December 1958 ostensibly on such familiar grounds as the protection of 'infant industries'. In reality there was in the whole of the Malayan Federation only one factory, employing 300 workers, to protect. This was the Malayan Weaving Mills Ltd in Johore, which had been opened a few months prior to the trade ban. But this factory did go on record as saying that it could compete with 'normal imports' from Hong Kong, India and Japan but not 'dumping' from China.[47]

Apart from the employment argument, Mr Tan also sought to justify the official anti-dumping measures on the basis of unfair practices of price-cutting by China. Tan argued that 'no commercial organisation, however efficient, could possibly compete with goods which are sold below cost'. He further cited the case of Hong Kong which had 'probably the most efficient textile industry', but had to 'shut down a fair proportion of its output as a result of large-scale and ruthless dumping by Communist China'.[48] But Mr Tan apparently avoided going into the full economic theory which would explain that the efficiency of Hong Kong's textile industry was precisely the result of open competition, not of protection!

Perhaps the most amazing aspect of official justification was its political self-righteousness. Hence Minister Tan stated:[49]

It will therefore be asked why we ban the one, that is Chinese textiles, and not the other, that is Indian, Japanese and other textiles.

The answer is simple. The one set of textiles comes in at commercial prices and the other comes in at prices which can reasonably be regarded as unfair competition. I say this because Chinese textiles have been known to be sold at prices which did not even cover the cost of the raw materials used in their manufacture. In addition, of course, under totalitarian regimes labour is employed under conditions hardly distinguishable from those of slavery and must accept whatever pittance as decided by the State.

Originally the ban was to operate for three months until detailed anti-dumping legislation came into force. The legislation would initially exclude Singapore on account of its free port status and also give special consideration to Penang for its entrepôt function. During the period, however, Singapore would have to work out its own legislative adjustments, eventually to follow the Malayan action.[50] This immediately aroused opposition from a wide segment of the Singapore community, which also criticised the Singapore government for 'blindly following the Malayan government in imposing similar measures of trade restrictions'.[51] Mr Yap Pheng Geck of the Chinese Chamber of Commerce urged the Singapore government not to be ruled by the policy from Kuala Lumpur on the trade ban. He argued that 'self-government will be meaningless if we cannot decide what we should do to protect our own economic interests'.[52]

In defence, Mr J. M. Jumabhoy, Singapore Minister for Commerce and Industry, pointed out that the Singapore economy was so closely interlinked with the Malayan economy that it was the 'clear duty of any Singapore government to do its best to prevent the undermining of the Malayan economy'. Siding with Tan Siew Sin, Jumabhoy further stated:[53]

It is quite apparent that the trading policy of China is strongly influenced by political considerations as is evidenced from the fact China has been selling those goods below the comparative producing cost of countries like Japan where there is a high degree of automation and where labour is cheap.

Jacob Viner has defined 'dumping' as price discrimination between two markets.[54] To speak of 'dumping' by a socialist economy is particularly ironical, precisely because 'dumping' has traditionally been used by the Marxist or Neo-Marxist writers as evidence of the 'anarchy of the market' under the capitalist system or as an inexorable consequence of the working of 'monopoly capitalism'. In reality, one can cite numerous examples of 'dumping' in the popular concept of the term by Soviet-type economies on the markets of non-Communist countries in the past.[55] In recent years, declining industries or depressed sectors of some advanced countries in the West have similarly complained of 'dumping' by such vigorous Asian NICs (Newly Industrialised Countries) as Hong Kong, Taiwan and Korea, in order to put pressure on the governments of the advanced countries to invoke protective measures.

Strictly speaking, 'dumping' by itself has no proper analytical meaning in economic theory. The fact that China exported low-priced textiles because they were produced by genuinely low-cost factors did not constitute 'dumping'. Chinese textiles had their own supply curves and cost structure which were necessarily different from those of Indian or Japanese textiles.[56] One has to establish the true resource cost of the export products before one can say if a particular export item is sold above or below the world prices. Just as it is almost impossible to compare relative prices across countries, it is also difficult to ascertain the real resource cost of the traded products. A case can legitimately be made that, as a centrally-planned economy, China is most likely to have an irrational price structure in the sense that its prices do not reflect scarcity relationships. If the Chinese were 'dumping' their below-cost products in the export markets, then the Chinese consumers at home would eventually bear the cost. This is not an uncommon practice among the dynamic, export-oriented countries: domestic consumers in Japan, Korea and Taiwan are known to have 'subsidised' the overseas buyers of their goods, when these goods are exported at very competitive prices.

The real issue, analytically speaking, should be on stability rather than on cost. The potentially harmful effects of a particular source of supply of goods, as Peter Wiles put it, should be judged not by the goods selling at lower prices but by the stability in their supply. It is 'dumping' associated with unpredictability and uncertainty of supply, and not 'dumping' in the sense of price-cutting, that should really worry the type of markets such as Malaya's.[57]

The Chinese complaint that their goods were being specifically discriminated against by the Malayan ban was certainly not without justification on the basis of the market shares argument. In 1958, the Chinese component in the Pan-Malayan textile import constituted only 9.3 per cent as opposed to 16.5 per cent of the Indian and 47.3 per cent of the Japanese shares. Similarly for cement, China's share was only 6.7 per cent as against Japan's 56.6 per cent and Britain's 31.9 per cent for the same year, as revealed in Table 3.2. Clearly, China was far from dominating the markets in the aggregate sense. If the Malayan authorities were really concerned with possible Chinese domination of their various markets, they should also ban the import of the equally cheap Chinese foodstuffs which amounted to as much as 45 per cent of Malaya's total food imports in 1958, with the shares for some individual food items being even higher – 50 per cent for eggs and 50 per cent for preserved vegetables.[58] It is therefore easier to see the Malayan ban as a political rather than an economic move, as Mr Yap Pheng Geck, Vice-Chairman of the Singapore Chinese Chamber of Commerce had bluntly put it:[59]

> I cannot understand how China can undersell the world suppliers in the Singapore market. It [the ban] must be a political measure.

Like many other politicians in defending a policy of trade restriction, Mr Tan Siew Sin actually drew most of his strength from non-economic arguments, including political emotionalism.[60] It may of course be added that a rational distinction between economics and politics was neither clear nor considered necessary in the heyday of Cold War. There was also a lack of proper understanding of the commercial practices and trade policies of Communist countries. Such misunderstanding was found even in the region's well-established *Far Eastern Economic Review*:[61]

> In a world where trade liberalisation is the order of the day China cannot expect to enjoy the advantages of other countries' liberalisation without on her side taking some steps in that direction; China restricts imports very rigidly indeed.

It may be asked what had really prompted the Malayan government to apply such drastic measures which were unprecedented in the commercial history of the country, especially since those measures were undertaken in the teeth of strong opposition from Chinese merchants and importers and, understandably, from a large segment of the Chinese community. To begin with, the significance of the Malayan government's perception of the issue of 'trade and subversion' was real and cannot be dismissed.[62] Kuala Lumpur still had clear memories of its combat with the predominantly Chinese insurgent movement. The Malayan government was apprehensive about the political implications of its trade with China. As Mr Tan

Siew Sin plainly put it, China's trading operations 'are completely controlled by the state and are often used as a weapon in their political armoury or in furtherance of their objectives or foreign policy'.[63] Beijing did not help matters by repeating its rhetoric on the inseparation of trade from politics, even though in practice it often tried to steer trade clear of politics.

At the back of its mind, the Malayan government was most concerned over the possibility of the Chinese government making use of trade to exert political influence on the ethnic Chinese in Malaya. It should be remembered that the decade of the 1950s presented a complicated scenario of fears, misconceptions and vague ideas about Beijing's potential involvement with the *Nanyang* Chinese.[64] Naturally the Malayan government felt great anxiety over the fast-growing China trade, which was always monopolised by Chinese traders and also appeared to have served mainly the needs of the Chinese community. In the 1950s, many Chinese in Pan-Malaya found the China-made products cheap, of good quality and familiar to their tastes. They actually referred to these products as *guo huo* or 'national products'.

In the economic perspective, the consistently unfavourable trade balance against Malaya had naturally added strength to the argument in favour of trade restriction. In much the same way many Western countries today are resentful of Japan for its persistent accumulation of trade surplus without opening up the domestic Japanese market. Sino–Pan-Malayan trade was often dubbed as 'one-way traffic'.[65] With the exception of rubber, the Chinese economy had limited demand for the main exports of Pan-Malaya. Even in respect of rubber, as will be discussed in the next chapter, the Chinese allowed their import demand to fluctuate in response to political requirement.

Besides, China's trade with Malaya was highly vulnerable to disruption on account of its special commodity structure. Apart from foodstuffs, Chinese exports to Malaya were made up of a wide range of textiles, household items and other consumer goods which were commonly considered 'non-essentials' with low income elasticities of demand. True, those commodity items could satisfy the consumption demand of the masses in the short run, but they were not regarded by the ruling elite as vital to the economy. Economically the most essential food item to be imported into Malaya was rice, as Malaya had a low degree of food self-sufficiency. But Chinese rice was imported in sizeable quantities only after 1959, that is after the trade dispute. In 1962 rice became the largest single item of Malaya's imports from China, representing some 15 per cent of the total, valued at M$172 million. It was rather ironic that such 'essential' food items as rice came into the Malayan market only in the aftermath of the trade ban and also at the time when China itself had to import a large amount of wheat from the advanced countries.

In retrospect, apart from the various underlying motivations, the introduction of the trade curb by the Malayan government had been prompted by the somewhat threatening posture of China's trade advance – the extremely fast rate of trade growth, the easy success by Chinese goods in breaking into certain established markets, the ruthless price-cutting, and some apparently unorthodox practices of offering a variety of non-price benefits to the merchants on the part of China's agents. Such an aggressive export drive on the part of a big economy would inevitably cause great concern to the government of the smaller importing country. To this must be added the fact that, nobody in 1958 could have foreseen that the Chinese trade advance in the late 1950s would dissipate of its own accord in 1959 owing to the collapse of the now discredited Great Leap Forward movement. In short, while the Malayan government appeared to have over-reacted in using somewhat high-handed measures to curb its China trade, the Chinese government also appeared to have over-exploited the Malayan market. The over-zealous Communist cadres in charge of China's various export corporations had yet to learn the capitalist way of exploiting an export market! Such a stormy period remains an important episode in Sino–Malayan relations, holding valuable lessons for both sides. Japan, as one of the interested onlookers of this mini 'trade war', stood to gain much from the beneficial spillovers of this drama. Japanese traders in Southeast Asia closely watched China's abortive 'trade offensive'[66] and they have profited enormously from the event and its outcome.

CONFRONTATION

Diplomatic achievement at the Bandung Conference had convinced the Chinese leadership that China could further its foreign policy advance by establishing friendly relations, or even alliance, with 'bourgeois' nationalist or capitalist regimes which were truly independent of the United States. Such view gained ground in Beijing rapidly towards the end of the 1950s as China's relations with the Soviet Union began to deteriorate. The 1963 Nuclear Test Ban Treaty further suggested to Beijing that the Soviet Union (the 'socialist imperialists') and the United States (the 'capitalist imperialists') had reached a tacit understanding on the need for political isolation, or even military encirclement, of China. The only diplomatic leverage left to China, to combat such super-power domination was for Beijing to cultivate better relations with the neutral nationalist states. Indonesia, the biggest country in Southeast Asia – led by the charismatic but highly nationalistic leader Sukarno – was an ideal partner in China's international 'United Front' strategy aimed at altering the power balance in Southeast Asia. This, along with factors already discussed in the previous chapter, had been the underlying incentive for Beijing to forge a very close relationship with Indonesia in the early part of the 1960s.

However Indonesia under Sukarno had the grand design of asserting hegemony over Malaysia and the Philippines. The formation of Malaysia in 1963 touched off open hostility from Indonesia, which viewed Malaysia not as an independent state but only a neo-colonial creation by Britain. Thus Sukarno launched the campaign, confrontation in order to 'crush Malaysia' (*ganjang Malaysia*).[67] China operated a double-faced policy during Confrontation. To support its Indonesian ally, China diverted its rubber purchases from Kuala Lumpur to Jakarta which were actually on a barter-buying basis. China also offered liberal trading facilities and generous inducements to Indonesian importers of Chinese goods. Above all, as already discussed in chapter 2, Beijing offered substantial economic and military aid to the Sukarno regime. Politically Beijing stood solidly on the side of Jakarta, stepping up from time to time anti-Malaysian propaganda in the Chinese media. Sino–Indonesian relations were so close that at one time the two countries came to form a kind of political axis. At the same time, China took great care to preserve its lucrative Malaysian market.

Given China's unfriendly attitude towards Malaysia, as clearly manifested in its open support for Malaysia's enemy, one would have expected that Malaysia would immediately have brought its trade with China to a complete halt, as in the case of Thailand with China in 1959, and Indonesia in 1967. But the Malaysian reaction to this challenge throughout confrontation was surprisingly moderate. Apart from re-asserting the partial trade ban on certain Chinese goods, the Malaysian government only sought to close the Bank of China in Kuala Lumpur and Penang, which was accused by Mr Tan Siew Sin of 'indulging in subversion'. Malaysia's continuing toleration of its 'suicide trade with Communist China' was a subject of amusement in its anti-Communist neighbour, the Philippines, where one of its newspaper editorials chided Malaysia for 'being fried in her own lard because her trade with Red China contributes to Indonesia's anti-Malaysia campaign'.[68]

Why had confrontation not killed the entire trade? One explanation from the Malaysian Prime Minister, Tunku Abdul Rahman, was couched in highly moralistic terms:[69]

Malaysia trades with China and in so doing it is hoped that the mutual benefits would in some way alleviate the internal economic difficulties of China so that she might be less prone to foreign adventures and interfering in the affairs of other countries.

Rhetoric of a similar nature was not lacking on the other side. Hence an equally self-justifying statement from Mr Liu Xi-wen, China's Vice-Minister for Trade:[70]

In conducting our trade with the Asian–African countries, our country has consistently pursued the policy of equality, mutual benefit and exchange of products needed by each other on the basis of the Five Principles of Peaceful Co-existence. We strictly respect the sovereignty of other nations; we never attach to a trade agreement any unequal conditions detrimental to the interests of the other party; and we certainly do not take trade as a means to interfere in the internal affairs of other nations or to place any political pressure upon them.

Apart from some solid economic rationale, which will be examined in detail in the following chapter, China's subsequent policy of steering politics clear of trade had certainly been the key non-economic factor in keeping the trade with Malaysia alive throughout the most difficult period in their relations since 1950. This is fully reflected in a revealing observation made by the *Far Eastern Economic Review*'s veteran correspondent:[71]

China's relations with Singapore and Malaysia are marked by these same pragmatism and ambiguities which largely govern Peking's treatment of Hong Kong. Trade is a powerful bait with which to overcome ideological antipathies. And, if trade can be conducted at one level, while various forms of propaganda appear at another, so much the better.

The economies of Malaysia and Singapore were basically open and outward-looking in terms of foreign trade. Emerging from the British political tutelage, Malaysia and Singapore were not, on the whole, ideologically committed to the US -dominated Cold War policy, which prevailed over such Southeast Asian countries as the Philippines and Thailand. It was the presence of these favourable institutional preconditions that had enabled Malaysia and Singapore to carry out trade with China largely on a non-ideological basis. Indeed, Malaysia and Singapore saw 'no sin in trading with China'.[72]

In a nutshell, the survival of the trade marks the triumph of pragmatism, and is a clear case of economics taking precedence over politics and ideology.

THE BANK OF CHINA INCIDENT

The Bank of China is officially a joint state-private bank subordinate to the People's Bank, China's central bank. The Bank of China operates as the foreign exchange arm of the People's Bank of China, and also as an agent in handling international settlements and China's foreign investments abroad. Before the Communist revolution, the Bank of China had 17 overseas branches. After 1950, only the branches in London, Hong Kong and Singapore continued their allegiance to the Head Office in Beijing, the rest being either closed or brought under the control of the Kuomintang government in Taiwan.[73] This made the three overseas branches particularly important for Beijing. In fact, the Hong Kong branch has long enjoyed status as China's unofficial mission in Hong Kong. As Singapore had no formal diplomatic relations with China, the Singapore branch of the Bank of China was also inclined to behave in the same manner.

Registered in Singapore in 1938, the Bank of China later expanded by opening two sub-branches in Malaya – Penang and Kuala Lumpur. The main functions of the Singapore branch were to handle the financial aspects of China's foreign trade with Pan-Malaya and to facilitate remittances to China by local Chinese.[74] In both functions, the Singapore branch had apparently performed well. In particular it had played a dominant role in opening up China's trade with Pan-Malaya throughout the 1950s. Apart from taking care of the credit and finance aspects of the trade, the Singapore branch also actively promoted Chinese products, behaving much like the familiar Japanese trading houses. The Penang sub-branch was known to be especially aggressive in its trade promotion activities. Bank officers were reported to have gone out to contact potential dealers and showed them samples of Chinese merchandise. Before any contracts were finalised, bank personnel would check competitors' prices in the market so as to adjust their own in such a way as to effectively undercut the potential competitors. Afterwards the sub-branch would continue to monitor the market.[75] Actually, there was nothing uncommon about these commercial practices, and many traders are familiar with this kind of hard selling, especially needed for breaking into a new market. But the Penang sub-branch was doubtless unwise in not setting up a separate trading firm to take care of these operations, so as to leave the sub-branch to concentrate on the legitimate financial activities.

As stated in the previous section, the two sub-branches in Malaya became the first casualties of the Sino–Malayan trade dispute when the Malayan government introduced the 1958 Banking Ordinance, designed specifically to outlaw them. The legislation did not then affect the branch in the self-governing Singapore. With the formation of Malaysia in September 1963, however, the Singapore branch was no longer legally immune and came under direct pressure from the Malaysian Minister of Finance, Tan Siew Sin, who had long viewed the continued presence of the Bank of China as 'an extremely serious threat to the security of Malaysia'.[76] As a correspondent remarked:[77]

> In fact Mr Tan had never concealed his intention to make the Bank of China liquidate its activities in Singapore where the bank had created for itself an important place in the island's economy.

Mr Tan first granted a temporary licence to the Singapore branch and then in April 1965 told the bank that its licence would not be renewed when it expired by the end of August 1965. The decision was in line with the banking regulations in Malaysia which prohibit the operation of any bank controlled by a foreign government. The Bank of China was advised to submit a plan to Bank Negara (Malaysia's Central Bank) for an orderly winding-up of its operations in Singapore.[78]

Understandably, this drew strong protest from Beijing. Mr Nan Han-Zhen, Chairman of the Board of Directors of the Bank of China issued a statement in Beijing condemning the 'Rahman regime' for its 'persecution' of the Singapore branch.[79] But reaction from the Chinese business community in Singapore was even stronger. Such organisations as the Singapore Chinese Chamber of Commerce and the Singapore Rubber Packers' Association were most vocal against the closure order. So was Singapore's opposition party, the Barisan Socialis, which actually condemned Kuala Lumpur's decision to close the bank as 'an attempt to shut off co-operation with Afro-Asian countries'.[80]

The Bank of China in Singapore had long established its position in the financial community of Singapore, not just because of Singapore's growing trade with China but also because the Bank provided financial services to many citizens. According to one report, as many as 75 per cent of the small businessmen in Singapore were served by the Bank.[81] It gave them credit on liberal terms and included those who were not directly involved in the China trade. There was also a sentimental attachment on the part of many Singapore Chinese, especially those from the Chinese stream of education, who viewed the Bank as the symbol of Beijing's physical presence in Singapore. In this sense, the closure of the Singapore branch would deeply affect 'an influential segment of the Singapore business community . . . from noodle hawkers to Chamber of Commerce executives.'[82]

In the event, the showdown never did take place. On 9 August 1965, less than a week before the scheduled closure date, Singapore was separated from Malaysia. Singapore's ruling PAP (People's Action Party) government, now free of political pressure from Kuala Lumpur and also eager to maximise consensus and support in days of crisis, immediately issued a new licence to the Bank of China for it to continue business. But this did not mark the end of trouble for the Bank.

Earlier, the manager of the Kuala Lumpur sub-branch of the Bank of China secured a loan from Bank Negara (apparently in violation of a standing directive from the Head Office in Beijing) for the purpose of clearing the outstanding debts of the sub-branch prior to its final closure. The Singapore branch, acting on instructions from Beijing, dismissed the manager and disclaimed the action of the Kuala Lumpur sub-branch as being 'illegal, invalid, null and void'. To recover its debt, Bank Negara then took legal action against the Singapore branch. In July 1968 a High Court ruling in Singapore ordered that the Bank of China's deposits with the local Chartered Bank be frozen in order to repay Bank Negara. China was then in the grips of the Cultural Revolution. With the radicals apparently in control, the Head Office of the Bank of China reacted strongly to the event and denounced the Singapore government for its 'acts of robbery'.[83] Hence flared up the Bank of China's dispute with Singapore government.[84]

At the risk of the further deterioration of Sino–Singapore relations, Singapore government served a summons on the Bank of China for having failed to maintain the legal minimum of 20 per cent liquidity ratio. As the Bank refused to face the litigation, its cheque clearing house facilities were withdrawn. In retaliation, the Bank obtained a promise from China that no letters of credits other than those issued by the Singapore branch of the Bank of China would be recognised by China's export corporations. The all-important China trade was finally drawn into the conflict.

The drama of the whole incident lay not in how it started but rather in how it ended. As soon as the China trade became involved both sides started to retreat, avoiding any further open clash. A major confrontation would certainly have jeopardised the trade, of which the Bank of China in Singapore was very much at the centre. After allowing for mutual face-saving both sides were content to let the matter drop quietly. The incident had brought home to both China and Singapore that there was much in their two-way trade that would benefit both parties – more than either had ever realised.

For two full decades, until their normalisation in the 1970s, China's economic relations with Malaysia and Singapore were ridden with political twists and ideological distortions. But in the end economics ultimately triumphed over politics and ideology.

4

Malaysia/Singapore's Relations with China – II

Transition to Normalisation

The separation of Singapore from Malaysia on 9 August 1965 brought a timely opportunity for these two countries to defuse their growing tension with China and to sort out the nature of their respective relations with Beijing. The separation triggered off a lot of political emotion and generated many new problems to engage the attention of the governments of the two countries in the immediate aftermath. Malaysia would now have squarely to face its many domestic problems such as economic development and racial and social issues, which clearly took precedence over any matters of foreign policy. The subsequent racial riots in Kuala Lumpur in May 1969 only confirmed that, however China had behaved in its relations with Malaysia, the basic problems were of domestic origin and not of the kind generated from external sources.

As for Singapore, the separation clearly gave it a free hand to trade with China and to deal independently with any related issue without being hamstrung by pressure from Kuala Lumpur. As a city-state with no natural resources, Singapore has to retain its open economy and keep within the free enterprise system. The basic economic interests of Singapore had never closely coincided with those of its more inward-looking neighbour, Malaysia. The separation brought into the open their inherent economic and social differences, and provided them with new impetus to cope with old problems from new angles and in accordance with their own perceived interests. In a sense, the separation had created a favourable precondition for Malaysia and Singapore to drift slowly and separately towards normalisation with China.

The hold-back this time came from China. At the time of the separation China was still a close ally of Sukarno's Indonesia, which had from the outset refused to accept the independent existence of Malaysia and had now even greater doubts as to the viability of Malaysia and Singapore as separate entities. With the collapse of the 'Beijing-Jakarta axis' following the coup in Jakarta in September 1965, and the subsequent liquidation of the Indonesian Communist Party (PKI) by the army led by Suharto, Beijing was no longer politically obliged to continue its propaganda attack against the 'Rahman-Lee Kuan Yew clique'. But with the advent of the Cultural Revolution China's foreign policy took an even more radical line, culminating in Beijing's open call to the Malayan Liberation Front to employ the thought of Mao Zedong to depose the 'Rahman-Lee Kuan Yew puppet governments'.[1] It was thus the Cultural Revolution, with all its radical tendencies, which held back the normalisation process. In the 1966 Commonwealth Prime Ministers' Conference in London, Malaysia's Prime Minister Tunku Abdul Rahman found occasion to condemn China's 'aggressive and adventurous policy':[2]

> China is the one country in Asia that aims to dominate the rest of the continent . . . the brand of communism which she is upholding and the population explosion which continually embarrasses her domestic programmes, dictates a policy of adventurism and expansion aimed at fulfilling her ideological crusade . . .

For Singapore it is quite clear that, but for the Cultural Revolution which compelled the officials of the Bank of China in Singapore to employ Red guard tactics of defiance, matters would have been resolved much more easily.

MALAYSIA

The foundation for a new turning-point in Malaysia's relations with China was laid in 1970 in the new foreign policy line of Tun Abdul Razak, who succeeded the Tunku after the riots of 1969. Tun Razak immediately set to work overhauling Malaysia's rigidly pro-Western foreign policy in favour of the neutralisation of Southeast Asia, to be guaranteed by China, the Soviet Union and the United States. Not only was the neutralisation proposal notable for its far-sightedness, but also its timing was good, for the political climate in the region was becoming more conducive to rapprochement as China, recovering from the foreign policy adventures of the Cultural Revolution era, was ready to mend its fences and assume a more moderate posture. Meanwhile, the United States was also de-escalating its war efforts in Vietnam.

In keeping with the new stand of non-alignment, Malaysia also reversed its overtly anti-China foreign policy based on the 'Tunku's black-and-white perception of China's profile in international relations'.[3] Specifically, Tun Razak declared that Malaysia was ready to establish a dialogue with China and even to consider an inter-state relationship based on peaceful co-existence and non-intervention. Thus Malaysia had taken the initiative in demolishing some of the Cold War barriers to its relations with China before the start of the 'Ping Pong Diplomacy' and before the announcement of President Nixon's visit to Beijing.[4]

China's initial response to Malaysia's gesture of rapprochement was to reduce its hostile propaganda against the Malaysian government and China's media started to use the correct name, 'Malaysia', instead of 'Malaya', a term still used by the Malayan Communist Party (MCP). More positively, when Malaysia was hit by a severe flood in February 1971, China – through its Red Cross Society – offered relief to the flood victims. But the first real breakthrough was achieved in May 1971, when the Chairman of Pernas (National Trading Corporation), Tunku Razaleigh bin Mohamed Hamzah, as Head of the nineteen-member Malaysian trade mission on an 'unofficial visit' to Beijing, was received by Premier Zhou Enlai in an unscheduled private audience. Razaleigh was very influential in Malaysia's dominant political party, UMNO (United Malay National Organisation); and Zhou's personal message, which Razaleigh carried back to Kuala Lumpur, was favourably received by Razak. Three months later a Chinese trade delegation returned on an historic visit to Malaysia – the first official mission since Malaysia's formation. Apart from making a purchase on the spot of 40 000 tons of rubber, the Chinese trade delegation also worked out details for more future contacts; the Malaysian ping-pong teams were invited to play in China, the Malaysian businessmen to take part in the Canton

Trade Fair, and the Malaysian Rubber Association to organise a technical mission to visit China.[5] In October 1971 the Sino–Malaysian détente advanced further with the Malaysian Cabinet deciding to abandon the hitherto 'One China, One Taiwan' policy in favour of a 'One China' policy. Above all, Razak personally went to the United Nations to cast Malaysia's vote for China's admission.

Through the foresight, patience and prudence of Tun Razak, Malaysia was already clearly on its way towards détente with China at the time when other ASEAN countries were still in the state of 'Nixon shock'. The main aim of the Malaysian efforts in 1972 was to strengthen the base of their economic relations with China. In March 1972 the Malaysian rubber technical mission visited China, and this visit was subsequently reciprocated by that of the Chinese technical mission to Malaysia.[6] In April 1972 Malaysia started to impose restrictions on the re-export of Chinese goods from Singapore in a move to reduce the latter's role as a middleman, and China supported the Malaysian move for more direct trade. In September 1972 the Malaysian pingpong and badminton teams went to China to join in competition. But the climax of China's 'ping pong diplomacy' was not reached until the middle of 1973 when the Chinese ping-pong team returned a visit to Malaysia. The Chinese sports team usually contained unofficial representatives from Beijing's Foreign Ministry.[7]

By 1973, Malaysia was well-ahead of all its ASEAN neighbours in their move towards normalisation of relations with China. The main thrust for Malaysia's efforts in 1973 was not trade growth but the formation of diplomatic relations. However, the negotiation proved to be quite protracted and was more complicated than had originally been thought.[8] Malaysia wanted to clear up two major obstacles before the setting up of diplomatic relations: (i) the question of the Chinese support for the Communist insurgents in Malaysia, particularly the issue of the China-based radio *Suara Revolusi* (Voice of Revolution); and (ii) the problem of ethnic Chinese.[9]

In particular, China's official attitude towards the national status of the ethnic Chinese in Malaysia was considered to be most crucial for this multi-racial country. At the time of the negotiation for normalisation there were over 4 million ethnic Chinese in the total Malaysian population of 11 million. In addition, there were about 220 000 stateless Chinese who had established permanent residence in Malaysia. As in other Southeast Asian countries, the issue of ethnic

Chinese had long complicated Malaysia's approaches to relations with China. Indeed, the previous Malaysian Prime Minister Tunku Abdul Rahman had once publicly accused some Malaysian Chinese of being 'subversive elements who owe loyalty to China'. In the Tunku's rhetoric:[10]

> China has thousands of her agents in this country whose sole aim and object is to try to overthrow the democratic government of this country by force of arms; for that reason we cannot have diplomatic or consular relations with her as this would be a help to these subversive elements, who owe loyalty to China.

As it happened, the obstacles were not insurmountable. In May 1974, just about two years after the start of negotiation, Tun Razak went to Beijing to formalise the establishment of diplomatic relations with China.[11] At a welcoming banquet in Beijing, Premier Zhou Enlai praised the Malaysian initiative in calling for a zone of peace and neutrality in Southeast Asia. In reply, Prime Minister Razak stressed:[12]

> differences in ideology, in our relative size, and in our approaches to some international issues, should not present obstacles to the development of fruitful relations and beneficial co-operation between our two countries.

After three days of talks and a long audience with Chairman Mao, the Malaysian delegate signed a joint communiqué which reflected some notable diplomatic success on the part of Malaysia. On the sensitive ethnic Chinese issue, for instance, the communiqué stated that both governments 'do not recognise dual nationality. Proceeding from this principle, the Chinese government considers anyone of Chinese origin who has taken up of his own will or otherwise acquired Malaysian nationality as automatically forfeiting Chinese nationality'.[13] With this, Razak went back to Kuala Lumpur to demand total loyalty from the Malaysian Chinese – 'there will be no future for fence-sitters and for people whose loyalties are divided'.[14]

Returning from his China trip, Tun Razak emphasised his other diplomatic achievement by claiming that both Chairman Mao and Premier Zhou had given him a 'categorical assurance' that they considered the problem of the Communist insurgents in Malaysia as 'a purely internal problem to be dealt with by us as we see fit'.[15] Instead of fearing the consequences of diplomatic relations with

China for Malaysia's own Communist movement, Tun Razak chose to confront the movement in the belief that the presence of a Chinese embassy in Kuala Lumpur could actually work to Malaysia's advantage. In this sense, Razak's recognition of China was a brilliant stroke designed to 'cut the ground from under the Maoist guerrillas who have been presenting a problem to his government'.[16]

Little wonder that Tun Razak considered his China diplomacy a personal triumph. He declared a public holiday to mark the success of his China visit immediately upon his return to Kuala Lumpur. In the general election a few months later, he shrewdly capitalised on his China visit, wooing Malaysian Chinese voters by appealing to their inherent pro-China sentiments. Until Razak's visit to Beijing, photographs of Chairman Mao and other Chinese Communist leaders were banned in Malaysia. During the general election in August 1974, however, the ruling National Front deliberately displayed pictures of Chairman Mao along with those of Tun Razak.[17] Razak was reaping domestic benefits from his recognition of China sooner than he had expected.

In the regional perspective, Malaysia's normalisation with China also had far-reaching consequences for other ASEAN countries in the sense that it hastened these countries to come to terms with China. Buoyed by China's endorsement of his own neutrality plan for Southeast Asia, Tun Razak said, in a euphoric moment, that as a result of his visit, 'the prestige of Malaysia has never been higher than it is today'.[18] Indeed, Malaysia was the first ASEAN country to recognise China since the international détente following Nixon's visit, at the time when the Philippines and Thailand were still dragging their feet in their normalisation process with China. As will be evident in the subsequent chapters, whereas Malaysia's recognition of China was the product of a well-conceived and carefully-calculated move – at least in the perception of the Malaysian leadership at that time – the decisions of the Philippines and Thailand to establish diplomatic ties with Beijing a year later were somewhat precipitated by the sudden deterioration of the region's political situation after the fall of Indochina to Communist rule.

SINGAPORE

The course of Singapore's normalisation with China was, in contrast, much less tortuous, Singapore's overall relations with China have been and will continue to be influenced by a set of conflicting forces. Singapore as a globally-oriented city-state, dependent upon trade and industry for its main livelihood, is always pragmatic in its approaches to foreign policy. Singapore is inclined to cultivate close relations with any country of any ideological shade provided this could lead to a further growth of trade or wider business contact. Such is Singapore's commercial approach to its relations with China. On the other hand, as a predominantly Chinese city-state, Singapore has to be wary of the political sensitivity of its neighbours in regard to its connections with China. Politically, insofar as dealing with China is concerned, Singapore cannot be ahead of other ASEAN countries or adopt a more independent foreign policy. (This explains why Singapore today still lacks 'full relation' with China.) In fact, it has to take great pains to demonstrate to its neighbours that it enjoys no special relations with China beyond the historical and cultural links. The Singapore government takes a stern view of any unwarranted spread of pro-China sentiments among its ethnic Chinese population. Such sentiments are officially labelled as 'Chinese chauvinism', which is severely dealt with, as evident in the purging of top executives of the two leading Chinese newspapers in 1971.

Sino–Singapore détente began where the Bank of China incident ended. Ever since, Sino–Singapore rapprochement has been part of the overall Sino–Malaysian normalisation process. When China, in the aftermath of the Cultural Revolution, started to accept the Malaysian proposal for the neutralisation of Southeast Asia and scale down hostile propaganda against Malaysia, it also dropped its attack on the 'Lee Kuan Yew clique'. Along with Malaysia, Singapore voted for the Albanian resolution to admit China to the United Nations. To follow the footsteps of the Malaysians, the Singapore Chinese Chamber of Commerce sent a trade mission to China in 1971, which held talks with Chinese Vice-Premier Li Xien-nien. Then, the 'Ping-Pong diplomacy' played its celebrated role. First, the Singapore table-tennis teams were invited, along with others from the region, to compete in the Afro-Asian table tennis tournament in Beijing in October 1971. Then the Chinese teams returned a visit to Singapore in July 1972.[19] The rapprochement was now clearly in process. In fact, between 1971 and 1976, some 16 Singapore delegations of various professional and business organisations visited China, culminating in March 1975 in the first official visit to China by

Singapore's Foreign Minister, Mr S. Rajaratnam, at the invitation of his Chinese counterpart, Mr Qiao Guanhua (Chiao Kuan-hua). By the time the Singapore delegates set foot on the Chinese soil, the Malaysians had already set up their embassy in Beijing.

Back in early 1973, as Malaysia began to hold talks with China on problems of establishing diplomatic ties. Rajaratnam was quoted as having stated in Bangkok that Singapore and Thailand had agreed to consult each other and their ASEAN partners on how they should 'individually and collectively deal with China'.[20] Later, in Jakarta, Rajaratnam told the Indonesian press that Singapore was in no hurry to set up diplomatic relations with Beijing, for this would restrict Singapore's diplomatic flexibility. He further explained that Singapore, with its Chinese majority, had been frequently mis-interpreted as a Third China so that hasty diplomatic relations with China could actually 'compound this misinterpretation'.[21] On the eve of starting his good-will journey to Beijing, Rajaratnam asserted: 'Short of the physical presence of Chinese diplomats here [Singapore], every form of co-operation will be explored'. But he also reiterated that Singapore would wait until its 'closest neighbours have established diplomatic relations with the People's Republic of China'.[22]

In Beijing, Rajaratnam had the opportunity of putting to his Chinese hosts the fact that Singapore is a multi-racial immigrant society, in process of developing its own national identity. He stressed that though Singapore was predominantly Chinese in ethnic content and culture, its political system and social outlook had been and would continue to be shaped by the Southeast Asian environment. He thus emphasised:[23]

> It is the consistent policy of the Singapore Government to ensure that the languages and cultures that the various communities brought with them to Singapore, as settlers as well as rulers, are kept alive and transformed to suit our needs.

That was apparently aimed as much at the governments of other ASEAN countries as at the Chinese leadership in Beijing. It was nevertheless in Singapore's own national interest to serve such notice, whoever the audience might be.

The climax of Rajaratnam's visit was the 45-minute audience with Premier Zhou Enlai in the hospital. Zhou said that China would be ready to establish diplomatic relations whenever it was convenient for Singapore, and that China was willing to wait.[24] With such understanding, Singapore's normalisation with China was as good as completed.

A year later Prime Minister Lee Kuan Yew was invited to visit China. By that time, Premier Zhou had already died, Chairman Mao was very ill, and China clearly had a leadership succession crisis. The next occasion for direct high-level contact was in November 1978, when China's Senior Vice-Premier, Deng Xiaoping, visited Singapore on the last leg of his Southeast Asian tour. In return, Prime Minister Lee Kuan Yew paid his second visit to China in November 1980. After Mr Zhao Ziyang became Premier of China, his first overseas trip was a tour of ASEAN in August 1981, which also included Singapore. The subject of all these visits was, however, an exchange of views concerning the many over-riding international and regional issues, such as the Kampuchea problem, which now dwarfed in importance any purely bilateral matter.

Sino–Singapore economic relations entered another new phase in December 1979, with Singapore Finance Minister, Mr Hon Sui Sen, signing a trade agreement with China in Beijing. Apart from agreeing to establish trade representative offices in both countries, the trade pact provided a legal basis for the expansion of mutual economic co-operation in the continuing absence of a formal diplomatic framework. Under the pact, both countries also committed themselves to extend to each other the 'most-favoured nation' (MFN) treatment.[25] In July 1981 China and Singapore formally exchanged trade representatives with the necessary diplomatic status. With the setting up of trade offices Singapore and China, for all practical purposes except in name, had established *de facto* diplomatic relations. In limiting its relations with China to less than the full ambassadorial status, Singapore was clearly acting 'out of respect for Indonesia', which had yet to resume its diplomatic relations with Beijing.[26]

The Pattern of Trade

GROWTH AND STRUCTURE

The durability of China's trade with Malaysia and Singapore is fully reflected not only in its ability to survive political intervention in the form of trade bans, as discussed in the previous chapter, but also in its potential to continue expanding even under adverse conditions, as during the Cultural Revolution. If political disruptions in China had not actually retarded its export growth in the region, the return to normality after the Cultural Revolution would certainly provide fresh impetus for further development. This was actually the case. As shown in Table 4.1, Malaysia's imports from China, having reached a high level in the late 1960s, rose markedly after 1972, when normalisation of relations between the two countries provided a favourable basis for growth. All political barriers to trade were now removed. Indeed, as a result of rapprochement, political intervention began to work in the reverse direction. In 1974, the year Malaysia recognised China, two-way trade registered a phenomenal increase, as agencies from both sides liberally placed orders for each other's goods. As much of the trade was conducted on a bilateral basis, it was susceptible to 'positive' political influence.

The rate of growth of Malaysia's imports from China has tended to slow down since the mid-1970s, with the annual increase being around 10 per cent in monetary terms, or just about staying ahead of the inflation. In 1968, the relative share of China's exports to Malaysia was 6.8 per cent; but it declined to 2.3 per cent in 1980. In other words, trade has obviously failed to take advantage of the buoyant conditions of the Malaysian economy throughout the 1970s, with the result that its market share has been sharply reduced. As for Malaysia's exports to China, its relative share – close to 2 per cent throughout the last decade – appears quite stable in spite of the fact that its commodity base is extremely narrow, being made up virtually of nothing but rubber.

The failure of Chinese exports to take advantage of the booming Malaysian economy in the 1970s, when political trade harassment had ceased, points to the long-term structural weakness of Sino–Malaysian trade which is very much evident in its commodity composition. As revealed in Table 4.2, the commodity structure of Malaysia's imports from China in 1952, being made up of 64 per cent food and 27 per cent sundry manufactures, was basically traditional in character. As the Chinese economy became industrialised under the thrust of its successful First Five-Year Plan, it introduced many non-traditional light manufactured goods into the Southeast Asian markets. Hence the so-called China's 'trade offensive', which eventually invoked an official trade curb from the Malaysian government.

After the period of slow growth in the early 1960s, China's exports to Malaysia picked up again later in the decade, at the same time showing some significant, though not conspicuous, structural change in the commodity composition. Although there was no basic change in the relative shares for the categories foodstuffs and manufactures, there was qualitative improvement in the Chinese merchandise, plus the addition of a new variety of manufactured goods such as iron and steel products and certain medium-level capital goods. Since then, until 1979, there was no further significant change in the overall commodity structure; nor was there much 'qualitative' improvement of the products. The range of products in a typical Chinese emporium in Kuala Lumpur in 1979 was virtually the same as in 1969 – even their designs, packaging and branding remained basically unchanged. But this happened to be the period when other dynamic East Asian economies such as Korea, Taiwan and Hong Kong were rapidly expanding their market shares in the booming Malaysian economy.

On the other hand, the organisation of Sino–Malaysian trade had undergone some significant changes since the start of the normalisation process around 1970. In the past, the great bulk of Malaysia's trade with China passed through Singapore, and this continued even after the separation. Most Chinese products were first imported by agents in Singapore and then re-exported after some handling to Malaysia. This was a time-honoured practice, arising from the fact that Singapore was from the start set up as an entrepôt centre for the Malayan hinterlands. In late 1969 the Malaysian government set up its own national trading corporation, Pernas (Perbadanan Nasional) originally for the purpose of fostering entrepreneurial trade and industry among the indigenous Malays, the *bumiputras*. In 1971 Pernas was directed into the lucrative China trade by Tun Razak, who made it officially the sole authority to implement the Sino–Malaysian trade agreement signed in August 1971. As already mentioned, Pernas's chairman, Razaleigh, was from the outset heavily involved in Malaysia's détente with China as he was the head of Malaysia's first 'unofficial' trade mission to Beijing in May 1971. Also, the bilateral nature of the China trade lends itself easily to state control.

Razak had two basic motives in putting Pernas in control of the China trade. First, this would help fulfil Malaysia's long-cherished goal of cutting out the middleman role of Singapore, and to some extent also of Hong Kong, in the China trade.[27] Secondly, the

Malaysian government, like many others in the developing market economies, found it advantageous to set up some kind of state organisation to take charge of trading with socialist countries – either for practical reasons, such as dealing with the state trading corporations of the socialist countries, or for political purposes, such as monitoring the trade with the view to controlling any undesirable political spillovers.

However, Pernas's attempt to monopolise the China trade soon ran into difficulties. Although Beijing was in principle inclined to deal with government representatives or state organisations, it was reluctant to drop existing agents from the private sector in Malaysia (or those in Singapore and Hong Kong), which had long been involved in the trade.[28] There was also rising domestic opposition, basically from the Malaysian Chinese, to Pernas's intended monopolistic role over the trade. In particular, discontent mounted after the government ruling, issued in December 1973, which required all Chinese imports except raw medical herbs and certain goods under quota control, to be channelled through Pernas. Individual merchants were also required to obtain a permit from Pernas in order to import Chinese goods, for which Pernas would charge half a per cent as commission.[29]

As high inflation struck the Malaysian economy in the mid-1970s, in the wake of the oil crisis, the government relaxed control over Chinese imports in order to encourage individual importers to bring in more consumer goods and foodstuffs. Since then the government has recognised the important role of individual Chinese merchants who, operating with their associates in Singapore and Hong Kong, have retained control over a sizeable portion of the Chinese consumer goods markets, despite Pernas's efforts to stimulate more *bumiputra* participation in the China trade. During the past ten years, Pernas has brought 11 *bumiputra* companies into the China trade and organised 127 *bumiputra* entrepreneurs to visit China for business contacts.[30] However, Pernas has not been conspicuously successful in monopolising the China trade. Its current efforts are aimed at establishing more direct trade links with China rather than at ending the participation of Malaysian Chinese private merchants, for it has realised that it wields little control over the distribution network in Malaysia, which is still largely in the hands of Chinese merchants. At the receiving end of the China trade are still thousands of small Chinese shopkeepers and retailers all over Malaysia.

For Singapore, the structure and growth trends of its trade with China, as might be expected, bear striking resemblance to those of Sino–Malaysia. Like Malaysia's, Singapore's imports from China reached the two-decade peak in 1968 with the volume of US$150 million, which accounted for about 12 per cent of Singapore's total imports. After that, the trade stabilised for a period until 1974, when Singapore's imports of Chinese goods resumed a steady upward trend (see Table 4.3). However, unlike Malaysia, Singapore since 1979 experienced a sharp increase in its trade with China, affecting both imports and exports, as the Chinese economy was opened up for more foreign trade and investment. This signifies a new role for Singapore, the significance of which will be examined in greater detail later.

Similarly, the growth of Singapore's imports from China over the past three decades has been closely related to the changing commodity composition of the trade. As shown in Table 4.4, the growth in the 1950s was accompanied by the transformation of a trade structure based entirely on foodstuffs and traditional products to one that included many manufactured items. The second period of growth in the late 1960s was supported by the diversification of manufactured goods and the inclusion of some new items. However, this commodity structure remained basically unchanged throughout the 1970s, and that has been, as in Malaysia, the main reason for the failure of the China trade to grow along with the booming Singapore economy. Consequently, the market share of Chinese exports to Singapore has fallen, from the high level of 11.8 per cent in 1968 to only 2.6 per cent in 1980.

The organisational aspects of Sino–Singapore trade are much less rigid than those of Sino–Malaysian. In Singapore, trading with China is basically a private sector activity involving 1200–1500 individual local traders, some of whom have been in the business for generations. In 1968 the Singapore government set up Intraco Ltd (International Trading Company), a semi-official trading corporation, to co-ordinate and oversee Singapore's trade with the socialist countries. Importers of Chinese goods had to have their import declarations endorsed by Intraco, which levied half a per cent commission, based on CIF value of goods to be imported, as a service charge. After 1 May 1976 this service charge was scrapped for Chinese imports, but the levies on imports from other Communist countries remained.[31] Chinese trade in Singapore has since been completely freed from all restriction, with Intraco currently directing its activities on promoting Singapore's exports to China.[32]

In 1968, as shown earlier, Chinese exports to Singapore and Malaysia reached the highest level of two decades, both in absolute terms and in their relative market shares. This was also the period which witnessed the rapid mushrooming of many Chinese emporia in both countries. In Singapore alone, eight big department stores were opened around this time – the number of Chinese emporia now amounts to 19, though they are not confined to dealing only in Chinese merchandise. Moreover, in this post-separation period Chinese products faced very little competition, as the local industries had not yet been developed. On account of their tremendous price advantages and popular appeal to wide segments of the local populations (including other non-Chinese ethnic groups), Chinese products immediately gained a strong hold in the local markets for foodstuffs and for a variety of daily household consumer products. Hence the economic and social – 'social' because of the broad-based nature of the China-product market – importance of the China trade to their respective economies. It was thus recognised that the 'Malaysian import bill would be considerably larger were the wide range of goods now bought from China purchased instead in Japan, Britain or other developed countries'.[33] Similarly in Singapore: 'A member of Singapore's influential Chinese Chamber of Commerce estimated that the cost of living on the island republic would go up as much as 15–20 per cent if trade with China were to cease'.[34] Indeed, but for the crucial importance of the China trade, the Singapore government, as discussed in the last chapter, would have certainly taken drastic action against the Bank of China during their confrontation.

A sample survey in September 1970 of the eight Chinese emporia in Singapore underlined some interesting economic and social characteristics of Singapore's imports from China.[35] Of the Chinese products, the most popular were canned foods (15.7 per cent), confectionery (9.3 per cent), daily household items (9.2 per cent), stationery and sports goods (8.1 per cent). The least popular items were, leather goods, cosmetics, electrical appliances and women's fashions (all below 2 per cent); these were 'bourgeois' items in which socialist China, just emerging from the Cultural Revolution, would not expect to have strong comparative advantage. Asked why they had patronised the Chinese emporia, 38 per cent of respondents said the goods were 'cheap', 20 per cent said 'good quality', 10 per cent said 'taste preferences' and only 10 per cent, 'stylist'.

In attitudes towards the Chinese emporia, the familiar local schisms between the 'Chinese educated' and the 'English educated' Singaporeans were apparent. As might be expected, 52.4 per cent of the respondents filling Chinese questionnaires felt that they preferred to buy Chinese products because they were Chinese, whereas 64.9 per cent of those replying in English questionnaires disagreed. Another finding which conformed to similar expectation is that 57.5 per cent of all the respondents felt that but for the availability of the low-priced Chinese products their cost of living would have greatly increased. Comparing most Chinese products of the late 1950s, when they first appeared in the Singapore market, most respondents (65.4 per cent) felt that the prices of Chinese goods in 1970 had increased. Significantly, the Chinese products in 1970 still retained the image of *jia-lian wu-mei* (inexpensive but fine quality).

Unfortunately, there is no new survey available to compare the operation of the current Chinese emporia in Singapore. It can, however, be reasonably surmised that the label of *jia-lian wu-mei* is unlikely to be an important selling point for the new generation of more affluent Singaporeans. To begin with, Chinese products are no longer distinctly cheap (or *jia-lian*) as a result of several upward price adjustments over the years. In a more prosperous market, it is not even the intrinsic quality of the product (or *wu-mei*) but rather how the product is presented to the customer, or how it adapts to the changing taste of the customer, that influences sales. Most Chinese products fall into the category of 'low income elasticity of demand', which also explains why they held strong appeal to a broad segment of low-income groups in the past. Per capita GDP in Singapore has since increased from US$900 in 1970 to over US$4000 in 1980 (at current prices). With growing economic influence and rising consumerism, Chinese products have simply lost out to their competitors supplying a different range of goods in the Singapore market. Ironically, it is not political interference but rapid economic and social changes which have eroded the dominant advantages of Chinese products and whittled down their market share in Singapore.

TRADE FLUCTUATIONS

How stable has been the China trade with Malaysia and Singapore? Since the normalisation process began in the late 1960s, China's trade behaviour with the two countries has also become regularised, particularly in respect of Chinese exports. During the 1950s and the greater part of the 1960s, however, when China's trade with Malaysia was beset by political intervention, Sino–Malaysian trade was subject to wide fluctuations. The instability of Chinese imports from Malaysia is sufficiently clear, as the trade was entirely a one-commodity affair – rubber. Moreover, China's behaviour in the Malaysian rubber market was extremely erratic, as will be seen in the next section. In contrast, Chinese exports to Malaysia have always been fairly well diversified. Have the Chinese exports to Malaysia behaved in a more regular way? What has been the actual extent of their fluctuations?

The question of trade fluctuation is significant for a variety of reasons. First, a pattern of wide fluctuation and high irregularity of Chinese exports to Malaysia would lend support to Malaysian charge of 'dumping' by China. As discussed in the previous chapter, 'dumping' becomes really serious when associated with unpredictability of supply. Secondly, since Malaysia is one of the few countries which have maintained uninterrupted trade flow with China during the Cold War period, an analysis of the stability (or instability) of Chinese exports to Malaysia may yield some significant generalisations in respect of China's typical trade behaviour at the time of high political stress. This, in turn, can reflect China's overall reliability as a source of supply. Thirdly, Malaysia has often been cited as a typical economy with a large measure of instability on account of its high commodity concentration in exports, particularly in the 1950s and the 1960s.[36] Past studies have shown that Malaysia's exports to socialist countries before 1965 were highly unstable owing to the frequent influence of politics.[37] This is quite ironic because the centrally-planned economies, by virtue of the absence of such capitalist phenomena as cyclical fluctuations in output and demand, are in theory more 'ideal markets' for the primary exports of developing countries. Furthermore, socialist countries tend to conduct foreign trade on bilateral arrangements, which should also, theoretically, contribute to greater stability in trade – provided of course the parties abide by the terms.[38]

In order to bring out the pattern and extent of Sino–Malaysian trade fluctuations, we can divide the trade before 1971 (or before the start of Sino–Malaysian détente) into three sub-periods, roughly in accordance with the cyclical movements over the twenty-year time series with their respective instability indices. As can be seen from Table 4.5, the middle sub-period (1958–65) gives the highest indices of instability for both Malaysia's imports from and exports to China, reflecting the full impact of adverse political influence on trade in this period – such as the Malaysian 'anti-dumping' measures and China's trade diversion policy during Confrontation. A second obvious feature is that, whereas Malaysia's exports to China display violent fluctuations (which situation also tallies with findings of other studies), Malaysia's imports from China on the whole have been relatively quite stable. Thirdly, the steep decline in the instability indices, especially for Malaysia's imports from China, in the last sub-period (1966–71) bears out a clear trend towards the increasingly stable trade relations between the two countries, reflecting the diminishing political pressure on trade after the ending of Confrontation.

In fact, Malaysia's imports from China had been very stable during 1966–71. Paradoxically, China scored the lowest instability index among the major countries exporting to Malaysia for the last sub-period, as can be seen from Table 4.6 – which incidentally gives Japan as Malaysia's most unstable source of imports for the same period. Since Malaysia's exports to China, though fluctuating violently, were negligible, and since Malaysia's imports from China were very stable, there is no evidence to suggest that the China trade had contributed to the instability of the Malaysian economy.

The statistical analysis has thus established China as a stable and dependable source of supply of goods to Malaysia even at the time of their high political tension. After the détente, there were even less grounds for trade fluctuations. Indeed, the dependability of Chinese exports to Malaysia was vividly demonstrated during the world food crisis in the early 1970s.

Malaysia was not self-sufficient in rice. Over the long term Thailand had been Malaysia's largest source of supply, providing 50–60 per cent of Malaysia's total rice imports annually, with China usually ranking second.[39] During the period of food crisis in Malaysia, 1973–75, rice imports from China shot up to 72 per cent in 1973 and 84 per cent in 1975, so that China virtually changed roles with Thailand to become Malaysia's dominant food supplier. This episode serves to indicate that China could be a valuable and reliable substitute when production from the main source tumbled.[40]

CHINESE DEMAND FOR RUBBER*

Before 1949 China consumed a limited quantity of natural rubber, amounting to only about 20 000 tons a year. In 1981 it was reported to have consumed 432 000 tons. Since China is estimated to produce only 100 000 tons or so a year domestically, the bulk of its rubber consumption has to be met by imports, making China an important factor in the world rubber market. In 1980, with the net import of 235 000 tons, virtually all from ASEAN and Sri Lanka – which combine to produce over 85 per cent of the world's supply – China absorbed 7.3 per cent of the world's traded rubber. These imports rank it far above such traditionally large rubber consumers as Britain, which imported only 3.9 per cent of the world's traded rubber in that year.[41]

Apart from its relatively large share in the world rubber market, the importance of China in the rubber trade merits attention for the following reasons. First, as a major current consumer with plenty of potential for future growth, China could affect world rubber prices as either a stabilising or de-stabilising force. In the past, China's sudden entry and withdrawal often created a 'stir' in the rubber market, especially in Malaysia and Singapore. Secondly, from the historical perspective, China's erratic pattern of behaviour in the rubber market, especially in the 1960s, is an interesting example of its trade behaviour, showing how it responded to non-market challenges. Last but not least, the economic viability of China's trade with Southeast Asia depends significantly on this strategic commodity. From the Chinese standpoint, a key motive for trade with Southeast Asia is the need to obtain such essential raw materials as rubber. For the Southeast Asian countries, rubber forms the single most important export item which helps to offset their chronic trade deficits with China. Indeed, for years exports to China from Malaysia and Singapore have consisted almost entirely of rubber – and even today rubber still constitutes close to half of Singapore's total exports, and about 90 per cent of Malaysia's, to China.

* Part of this section is based on John Wong, 'Chinese Demand for Southeast Asian Rubber, 1949–72', *China Quarterly* (September 1975).

The rubber trade was very much the pivot of China's economic relations with Malaysia and Singapore, particularly during the 1950s and the 1960s. The first substantial trade deal between Malaya and the newly established People's Republic happened to be for rubber. In 1950 China made a very impressive entry into the Malayan rubber market with a heavy purchase in anticipation of the increased strategic demand during the coming Korea War. Later, rubber was in the list of strategic commodities included in the UN embargo imposed against China. In order to obtain its vital supplies, China had to seek a new source of supply.

In December 1952 Ceylon (now Sri Lanka) signed a five-year rubber-rice trade pact, which has since been renewed more than five times. This was basically a form of barter under which China agreed to purchase rubber from Ceylon at above the world price and supply Ceylon in return with rice at below world price. Up to 1956 Ceylon was the major source of rubber supply to China, but the lifting of the embargo in that year caused a sharp decline in the amount it exported to China, and the decline has since continued. By 1979 Sri Lanka's share in China's total rubber imports came to only 18 per cent (see Table 4.7).

The removal of the trade embargo not only brought China back to the Malayan (Malaysia plus Singapore) rubber market but also paved the way for the rapid expansion of Sino–Malayan trade in general, until the Malayan government atttempted to curb the growth of Chinese imports with its 'anti-dumping' legislation of 1959. Up to that point the Malayan share in China's total rubber imports increased steadily along with the overall growth of trade between the two countries. To retaliate against the Malayan sanction, Beijing started in 1959 to shift its rubber purchases away from Malaya in favour of Indonesia, and this process of market substitution was carried further during Confrontation. In 1963 China bought only 9000 tons of Malaysian rubber, and in 1964 the amount was reduced to a trickle of 114 tons, as China virtually diverted its demand to the Indonesia market. It was only after the suspension of Sino–Indonesian relations in 1966 that China returned again to the market of Malaysia and Singapore. Its demand for Malaysian and Singapore rubber has since grown steadily, as can be seen from Table 4.8.

Like the Chinese 'Ping Pong Diplomacy', Malaysia's 'Rubber Diplomacy' had also played a role in spearheading Malaysia's rapprochement with China. Hence there was the exchange of visits by their respective rubber technical missions in 1972, and on other appropriate occasions Beijing made 'good-will rubber purchases'. Throughout the 1970s Sino–Malaysian rubber trade rode high on the tide of the détente between the two countries. In recent years, Malaysian/Singapore rubber has firmly established its dominant position in the Chinese market, with an average share reaching over 60 per cent.

In the past, the Malayan rubber had a number of distinct advantages for the Chinese buyers, despite an adverse political climate. First, whereas the Chinese rubber trade with Ceylon and Indonesia was based on binding bilateral agreements, Chinese purchases of Malayan rubber were basically free market operations with deliveries made against hard currency. The open Malayan rubber market gave China the freedom of entry and exit at will without political complication, and at the same time provided a ready alternative from which to make up for any deficiencies in supply from its fixed sources. From the Chinese standpoint, therefore, the free market ironically proved to be a more reliable source of supply. This is because Ceylonese rubber output (half of which was sold to China in the 1960s) was too small to satisfy China's growing but fluctuating demand, while the supply from Sukarno's Indonesia was often irregular and less dependable owing to low efficiency in processing and handling. Secondly, since prices for Malayan rubber were largely determined by the forces of demand and supply, China had neither to pay a premium price nor to add economic aid to the transaction as it so often had to do when obtaining supplies through bilateral deals. Finally, China could not have obtained high-grade and quality-consistent rubber with the required technical specifications (the SMR or Standard Malaysian Rubber and SSR or Standard Singapore Rubber) from sources other than Malaysia and Singapore. In addition, Singapore also offered efficient handling, and good shipping and financing facilities. The détente has brought out the technical and economic advantages of rubber from Malaysia and Singapore. Hence its domination of the China market.

From the standpoint of the market operators in Kuala Lumpur and Singapore, the overriding concern is with the trends of China's future import demand for natural rubber. Will the Chinese purchasing behaviour continue the relative predictability started with the détente? Will there be another spurt in the growth of demand from China in the 1980s to meet its increasing requirement for the Four-Modernisation programme?

Natural rubber is a notoriously volatile trade commodity due to its low elasticities of both supply and demand, especially in the short run. For the two decades before détente, the 1950s and the 1960s, Chinese overall import demand for natural rubber has shown a record of violent fluctuations, as can be seen in Table 4.7. The actual extent of these fluctuations for China's three main sources of supply during this period is worked out in Table 4.8. It can be seen that fluctuations of Chinese rubber imports from Ceylon have been very mild, those from Indonesia not great, but those from Malaysia and Singapore extremely violent, as reflected in their respective instability indices. Clearly, the relative stability of China's import behaviour with Ceylon and Indonesia was largely due to the bilateral trading arrangements, while its instability in Malaysia and Singapore had been the outcome of the free market mechanism aggravated by frequent political intervention such as trade disputes.

More significantly, as in the case of China's overall trade with Malaysia and Singapore analysed in the previous section, there is a strong tendency for China's total rubber imports to become more stable, as manifested in the sharp fall of the instability index, for the sub-period 1961–72. The drop in the instability index for China's rubber imports from Malaysia and Singapore is even more pronounced – from 105.46 for 1956–63 to 32.67 for 1966–72. This means that Chinese demand for rubber from Malaysia and Singapore had already begun to stabilise before the détente decade of the 1970s. In fact, the pattern of Chinese demand for Malaysian and Singapore rubber in recent years is no different from that of other major buyers from market economies.

For lack of information regarding the structure of rubber demand in China, particularly the relevant cross-sectional data on domestic industrial end-uses and output of synthetic rubber, it is difficult to make any rigorous projection of Chinese future import demand for Southeast Asian rubber. But broad generalisations can be attempted on the basis of the past trends. First, China's import demand for rubber showed one of the world's highest growth rates for the 1950s and 1960s, but levelled off in the 1970s. It is likely that the demand growth could pick up again in the 1980s once the Four-Modernisation programme gets underway. Secondly, the overall demand for rubber is closely related to income and population growth of a country. As in other countries, the most important area of rubber usage in China is in tyres, not necessarily for the automobile as in the industrially advanced countries, but also for the millions of bicycles in Chinese cities and the millions of carts in the Chinese countryside. The per capita level of rubber consumption in China is still very low: it works out at around 3–4 kilograms for 1980, as compared with over 30 kilograms for Japan. This allows enormous room in future for the further growth of demand for Southeast Asian rubber.

Issues and Problems

In the immediate aftermath of Tun Razak's trip to Beijing to seal Sino–Malaysian diplomatic relations, the Malaysian leadership was inevitably infected by a sense of euphoria. Razak, in particular, took great personal pride in having blazed 'the Peking [Beijing] trail' for Malaysia's ASEAN neighbours.[42] But Razak's great diplomatic feat was not without its backlash. To begin with, on the economic front, Malaysia has been constantly irritated by its persistent trade imbalance with China, even though the annual trade deficits are quite small and do not pose any serious problem to the Malaysian economy, which generally faces no balance of payments difficulties. The irritation has rather been associated with the Malaysian belief that China could have easily reduced or wiped out such trade surplus by increasing its imports of natural rubber.[43]

As in other ASEAN countries, the more serious frictions or potential conflicts between Malaysia and China stemmed from domestic political and social origins, not directly related to trade or economic matters. Despite mutual efforts to upgrade diplomatic representation with high-level appointments – China's first Ambassador to Kuala Lumpur was Mr Wang Yu-ding, formerly Chinese Ambassador to North Vietnam, and Malaysia's envoy in Beijing was Mr Hashim Sultan, Deputy Secretary-General of Malaysia's Foreign Ministry – Sino–Malaysian relations remained 'cool and correct', which was clearly not enough to be regarded by either side as much of a diplomatic gain. In moving ahead of other

ASEAN countries to normalise relations with China the Malaysian leadership reckoned that they had taken a political risk; but post-recognition developments inside Malaysia did not suggest to them that the gamble had paid off. Opposition to détente with China from the conservative wing of Razak's UMNO party soon began to surface. The dissenters, who were also strongly anti-Communist, were mainly from the state of Perak. As is often the case in the Malaysian context, anti-Communism on the part of the Malays is frequently entangled with emotive anti-Chinese feeling which could easily draw Beijing into the picture.[44] The opposition was further reinforced by a rising spate of sabotage activities by the Communist insurgents as well as by the continuation of anti-government radio propaganda broadcast from the Voice of the Malayan Revolution. True, the Chinese diplomats in Kuala Lumpur had behaved impeccably by taking an inordinately low profile; but this did not help the situation so long as Beijing adhered to the principle of separating state-to-state relations from (communist) party-to-party relations in its general approach to foreign relations with the ASEAN countries. Consequently, there was a growing feeling among the younger UMNO leaders that Razak's historic diplomatic venture with China, however pioneering in nature, had simply failed to achieve its original objective of developing a better leverage for the government to reduce its internal security threat.

The Malaysian frustration was conveyed to Chinese Senior Vice-Premier Deng Xiaoping during his 1978 Southeast Asian tour. To counteract the Vietnamese diplomatic manoeuvre, Deng made a similar diplomatic trip to ASEAN in November 1978 close at the heels of Vietnamese Premier Pham Van Dong. In Kuala Lumpur, Dong did not hesitate to acquiesce to the demand of his host and readily made a public pledge that Vietnam would not give any support to the Communist guerillas in Malaysia for the obvious reason that the MCP were Beijing-oriented.[45] Deng, however, refused to make a similar statement on the grounds that it was 'an important point of principle for China and to change it would have serious international implications'.[46] However, Deng did made a concession by paying respect to the Malaysian National Monument for those killed in suppressing the Communist insurgents.

In retrospect, Deng's visit actually sparked off a renewed debate among the Malaysian leadership on the two critical issues with which Beijing was involved directly or indirectly: China's support for MCP, and Chinese policy towards the Malaysian Chinese. These two perennial issues in Malaysian politics had been put aside temporarily by Razak in his thrust for normalisation with China but had now reappeared in a new guise as 'structural problems' in the Sino–Malaysian relationship. Datuk Hussein Onn, who succeeded Tun Razak as Malaysia's Prime Minister, bluntly told Deng that Malaysia would not compromise its fight 'to eliminate the threat posed by the Communist terrorists and other subversive elements'.[47] The equally blunt Chinese Vice-Premier emphasised that China would not publicly disown MCP but preferred 'to be judged by its actions'. In the end, Malaysian frustration remained, as reflected in Datuk Hussein's statement:[48]

> It takes two to have an agreement. If one cannot agree, what does the other do? Do we have no diplomatic relations at all or do we have diplomatic relations? Or do we say we understand what to us sounds a bit illogical, but to them is logical?

Deng also touched off an issue concerning the Malaysia Chinese which struck the raw nerves of the UMNO leadership. Prior to Deng's arrival, a leading UMNO member virtually warned the Malaysian Chinese to stay away from Deng.[49] In the event, most Malaysian Chinese were 'indifferent' to Deng's visit, in part due to the deliberately tight security measures, which insulated Deng from the masses of the Malaysian Chinese.[50] Referring to the status of the Malaysian Chinese, Deng restated China's well-known policy on overseas Chinese, namely, that of encouraging them to take up the citizenship of their residence and abide by the local laws. However, Deng also emphasised that the Chinese in Malaysia, while having the same duties as other ethnic groups, should also enjoy the same 'equal rights' and that their 'proper rights and interests should be protected and guaranteed'. Championing 'equality', an internationally accepted principle, might appear to be a harmless statement on the part of Deng. But it touched the most sensitive spot in Malaysian politics. This is because the New Economic policy, introduced after the 1969 riots, was deliberately designed to bias the political, economic and social opportunities in favour of the *bumiputras*. Most Malaysian Chinese certainly felt that in many ways they were not treated as first-class citizens, but the *bumiputras*, who controlled the political power, would continue to argue that some initial discrimination is necessary to achieve equality for the Malays. Hence the endless polemics that have since divided Malaysia's domestic politics. Suffice it to say that Deng's apparently unintended intrusion into the controversy through an oblique reference to the racial issue in Malaysia only served to reinforce the deep-rooted distrust of Beijing by many UMNO leaders. Deng thus left Kuala Lumpur with Sino–Malaysian relations 'friendly, proper and correct', but he did not achieve the increase in good-will that he had originally intended.[51]

Sino–Malaysian relations after Deng's visit in fact grew cooler, partly due to the aggravation of the unresolved problems facing both sides, and partly because of the emergence of new factors in Malaysian domestic politics. A new generation of Malay leadership had taken over the government and UMNO, and they had not been originally involved in Razak's normalisation process with China. The young, Dr Seri Mahathir Mohamad, who succeeded Datuk Hussein Onn as Malaysia's Prime Minister, openly departed from the established policy on China set by his two predecessors. To begin with Dr Mahathir, who, before coming to power, used to hold strong (Malay) chauvinist views and be strongly resentful of the economic influence of Malaysian Chinese, appears to be less broad-minded than Razak and therefore less likely to be well-disposed towards Beijing. Mathathir also broke away from the previous ASEAN stand on Vietnam and regarded China as a more dangerous long term threat to the region than Vietnam. He saw China as a country with 'potential expansionism southwards', so that China in the long run would be as disruptive to ASEAN's stability as the Soviet Union, even though Beijing has openly pledged firm support for ASEAN.[52]

The new Malaysian Foreign Minister, Tan Sri Ghazali Shafie, was also publicly critical of China for its continued support of the Communist insurgents in Malaysia. In January 1981 Beijing gave permission to the Chairman of MCP, Musa Ahmad, to return to Malaysia. This appeared to the Malaysian public as a form of defection, dealing a disastrous blow to the MCP. Instead of interpreting Musa's return as a sign of Beijing's reduction of support for the MCP, Ghazali declared that the Malaysian government would continue its war against subversion and pointedly added: 'In seeking a solution, we felt we must go to the source – which is in Beijing.'[53]

Not surprisingly, Chinese Premier Zhao Ziyang's goodwill visit to Malaysia in August 1981 achieved even less than Deng's. Zhao's reaffirmation of Chinese policy of not interfering in the internal affairs of ASEAN countries was not regarded as sufficient, and he was under strong pressure to clarify further China's official stand on the local Communist movement. Zhao pleaded that China's relations with the MCP were purely 'political and moral' and China would do its utmost to deal with those 'questions left over from history'.[54] But the Malaysian leadership was still not satisfied.

In the circumstances it is difficult to see how China could possibly act to resolve the two fundamental issues endemic in its relations with Malaysia without drastically revising the political and ideological premises for its foreign policy. However, without a solution of these two problems, the present Malaysian leadership (which is likely to stay in power for a long time), would clearly be unwilling to develop cordial relations with Beijing, such as China currently enjoys with the Philippines and Thailand. On the other hand, barring a sharp shift in the region's geo-political balance or an abrupt turnabout in China's domestic politics, Sino–Malaysian relations are not likely to grow much cooler. Whatever the political relationship, Sino–Malaysian trade will continue to expand steadily. It has weathered the worst political interference in the past, and its future viability should remain in no doubt.

By and large, the range of problems that has plagued Sino–Malaysian relations has also operated in the Sino–Singapore sphere, but in Singapore the problems were naturally seen in a different light and took a different shape. On the economic front, Singapore has similarly suffered from trade deficits with China. But unlike Malaysia, it is not the least concerned with its trade imbalance with China. This is not just because Singapore's economy is consistently in surplus in its balance of payments, but also because most of Singapore's important trade partners have also recorded large surpluses in their trade with Singapore.

In its traditional entrêpot role, Singapore overcomes its trade deficits with the export of services as well as through various forms of invisible earnings. In the case of trade with China, a great deal of Singapore's imports are re-exported to Malaysia and Indonesia. In Singapore, re-exports of goods to Indonesia are unrecorded. So are the numerous tourist purchases. Accordingly, the trade deficits with China have never been a matter of real concern to the Singapore authorities, except as a tactical starting point from which to urge China to buy more Singapore-made goods.

What has really annoyed Singapore traders, however, have been the persistent discriminatory pricing practices of China against the Singapore (and also Malaysian) markets. All along China has been quoting lower prices for its exports to Hong Kong than for the same goods exported to Singapore and Malaysia. The price differentials are so wide that Singapore importers find it cheaper to buy Chinese products from the Hong Kong agents than to import directly from China. The Singapore Federation of Chambers of Commerce and Industry has been for years urging China to discontinue such unfair practices.[55]

On the political level, Singapore government has similarly watched closely over China's policy towards the 'overseas Chinese' and towards the local Communist movement. During Mr Deng Xioaping's visit to Singapore as the last leg of his Southeast Asian tour in late 1978, Mr Lee Kuan Yew made it clear that Singapore was determined to remain non-Communist and that Chinese Singaporeans did not regard themselves as 'overseas Chinese' any more. The Singapore official statement issued after Lee's talks with Deng thus emphasised:[56]

We explained (to the Chinese visitors) our efforts to create a Singapore identity and that we do not regard ourselves as overseas Chinese and part and parcel of the overseas Chinese problem.

As a result of sustained material and social progress over the past two decades, Singapore's government has in the main achieved its goals of inculcating among Chinese Singaporeans a sense of national identity, which provides them with a different outlook from those on mainland China. Similar progress has also strengthened the political muscles of the ruling PAP government and provided the best insurance against Communist insurgence. This prompted an observer to remark that Lee's message for Deng was actually aimed at Singapore's suspicious neighbours, an 'understandable compulsion here to be "more Catholic than the Pope" '.[57]

So minimal were the areas of real conflicts that Zhao's visit to Singapore in August 1981 was both cordial and low-keyed, in sharp contrast to his near-confrontation with the Malaysian leadership in Kuala Lumpur.[58] In Singapore the main focus of Lee's talks with Zhao was on the regional issue rather than on bilateral problems, such as the Kampuchean issue, the Soviet menace to the region, and China's dilemmas over its past relations with the Communist parties in Southeast Asia.[59]

A number of factors have contributed to the difference between Singapore and Malaysia in their respective reaction to China's approaches to Southeast Asia. Obviously, as a predominantly Chinese society, Singapore has no psychological antipathy towards China or pathological fear of China's ulterior motives now that post-Mao China has discarded its rigid ideological stance and revolution-ary zeal. Singapore currently faces no Communist insurgent activities and its continuing economic prosperity has effectively immunised it against any such threat in the future. The Singapore leadership is also more flexible and perceptive. Mr Lee Kuan Yew shares the prevalent view that China can be an effective counterweight to the Soviet ambition in the ASEAN region. Further, China is seen to be a stabilising influence in the region as long as the Indochina problem remains unresolved.[60]

Singapore's Role

As the commercial and financial hub and the entrêpot centre of the region, Singapore is apt to play a vital and even a catalyst role in China's expanding economic relations with Southeast Asia. Such a role is perceived to be of mutual benefit to both China and Singapore, and not inimical to the interests of other ASEAN countries. As a predominantly Chinese city-state, Singapore would hesitate to develop an intimate or overtly friendly political relationship with China in deference to political hyper-sensitivity on the part of Singapore's neighbours. However, other ASEAN countries would understand and accept Singapore's efforts to develop close economic ties with China on an open basis. This is not just because Singapore owes its very survival and prosperity to its ability to seize new commercial opportunities and open new markets anywhere in the world, but also because growing Sino-Singapore economic relations may even have beneficial results for the ASEAN region as a whole. Both China and Singapore are pragmatic nations; they have shown that their expanding economic relationship can be operated in-dependently of their political relationship.

There are three major components in the emerging Sino–Singapore economic relationship. The first is the all-important two-way trade, which is in fact the main sinew of China's trade with Southeast Asia. The two-way trade between Singapore and China did not grow much in the first part of the 1970s, after its spurt in the late 1960s. In 1976, the trade actually experienced a slight decline, even though Sino–Singapore normalisation process had officially begun in March 1975 with the visit of Singapore Foreign Minister, Rajaratnam, to Beijing. The poor performance of Sino–Singapore trade throughout most of the 1970s indicated that it lacked underlying strength for its further growth.

It was not until 1979, when China launched its programme of economic modernisation, that Sino–Singapore trade resumed its growth and then it rapidly built up momentum in 1980. As shown in Table 4.9, the growth of trade since 1979 has been phenomenal, with a more than two-fold increase in the short span of three years. Much of the increase was due to the rise of Chinese exports to Singapore. However, there has also been during the same period a sharp increase in Singapore's exports to China, clearly indicating that Singapore, among a handful of countries in the Third World, has been successfully penetrating the much-coveted China market.

The rise of Singapore's exports to China not only helps, to reduce Singapore's trade deficits with China but also carries some far-reaching implications. As shown in Table 4.10, Singapore's exports to China used to be dominated by rubber, but since 1980 they have included many non-traditional items, noticeably, TV sets, oil rigs and some capital equipment, mostly produced and marketed by the multinational corporations based in Singapore. This has raised the exciting prospects of increasing Singapore's exports of medium-technology goods and certain specialised capital equipment needed by China's economic modernisation, such as off-shore and on-shore equipment for oil exploration. With regional supremacy in oil and gas services, Singapore is eyeing intently oil exploration activities off the China coasts, and hopes to cash in if the offshore oil boom in China materialises in the second part of 1980s.[61]

Apart from trade, the financial aspects are also critical to Singapore's future participation in the China market. This involves not only financing trade covering exports to China but also the financing of development in China such as project loans and joint ventures. In recent years, China has abandoned its time-honoured policy of financial self-reliance. Beijing has realised that, to finance its economic development programme, China cannot stand entirely on its own but has to borrow from foreign sources. In the short run, China needs export credits; but it also needs long-term financing from external sources for huge investment projects with large capital outlays.

When China first unveiled its massive modernisation programme in 1979, the world finance community initially responded with great enthusiasm. China immediately secured substantial credit lines totalling US$ 23–30 billion. By 1981 it was reported that China had actually drawn US$8.78 billion in foreign funds.[62]

As a financial centre in the region, Singapore obviously has a potentially important role to play in financing China's trade and development. In Asia, Singapore is a centre for funding, as opposed to loan syndication for Hong Kong. At present, Singapore's current exports to China are too small for significant financing operations. Also, if China were to go for syndicated loans now it would probably benefit the European financial markets rather than those in the region.[63] However, as Sino–Singapore trade continues to expand rapidly, Singapore's financial institutions could be more extensively involved. In the long run, one cannot rule out the possibility of China coming directly to financial markets in Singapore, and this would provide all the preconditions for closer financial co-operation. And more than financial services alone would be involved. As the only economy in the region with an export-oriented service sector, Singapore can provide other ranges of economic services such as management and technical consulting, technology transfer, and transport and telecommunications, which will be highly valuable to China's economic modernisation efforts.

The third component in the growing Sino–Singapore economic relations is concerned with Singapore's direct involvement in China's internal economic development through various forms of co-operation such as joint venture, co-production or compensation trade schemes. Unlike some ASEAN governments, the Singapore government does not frown upon Beijing's plans to attract capital and expertise from the ethnic Chinese to participate in China's economic modernisation efforts. Singapore takes a more positive view that direct economic involvement in China by local and Singapore-based foreign firms will enable them to gain a foothold in the Chinese economy that will ultimately enlarge Singapore's share in the China market and will work to the mutual advantage of both countries. Currently, Singapore interests are widely involved in various joint ventures with China, including hotels, textiles, shipbuilding and food-processing. The government's Economic Development Board (EDB) has in fact promoted some of these projects.[64] The semi-government Intraco has also been very active in the China market, and has recently secured the agency rights for direct distribution of some China products.[65]

Well equipped with the necessary institutional and material resources, Singapore is thus actively responding to rising economic opportunities in China. In strengthening its economic ties with China, Singapore is also opening up avenues eventually for other ASEAN countries to participate in the Chinese market and also for China to be more involved in economic development of the region. In future, when business concerns from other ASEAN countries, particularly those run by ethnic Chinese, set about entering the China market, they will find it more convenient to go through the established 'Singapore connection'.[66]

In conclusion, it may be reiterated that both Malaysia and Singapore will continue to be the mainstay of China's overall economic relations with ASEAN, with the bulk of China's trade with the region centred on this sector. Both Malaysia and Singapore will be in a better position than other Southeast Asian countries to respond to new economic opportunities arising from China. In particular, Singapore's advantage over all the other Southeast Asian countries is even more clear cut.

5

The Philippines' Relations
with China

Introduction

Among the ASEAN countries the Philippines is geographically the closest to China, with the two countries being separated only by a stretch of 600 miles of the South China Sea. 'So physically close are the Philippines and China that ancient stories tell of land bridges connecting the Philippines and China'.[1] Historically, contacts between the two countries can be traced back to ancient times. It was reported that the tributes from the Luzon island were sent to Chinese Imperial Court as early as 3000 years ago, although significant contacts started much later.

Despite the imperatives of geography and history, however, the Philippines and China experienced a long period of lopsided relationship during the two decades of 1950s and 1960s, starting with the Communist revolution in China in 1949. This was a clear example of an extreme form of Cold War diplomacy, in the context of which both governments developed mutual misperceptions of each other's intentions and at times even indulged in diatribes against each other. Thus the staunchly anti-Communist Philippine government imposed a strict diplomatic quarantine against any form of contact with any socialist country, lest such contacts should open an avenue for 'Communist subversion'. On the other hand, the Chinese government from time to time haughtily dismissed the Philippines as not being an independent state but merely a 'puppet' of American imperialism. It was not until the turn of 1970 when the Cold War in

123

Asia started to thaw, following the announcement of President Nixon's visit to Beijing, that both the Philippines and China made serious endeavours to approach each other. Later, the process of Sino–Philippine detente was quickened by fundamental foreign policy changes in both countries. Apprehensive of the rapid disengagement of the United States from Southeast Asia, the Philippines became alive to the political liability of operating a rigid foreign policy based on almost total identification with American policy objectives, and decided to pursue a more pragmatic attitude towards relations with the Communist world. At the same time, China, emerging from the turmoil of the Cultural Revolution, started to mend its diplomatic fences damaged by the radical 'revolutionary foreign policy' of the 1960s and took new initiatives to widen foreign contacts by launching the 'Ping Pong Diplomacy'. Hence both countries drifted towards rapprochement, which eventually crystallised in the establishment of diplomatic relations in 1975.

Since 1975, Sino–Philippine relations have continued to improve. Over the years the Philippines has become China's most friendly country in the ASEAN region, with very few outstanding political issues that are likely to upset their cordial relationship in the foreseeable future. This is a far cry from the Cold War days when the Philippines was China's most hostile country in the region. In the views of a senior Filipino diplomat, this 'confirms that geography is truly an inescapable factor in Philippines' foreign relations'.[2]

Trade between the Philippines and China started in the early 1970s, before formalisation of diplomatic relations. Taking advantage of some favourable structural factors, Sino–Philippine trade has since grown rapidly and has in fact provided a strong economic impetus for the Philippine government to move towards finalising its diplomatic ties with China. The present level of Sino–Philippine trade is still small in quantitative terms but is regarded to be mutually beneficial by both sides. Moreover, the trade is conducted apparently on a sound base, holding good potentials for further growth. The trade will continue to add significant economic muscle to the burgeoning overall Sino–Philippines relations.

Early Commercial Relations

Chinese records of the Sung Dynasty (960–1278) already referred to flourishing trade between China and the Philippines. By the Ming Dynasty (1368–1644) this trade was firmly established on a regular basis.[3] With the arrival of the Spanish in the Philippines in 1521, Chinese merchants began to settle there. To the Chinese in the Philippines the three and a half centuries of Spanish colonial rule was a period of prolonged struggle for survival in the face of frequent massacres, expulsion, and economic and legal discriminations.[4] The trade soon became stagnant, particularly during the closing years of the decaying Spanish rule when numerous trade restrictions were imposed. From the Chinese sources, Sino–Philippine trade started to dwindle from the peak of 440 000 Hk taels* in 1868 to 100 000 Hk taels in 1898, which was the last year of Spanish sovereignty in the Philippines.[5] None the less, Sino–Philippine trade had not only survived the adverse commercial climate but also managed to maintain its relative predominance. In 1899, when the trade fell to its lowest level for decades, it still occupied 36 per cent of the Philippines' total trade, with China ranking as the Philippines' biggest trade partner, followed by Great Britain and the United States, with their relative shares of 20 per cent and 15 per cent respectively.[6]

A marked change took place in the general pattern of Philippine foreign trade after the Islands were annexed by the United States in 1898. The American administration was more disposed to free trade and afforded the Philippine economy more opportunities to grow and develop. Trade with China soon increased to one million Hk taels in 1902 and continued to grow until it reached the record 12 million in the early 1930s.[7] During the same period, the Philippines' trade with the United States had grown even faster, both absolutely and relatively, taking advantage of the special status of the United States as a rich metropolitan country. Ten years after the commencement of American rule, the United States accounted for one-third of the

---

* Hk taels or Haikwan taels (meaning 'Customs' monetary unit). It was actually not an existing currency but purely a money of account, with each unit calculated to have 583.30 grams of silver 1000 fine. In the late nineteenth century and in the 1930s, each Hk tael was roughly equal to US$1.20. (Cheng Yu-Kwei, *Foreign Trade and Industrial Development of China*, Washington, D.C., University of Washington Press, 1956).

Philippines' total trade and its share continued to rise to over 70 per cent in the 1930s. The American domination of the Philippine foreign trade sector became the most conspicuous feature of Philippines' external economic relations and lasted well into the years after the Philippines gained independence. With the Americans taking up such an overwhelming share of the Philippine market – as high as 80 per cent on the eve of the Pacific War in 1941 – there was naturally little room left for other countries. But China seemed to be an exception. She continued to carve for herself a relatively significant slice of the Philippine market. In the 1920s, the Chinese share in the Philippines' total trade stood at 5 per cent but it dropped to 3–4 per cent in the early 1930s. In view of the American predominance, such a proportion was actually not small, for it still ranked China as the Philippines' third biggest trade partner, just next to Japan. Historians have since brought to light the fact that both China and the Philippines had played a joint role in the US 'imperialist' expansion into Asia. The Philippines was originally acquired by the United States as a strategic base for the 'illimitable China markets'.[8]

The trade was only of marginal significance from the standpoint of China, for the Philippines' share in China's overall trade never exceeded 1 per cent of China's total foreign trade in the prewar period. The balance of trade was, however, invariably in favour of China. The Philippines imported from China mostly foodstuffs – eggs, meat and lard – and later some textile goods. China imported from the Philippines mainly coconut products, tobacco and timber, which were not really in high demand by the Chinese because of their economic backwardness at that time. Likewise, the generally low levels of income of the Filipinos had also restricted their demand for such staple Chinese exports as silk and tea.[9] Despite some strong favourable historical and geographical preconditions, industrial backwardness in both China and the Philippines was a basic constraint on the growth of Sino–Philippine trade before the war.

The Cold War Era

After the People's Republic of China was proclaimed on 1 October 1949, Premier Zhou Enlai sent a message to the Philippine government inviting diplomatic relations. The initial reaction of President Quirino was one of ambivalence. Earlier, the Philippine Consul General in Shanghai had urged the Philippine government to take a more realistic attitude towards the new Communist government in China, but his advice was not taken seriously. The presidential candidate Jose Laurel also openly cautioned against recognition. Nevertheless, there were moments when it seemed that the Philippines might extend recognition to the People's Republic of China. A strong hint was contained in the inaugural speech of President Quirino on 30 December 1949:[10]

> We respect the right of our neighbours to choose freely their own system of government. In our relations with the Chinese people, with whom we had such close contacts over many centuries, we shall maintain an open mind, giving due heed to the requirements of our national security and the security of Asia as a whole.

In the event, the hesitation resulted in the delay of 25 years. Both the internal and external situations deteriorated so rapidly in the following months that the Philippine government eventually dropped the idea of recognition.

To begin with, most of the Philippine ruling elites, with their American education, Catholic background and landlord origins, were unlikely to be well-disposed towards any Communist regime. They were further shaken by rising insurrection of the Communist–led Hukbalahap (People's Anti-Japanese Army), which was a peasant-based organisation, initially with considerable grass-roots influence in the rural areas. Inspired by the victory of the Communist revolution on mainland China, the Huks stepped up their armed struggle in the early 1950s. Although the Huks movement was quickly put down, it had instilled enough fears into the Philippines leadership of the potential Communist threat. In addition, the Philppine government was apprehensive of possible external moral and material support to the Huks, particularly from the newly-established Communist government in China, which was then espousing revolutionary missions in Asia. There already existed in the Philippines a sizeable number of overseas Chinese who, so it would appear, might become susceptible to 'subversive influences' from Beijing. Thus, increasingly, the Philippine leaders were viewing the 'China question' within the context of the Philippines' own security considerations.

Then there was the Nationalist China factor, which further complicated the whole China issue. Up to April 1949, Nationalist China was the only Asian state with which the Philippines had formal diplomatic relations. Shortly after the Communist liberation of Shanghai, Jiang Jieshi (Chiang Kai-shek) struck a major diplomatic coup by exploiting the Philippine leaders' fear of Asian communism. In July 1949, Jiang paid his first state visit to the Philippines and held talks with President Quirino in Baguio. Even though Jiang failed to persuade the Philippines to commit itself openly to the immediate formation of an Asian Anti-Communist Alliance, he had cultivated good understanding with the Philippine leaders, thereby laying the cornerstone for what was to last for over two decades – a close relationship between Nationalist China in Taiwan and the Philippines. The Baguio meeting produced a joint communiqué, which served warning of the potential danger of Communist expansion in Asia. Understandably, the communiqué was enthusiastically endorsed by Syngman Rhee of South Korea but at the same time viewed with great displeasure by Beijing. China was already irritated by Manila's decision to allow its diplomatic mission to evacuate along with the Nationalists to Taiwan when Shanghai fell. It can thus be seen that diplomatic relations between Beijing and Manila did not start on a really clean slate even at the very beginning.[11]

The outbreak of the Korea War in June 1950 and the subsequent Chinese intervention dispelled whatever ambiguities Manila might have felt towards the question of recognising Beijing. The Korea War brought the Cold War to Asia and led to active American political and military involvement in the region. In the 1950s, Cold War politics divided most Asian countries simplistically into two groups – the American-led 'Free World' versus the Communist 'Iron-Curtain Bloc', with only a handful of neutrals such as Burma and Indonesia standing 'between two camps'.[12] The choice for the Philippines was clear-cut. Political independence of the Philippines did not free it totally from other forms of neo-colonial dependence on the United States. From the outset, the Philippine leaders had committed their country to 'an almost total identification of interest with the United States' and plunged their country straight into the American alliance system.[13] Thus the Philippines was one of the first countries to send combat battalions to South Korea. It also signed a Defence Treaty with the United States and let the US armed forces use its air and naval bases. Above all the Philippines, in September 1954, played host to the formation of the Southeast Asia Treaty Organisation (SEATO), the charter of which was known as the 'Manila Pact'.[14]

Throughout the 1950s, the Philippines' policy towards China was a simple extension of the US Secretary of State John Foster Dulles' anti-China containment policy. Indeed, the Philippine government did Dulles 'one better by shunning contact with all Communist countries'.[15] Manila's policy of upholding non-recognition and banning trade with any Communist country was much more thorough and stringent than that ever implemented by any of the other Southeast Asian countries, including Thailand. Within such a rigid foreign policy framework, the Philippines had few alternatives but to cling to a few like-minded anti-Communist (so-called 'free') Asian countries such as Taiwan, South Korea, South Vietnam and Thailand, leading to the founding of the right-wing Asian People's Anti-Communist League (APACL).

Specifically with Taiwan, the Philippines had developed a special relationship. Thus, the Philippine representation in Taipei was upgraded to full ambassadorial level as soon as the Philippine government decided against recognition of Beijing. In 1957, the Philippines signed a trade pact with Taiwan. The two sides also put up a series of exchange programmes including the frequent exchange of visits by dignitaries, culminating in the first state visit to Taiwan by President Garcia in 1960 and the return visit to the Philippines by the Nationalist Vice-President Chen Cheng in 1963.[16] During the Taiwan Straits crisis in 1960, Garcia went as far as stating publicly that the Philippines would 'react actively, militarily or otherwise' in the event of a Communist attack on Taiwan.[17] The climax of the Philippines' relations with Taiwan was reached when President Marcos declared 1966 as the 'Philippines-China Friendship Year'.

The more the Philippines gravitated towards Taiwan, the further it drifted away from China. However, the Chinese official reaction to Philippines' total commitment to the anti-Communist alliance system was surprisingly mild. Beijing's official remarks on the Philippines were often confined to deriding the Philippine ruling elites for pursuing a 'subservient' foreign policy as though the Philippines was a 'client state' of the United States, its former colonial master. After 1954, the Chinese propaganda machinery stopped openly advocating insurgent activities in the Philippines, in line with its 'smiling diplomacy'. Basically, China, at least up to 1958, was making an effort to present a 'benign face in Southeast Asia'.[18] This was most evident during the Bandung Conference in 1955, at which Premier Zhou Enlai, through his exercise of consummate diplomacy, was able to make a deep impression on the Philippine delegates, led by Carlos Romulo, with regard to the 'reasonableness' of China's basic policy towards the Philippines. Zhou repeatedly assured the Filipinos that 'China entertained no aggressive designs on the Philippines'.[19] Romulo was invited to visit China and to roam about freely to see for himself 'the good, the bad, and the in-between'.[20] When Romulo later returned to Manila he deleted all official references to his contacts with Zhou.[21] This clearly indicates that the international Cold War atmosphere at that time was too forbidding for any possible rapprochement between the Philippines and China, regardless of their true intents, once the two countries were locked into opposite camps.

After 1958 China started to draw away from the Soviet Union and increasingly assumed a role of leadership in Third-World communism. Consequently, China's policy towards the Philippines became more abrasive, in keeping with the hardening of China's overall foreign policy towards Southeast Asia. Specifically, China stepped up hostile propaganda against the governments of Southeast Asia. In the 1950s it was often not easy for the Philippine government to justify its Cold War approaches to China, and at times the Philippine government had to resort to moral and religious arguments (the 'godless ideology of Communism'). With China now abandoning its moderate image, based on the policy of peaceful coexistence, and supporting local revolutionary movements in Southeast Asia, the Philippine government was in effect conveniently given a *raison d'être* for prolonging its inflexible China policy.

Meanwhile the escalation of the Vietnam War deepened the American involvement in the conflict, bringing the Cold War in Asia to a new climax. In 1966, soon after assuming his first term in office, President Marcos dispatched a contingent of army engineers and security troops to South Vietnam to boost the many flags image of the American war effort. This served to sharpen Sino–Philippine antagonism, because China was not only a close ally of North Vietnam but was also feeling threatened by increasing American military presence in the region.

Towards the end of the 1960s there emerged in the Philippines a splinter group of young Philippine Communists who organised themselves into the new People's Army' and openly paid ideological homage to Mao Zedong's Thought. This further strengthened the hands of the Philippine conservatives, particularly those in the military and intelligence circles, who had long suspected China of conducting subversive activities inside the Philippines. In short, there were simply too many stumbling blocks for any improvements in Sino–Philippine relations in the 1960s.

Consistency was the one admirable feature of the Philippines' China policy throughout the two Cold War decades. All along, high-ranking Philippine leaders were frankly and unequivocally against the recognition of China and its admission to the United Nations. Trade with China was strictly prohibited. So were travel and other forms of contact. China, Asia's biggest country just 600 miles across the South China Sea, was in effect non-existent to this archipelago. In the context of the Cold War, trade with any Communist country was regarded as affording a convenient avenue for 'Communist infilt-ration'. Such thinking was vividly reflected in a statement by President Garcia in 1958:[22]

> I am not prepared to engage in even limited trade with Communist China. We would be on the losing end because in the long run we would spend more to combat the trouble Communist agents would stir up once we let them in as traders than we would ever realise in profits from the trade.

The Road to Normalisation

In the Philippines there was no shortage of enlightened individuals who would from time to time question the general wisdom of their country's US–dominated foreign policy as well as the basic ratio-nality underlying the rigid, blanket anti-Communist approach to international relations. The foremost of these liberal sceptics was Senator Claro Recto, who from the beginning had been outspoken against Magsaysay's all-embracing relationship with the United States and had urged the Philippine government to adopt a more flexible foreign policy, not totally identified with the Western bloc but moving towards 'Asia for Asians', then a popular advocacy by such neutrals as Burma and Indonesia. The liberals maintained that differences between countries in their political and economic systems should not constitute an obstacle to their peaceful coexistence, which was a basic tenet of the Bandung spirit. They maintained that diplomatic relations between the Philippines and a Communist country would not necessarily imply that the Philippines had an obligation to endorse the Communist ideology. The liberals put up an even stronger case for opening up commercial relations with a Communist country as a more pragmatic approach. [23] But the liberal protest in the stifling Cold War atmosphere of the 1950s was no more than a voice in the wilderness. Magsaysay himself had declared that 'Neutralism is un-Filipino'. [24]

The budding nationalism in the Philippines continued to grow during the 1960s. [25] When Marcos first took office, he was under mounting pressure to introduce some flexibility into the Philippines' China policy. In March 1966 he made it legal for the first group of Filipinos, led by the woman Senator Maria Kalaw Katigbak, to visit China. The group returned to Manila calling for the opening up of both diplomatic and trade relations with China. [26]

In the same year, the Philippines experienced a very bad rice harvest, owing to severe natural calamities, and had to import a large quantity of rice to make up for domestic shortfalls. China, a regular and significant rice exporter, immediately responded and offered to sell 200 000 tons of rice at prices 20–30 per cent below the world market price. [27] This at once touched off a great political controversy. While the Philippine National Rice and Corn Administration was in favour of importing rice from China because it was 'cheap and of better quality than the rice from Thailand, Burma, Cambodia or Egypt' [28], the foreign affairs establishment, still under strong American influence, was opposed to the deal. Eventually Marcos, in March 1967, gave the green light for the Chinese rice to be imported, not directly from China but in a roundabout way, via Hong Kong. [29]

President Marcos was quick to spot the changing international and domestic political mood. In 1968 he revealed at a news conference the first sign of foreign policy change in a statement: 'It is my proposition that it is about time that perhaps we establish trade relations and perhaps diplomatic relations with some of the socialist countries'. [30] He was, however, quick to add that this did not include bigger socialist countries like the Soviet Union and China. A few months later, in January 1969, the staunchly anti-Communist Foreign Secretary Romulo echoed the new policy line more explicitly by calling for a 'positive and open-minded approach' towards trade with Communist countries. In regard to relations with China, Romulo further said that this 'will depend on whether the latter will commit itself to a policy of friendliness and mutual respect'.[31] A crack thus opened in the Philippines' two-decade old 'no-trade and non-recognition' China policy.

However, as seems quite natural for a country with its foreign policy locked into a 'special relationship with the United States', no real initiative for a radical policy change would be possible without prior change in the Americans' own policy. The signal for the American detente with China finally came in May 1971 with President Nixon's announcement of his intention to visit China. This rendered the Philippines' Cold War oriented China policy obsolete overnight. A real turning-point in the Philippines' relations with China was contained in Romulo's speech towards the end of 1971:[32]

> The vital question of the 'People's Republic of China' and its future role in international relations can hardly be avoided in any consideration of the prospects for peace and stability in Asia. The policies of Peking – good, bad or indifferent – inevitably touch on the life of the countries of the region. The sheer fact of geography and the imperatives of the political life made it difficult if not impossible to adhere permanently to a negative policy of isolation from a government which exercises control over a population that approaches a billion in number.

China was no longer a non-country but as Marcos admitted in late 1973:[33]

> It is not only unwise but certainly the highest form of indiscretion and avoidance not to take into account the People's Republic of China in all matters pertaining to security as well as the economic development of our country.

However, changes in the Philippine official perception of China did not lead to immediate diplomatic relations, which materialised only after a rather long and tortuous period. To begin with the Philippine government found it quite difficult to shake off links with Taiwan, while Beijing always insisted on severance as a precondition for any direct diplomatic relations with China. For more than two decades Taiwan had been a close ally of the Philippines, and their cordial relationship had further been cemented in the 1970s by rising trade and programmes of exchange and development cooperation, including a generous rice loan from Taiwan in May 1971.[34] Furthermore, the Nationalist Chinese had cultivated a strong lobby inside the Philippines, with support from some influential and wealthy Chinese businessmen. The waves of terrorist bombings in down-town Manila by the Maoist–inclined New People's Army around 1970 also added convenient propaganda benefits to the Taiwan lobby. For a time, it seemed as though the Philippine government wanted to follow an easy option of going for a two-China policy, as strongly hinted in Marcos' 1971 State-of-the-Nation address: 'We must reorient foreign policy to gain new friends while strengthening the ties with old ones'.

The road to rapprochement with Beijing was therefore destined to be a rather long one. Taking advantage of the relaxation in government restrictions on travels to China, many Filipino journalists, businessmen, academics and civic groups joined the increasing streams of foreigners visiting China since 1970. In September 1971, the Philippine Chamber of Commerce sent its first trade delegation to Beijing, where Premier Zhou Enlai told its members that 'the only thing obstructing the opening of trade between the Philippines and China is the Philippine government'.[35] In October 1971 Marcos dispatched his Executive Secretary Alejandro Melchor to lead a mission to Moscow, and Melchor returned to Manila a convinced advocate of normalising relations with the Soviet bloc. Such normalisation process actually started in early 1972, first with Yugoslavia and Rumania, and then with other East European countries. At the same time Marcos sent off brother-in-law Benjamin 'Kokoy' Romualdez, Governor of Leyte Province, on a secret mission to Beijing to have a private meeting with Zhou Enlai. Romualdez was told that China could trade with the Philippines without the benefit of diplomatic relations but that the Philippines would have eventually to sever all ties with Taiwan before there could be real progress towards normalisation.[36]

On 11 March 1972, a new land-mark was registered in the Philippines' foreign policy, when Marcos signed the Presidential Executive Order No. 384 formally to legalise trade with a socialist country.[37] Meanwhile, the Philippines was once again struck by rice shortages, despite the early euphoria over the success of the Green Revolution. The new rule came in a good time to formalise the import of 10 000 tons of rice from China in exchange of 3000 tons of Philippine coconut oil.[38] Thus, the Philippines and China were already in active rapprochement even before Nixon made his historic journey to Beijing.

To foster further growth of Sino–Philippine trade, which now seemed to appear quite promising, the Philippine Department of Commerce proposed the formation of a special trading corporation to handle its China trade and the assignment of trade representatives to be stationed permanently in Beijing and Shanghai. But Marcos would only agree to the setting up of the semi-government National Export Trading Corporation and would not go as far as setting up trade offices in China, which could precipitate progress toward hasty diplomatic recognition of China. By the end of 1972 Marcos was still too cautious to consider taking such a drastic move. Several developments had in fact occurred to slow down the normalisation process.

Both China and the Philippines had been used to avoiding each other for so long, and the detente seemed to have unfolded itself so rapidly, that the Philippines needed time to study the change as Romulo remarked in the middle of 1971. Close relations with a Communist country like China represented an uncharted course for which the Philippine government had gradually to re-orient itself. After all, even the United States, to which the Philippines still looked for new diplomatic initiatives, did not declare recognition immediately after Nixon's visit. Further, the road to Beijing meant sacrificing Taiwan. Meanwhile, the Taiwan lobby had been stepping up pressure against such a move. In trying to maintain the status quo for as long as possible, Taiwan's new envoy, Dr Liu Chieh, had attempted to mobilise all the conservative forces in Manila, including some religious leaders, to block the normalisation process.[39] Above all, the Philippines was in the grips of growing social unrest – so much so that Marcos had to declare martial law for the country. Faced with mounting opposition to his rule, Marcos had to give top priority to urgent domestic issues and was not inclined to be venturesome in foreign policy. Earlier on Mrs Imelda Marcos' trips to East Europe, undertaken without prior consultation with the Philippine Senate, had already aroused strong criticism from the opposition leaders.[40] Thus Marcos had to be extremely cautious in any new China venture.

With these obstacles existing in 1972, the outlook for Sino–Philippine relations in 1973 did not seem to be promising for anything more concrete than diplomatic overtures. In the long run, of course, diplomatic overtures are no less significant as they can lay down the necessary groundwork for the final breakthrough. Thus, in January 1973, Marcos approved the sending of the first official Philippine Trade Mission to China, comprising mainly members of the Philippine Chamber of Commerce.[41] The Trade Mission, led by Dr Wigberto Clavecilla, went to Beijing in May 1973. Although no trade agreement was signed Zhou Enlai told Clavecilla that China was ready to increase trade and enter into various forms of cooperation with the Philippines as a prelude to diplomatic relations, including the possibility of letting the Philippines set up a trade liaison office in Beijing, like that of the United States. Clavecilla called the trade mission a success and he was 'impressed by Premier Zhou Enlai's understanding attitude towards the Philippines' dilemma of recognition of China at the expense of Taiwan'.[42] Following the visit of the Philippine trade mission, Marcos' public stand on China became more conciliatory. When interviewed by a Hong Kong newspaper in May 1973, Marcos said that domestic dissension in the Philippines, which he had once attributed to the work of Maoist terrorists, would not be allowed to impede the Philippines' move towards normalising relations with China. He further denied the possibility of Beijing supporting any 'subversion' in the Philippines.[43] This was a remarkable change of official attitude!

Before 1973 was over a Chinese trade mission returned a visit to the Philippines. The Chinese left Manila with a public offer to purchase US$40 million worth of Philippine goods as well as agreeing to the Philippine government's proposal for a trade office to be set up either in Guangzhou (Canton) or in Beijing.[44] The Chinese trade mission also made an agreement to conduct direct trade between the two countries instead of dealing through Hong Kong.[45]

Meanwhile, conditions favourable for the normalisation of Sino–Philippine ties rapidly emerged. Towards the end of 1973 the OPEC began to cut back oil production and this led to the development of the world's first oil crisis. The international oil companies served notice to Manila that the Philippines would face a delivery cutback of 12–34 per cent. At the same time, China's oil industry was booming, having enjoyed over 20 per cent rate of growth during the early 1970s. Furthermore, China started to export oil to Hong Kong and Japan. When the Philippine trade mission was in Beijing, China had offered to supply oil to the Philippines at prices much lower than those offered by the American oil companies.[46] With the oil crisis spreading to the Philippines, the immediate hope of easing the problem appeared to hinge on China as a new source of supply. In September 1974 the first lady, Mrs Imelda Marcos, visited China and the climax of her trip was the conclusion of an oil agreement with China. Under this agreement, China would sell to the Philippines 'considerable quantities' of crude oil in exchange for such Philippine products as sugar, lumber, copper and coconut products.[47] About a month later the first shipment of the much-needed Chinese crude oil to the Philippines totalling one million tons arrived in Manila.[48]

Following closely on the heels of the oil crisis came the 'food crisis'. It has now come to light that the Philippines could have been hit in the early 1970s by the long-term adverse weather cycle, leading to a series of bad rice harvests, which in turn had set back the Philippine government's goal for rice self-sufficiency. In 1973, however, bad weather had also affected rice output in Thailand, the region's traditional granary. This prompted the Thai authorities to cut back rice exports, even to their traditional buyers. In the circumstances, the Philippines had to look for new sources of rice supply from the United States and China. Actually, ever since the late 1960s when Chinese rice was first imported into the Philippines via Hong Kong, it had become obvious to the Philippines that China could be an attractive source of rice imports. Indeed, it was with the rice trade in mind that the Philippine Secretary of Agriculture was among the strong advocates for opening up direct trade with China as early as in January 1972. In August 1972 China also donated one million yuan worth of rice and medicine to aid the flood victims in Central Luzon. Therefore, rice, like petroleum, was another strategic commodity which had greatly helped to pave the way for diplomatic normalisation with China.

The world economic crises during the early 1970s had made a profound impact on the Philippine leaders. The events clearly demonstrated to them that the Philippines could enlist the co-operation of China to help cope with its domestic economic problems. The Chinese supplies of rice and petroleum at the time when these two essential commodities were most needed had added tremendous weight to the argument that the Philippines' normalisation of relations with China was not just motivated to meet the requirement of international politics but was also rationally based on pragmatic economic grounds. Prior to the world crises, the economic dimension was not so obvious in the Sino–Philippine relations, which had always been couched in geo–political terms. The new 'pragmatic' view must have urged Marcos to make up his mind on the China question. Hence in August 1974 he formally advised the United States and the other ASEAN members that the Philippines had decided to recognise China 'soon'.[49]

The world economic crises also brought to the fore the many structural defects inherent in the economic systems of both the advanced and less developed countries. For the industrially advanced countries, the focus was on pollution and environment, the wasteful consumption of depletable resources, and similar problems. For many underdeveloped countries, the combined energy and food crises compounded their plight. Amidst such great uncertainty and gloom on the international economic scene, China seemed to be a new source of inspiration for many Third World countries, partly out of myth and partly because China then stood out clearly as one of the few countries which seemed, thanks to the application of the Maoist self-reliant development strategy, to have successfully averted the major economic woes that were then plaguing the rich and poor countries alike. A sort of crisis of faith with the West prevailed in many Third World countries whose leaders were beginning to question the viability of the materially-oriented western civilisation. The New International Economic Order was about to emerge, with different political and economic assumptions from the past. In the case of the Philippines, the new mood was reflected in the termination in 1974 of the Laurel-Langley Agreement, bringing to an end the special trade relations between the Philippines and the United States.[50]

The sentiments of the Philippines were reflected in Marcos' somewhat emotive statement made at the time of the visit by the Chinese basketball team to the Philippines in May 1974:[51]

> Chairman Mao Tse-tung's [Mao Zedong] success in binding together the Chinese people, once fragmented and colonised by alien powers, is an achivement which peoples all over the world must admire and respect . . . .
>
> As a small developing nation, the Philippines looks to the People's Republic of China not only for inspiration but also for support of its legitimate objective of attaining its own destiny through self-reliance and through its own efforts.

About a year later, in Beijing, Marcos poured out such feelings to an even greater extent. Speaking at the banquet held at the People's

Great Hall on 9 June 1975, Marcos, after having chastened the West for 'the destructiveness of Western industrial civilization', lavishly praised China as follows:[52]

China's development, unlike the development of other countries has not alienated man from nature, nor science from the world with all its attendant ills, waste and pollution. In this respect, therefore, China may be a model and inspiration of all the world and mankind.

With the political and social climate developing rapidly in favour of normalisation, the year 1974 saw more frequent contacts and exchanges between the Philippines and China. Among the more publicised events was the visit to Beijing in September 1974 by the First Lady, Mrs Imelda Marcos, at the invitation of Zhou Enlai as already mentioned earlier.

Shortly after Mrs Marcos' visit to China, the Philippine National Security and Foreign Policy Councils met jointly on 5 October 1974. Having considered all the interrelated matters, which included the enforcement of the Anti-subversion Act, the Chinese nationals in the Philippines, and the military bases and defence arrangements with the USA and SEATO, the joint meeting published its decision to endorse full diplomatic relations with China.[53] The internal barriers had thus been cleared for the final move.

On the matter of Chinese nationals, who numbered more than 500 000 if the Philippine-born Chinese were included, the prevailing view was that the issue must be resolved before diplomatic ties with China in order to ensure that the resident Chinese owed their allegiance or loyalty only to the Philippines. An attempt to clear this hurdle was finally made in April 1975 when Marcos issued the Letter of Instruction No. 270, which simplified the naturalisation procedures and authorised the granting of citizenship to deserving Chinese residents in the Philippiness en masse. Under the old regulations it was an extremly complicated matter for a Chinese resident to become a citizen, even if he was born in the Philippines. The process of application would take at least three years and he had to pay a hefty sum of P30 000 (or about US$ 4500).[54]

On 20 May 1975, China issued a formal invitation in the names of Chairman Zhu De and Premier Zhou Enlai to President Marcos for a state visit to China. At midnight of 31 May 1975, Malacanang formally announced the acceptance of the Chinese invitation. On 7

June 1975, Marcos flew to Beijing with a large entourage, which included his own family members and seven Cabinet ministers. At an euphoric moment, Marcos publicly repudiated the Philippine past Cold War attitude towards China as a 'misconception in the past imposed [upon] us by the tyranny of circumstance'.[55]

The climax of Marcos' state visit was the signing of a joint communiqué which formally established diplomatic relations at ambassadorial level between China and the Philippines. The joint communiqué also stressed that 'differences between the economic, political and social systems of the People's Republic of China and the Republic of the Philippines should not constitute an obstacle to peaceful coexistence and the establishment and development of peaceful and friendly relations between the two countries'. Before Marcos completed his memorable visit, he concluded a trade pact with China which listed a number of key commodities from both sides which could be used as a basis for the promotion of more trade.[56]

Returning to Manila Marcos remarked that his historic visit to China merely reflected the Philippines' attempts to relate itself to the 'imperatives of change in today's world.'[57] Some observers held the view that the Philippines' rapprochement with China began with the American initiative and was completed with the fall of Vietnam. But Marcos in his Independence Day Message defended:[58]

> The decision to normalise relations with the People's Republic of China is part of all our present efforts at complete political, economic and cultural independence and total self-reliance. We did not arrive at such decision overnight. Neither was it simply in response to the developments in Cambodia, Vietnam, Laos; nor have we embarked upon it simply to follow the steps of others or to react to the decisions of others.

To Marcos' predecessor, China had been a non-country. To Marcos, the same China was a big country only 600 miles north of the Philippines; finally he had to yield to the dictates of the new geopolitical balance and its concomitant economic forces.[59]

Sino–Philippine Trade

Officially the Philippines had no records of trade with Communist China until 1971. But there was no lack of sale of Chinese-made products in Manila even in the early 1950s when the Philippine government viewed trade as a vehicle for 'Communist subversion' and imposed a strict ban on the import of any Chinese product. Many Chinese 'traditional products', for example Chinese herbs, were known to have been smuggled into the Philippines through Hong Kong, amounting to several millions of dollars a year.[60] This prompted the Philippine Congress in 1954 to investigate the illegal inflow of Chinese products, and resulted in the further tightening up of restrictions, with a bad effect on the Philippines' trade with Hong Kong. But Chinese goods still filtered in via Singapore, Sabah and even Japan. In 1958, the Philippine House Committee on Anti-Filipino Activities created a special watch-dog group to oversee the Chinese drugstores in Manila in an attempt to stamp out the many made-in-China drugs.[61] Then, in 1966, as shown earlier, Chinese rice was 'officially' exported for the first time through Hong Kong.

Direct trade between the Philippines and China officially commenced in 1971 with the Chinese purchase of US$0.4 million worth of Philippines crude coconut oil. But the trade became 'legal' for the Filipinos only in March 1972 with President Marcos' promulgation of the Executive Order No. 384, which set out guidelines for trade with all socialist countries. The trade has since started to grow rapidly, reaching US$37 million in 1974 and US$72 million in 1975, as can be seen in Table 5.1. The trade was further boosted by the conclusion of a trade agreement in June 1975 so that in the following year the trade turnover jumped to US$93 million, making China the Philippines' ninth trade partner. In 1979 the two-way trade between Philippines and China stood at US$173 million, which ranked China as the Philippines' fifteenth trade partner.

The most conspicuous feature of the Philippines–China trade, as clearly shown in Table 5.2, is its extreme commodity concentration throughout. In the first few years of direct trade, the two-way traffic was basically one of barter exchange between Philippine coconut oil and Chinese rice. After 1974, Chinese petroleum began to appear and ever since it has dominated the import structure. As for the Philippines' exports to China, after 1975 coconut oil gave way to sugar and copper. Today, the trade is still dominated by a few commodity items, even though there are signs of commodity diversification in recent years.

Another notable feature of the Philippines–China trade, as shown in Table 5.1, is that the balance of trade is, with the exception of 1975 and 1977, largely in favour of China. The trade deficits for the

Philippines are caused by its imports of high-value products, petroleum and rice. Fortunately the size of deficits was not alarming in either absolute or relative terms; but a consistently unfavourable trade balance can be a source of irritation for any country. Since the trade was made up of only a few commodities and conducted largely within a bilateral framework, it was susceptible to political pressure to swing the balance in favour of the Philippines. The favourable trade balance for the Philippines in 1975 and 1977 was largely the result of the Philippine government's efforts to persuade the Chinese to increase purchases of Philippine copper. In future, as the trade gets more sophisticated and the commodity structure becomes more diversified, it would be more difficult for the Philippines to manipulate the trade politically in order to obtain a favourable balance with China. Trade deficits, if sustained, would become a structural problem, as in the case of the Philippines' trade with other major industrial countries.

In the trade pact signed in Beijing in June 1975 during Marcos' visit to China, both sides pledged to encourage the exchange of goods listed in Schedules A and B. Schedule A laid down the possible exports from the Philippines to China, which included logs and lumber, coconut products, sugar and tobacco, copper, and textiles. Schedule B indicated possible exports from China to the Philippines, which included petroleum, rice and foodstuffs, textiles, chemicals and machinery, together with a wide range of intermediate-technology manufactured products. Thus, by and large, the commodity base of the Philippines-China trade is potentially complementary, with the Philippines exporting to China its geographic-specific primary products and minerals, in return for Chinese light manufactured goods as well as energy and foodstuffs.

No discussion of Philippines–China trade would be complete without singling out rice and petroleum for special discussion. These two items, as evident from the foregoing discussion, were the 'strategic' commodities which had played a key role in instituting the Sino–Philippine diplomatic relations. Rice was the commodity which spearheaded the opening up of direct trade, and petroleum later came in to sustain and expand that trade. The Chinese supply of petroleum to the Philippines at 'friendship prices' during the oil crisis was a splendid diplomatic overture which served notice to the Philippines that China, the big neighbour to its northwest, had considerable economic leeway in dealing with the smaller Southeast

Asian countries. Full credit was given to the importance of petroleum in the breakthrough of Sino–Philippine relations in the official *Philippines Yearbook 1979* which stated: 'Ties with the People's Republic of China started with the Chinese pledge to supply the country with crude oil'.[62]

Ever since 1974 China's 'super heavy Shengli crude is doing very well in the Philippines.'[63] Before the world oil crisis, 95 per cent of the Philippines' oil imports came from the Middle East. After 1974, the Philippines' oil imports have gradually been diversified with a view to reducing its total dependence on the Middle East, regarded as a potentially unstable source of supply. Thus, by 1978, the Philippines' oil imports from the Middle East had been reduced to 72 per cent while the shares for Indonesia and China increased to 15 per cent and 11 per cent respectively. In July 1978 the Philippine oil representatives went to China and secured a five-year agreement from China to supply oil to the Philippines, totalling 6 million tons again at 'friendship prices'.

At the turn of this decade, the petroleum outlook has changed somewhat. With production levelling off and domestic demands rising, China started to cut back its export commitments to Japan. Since the amount earmarked for the Philippines was relatively small, China could still easily fulfil its export commitments in accordance with the agreement. Meanwhile the Philippines had also been stepping up its efforts in offshore oil exploration, with some promising finds. But the recent oil discovery would not substantially reduce the Philippines' import dependency, and the Philippine economy would still rely on imported oil for the greater part of this decade. For many years to come Chinese petroleum products will therefore remain strategic items in the growing Sino–Philippine trade.

How does the China trade stand in the Philippines' overall foreign trade sector? For the period starting from 1975, when the Philippines recognised China, to 1978, the average share of the China trade in the Philippines' total trade was 1.9 per cent, admittedly a very small proportion especially when compared with 26.9 per cent for Japan and 26.3 per cent for the United States (see Table 5.3). However, such a proportion is not all that small when viewed in the historical context of the Philippine foreign trade development. One salient feature of the Philippines' foreign trade structure is that it has all along been so heavily dependent upon one or two trade partners that growth of trade with other countries has tended to be stifled. As pointed out at the beginning of this chapter, China was ranked as the third most important trade partner of the Philippines (after the United States and Japan) in the 1930s with something like a mere 3 per cent share. The present 1.9 per cent for China is exactly the same as for Taiwan but puts China ahead of such export-oriented Asian economies as Hong Kong, Singapore and South Korea. In ASEAN, only Indonesia achieves a 2.2 per cent share in the Philippines' total trade because of the Indonesian oil exports; but both Malaysia's and Thailand's trade shares in the Philippines are virtually insignificant. Indeed, one underlying motive for the Philippines to develop stronger trade ties with China as well as with other ASEAN member countries was its desire to diversify its historically over-concentrated market structure. Viewed from this angle, the Philippines-China trade should hold good potentials for future expansion.

Finally, it should also be recorded that ever since the Philippines started to open trade with socialist countries in 1972 under Executive Order No. 384, its trade with China constituted the bulk of its overall trade with all the socialist countries. In fact, between 1975 and 1978, the Philippines' trade with China took up 61 per cent of the Philippines' total trade with all the 14 socialist countries put together.[64]

It can reasonably be stated that Sino–Philippine trade is being conducted on a healthy base, with good potentials for further growth. If the benefits of the trade are still only of marginal significance to both countries, it is at least unlikely to turn into an issue to sour the overall Sino–Philippine relationship, in the sense that huge trade deficits with Japan have already posed problems in the Philippines' foreign relations with that country.

Issues in Sino–Philippine Relations

What then are the potential sources of conflict between China and the Philippines? The fact that their overall relationship appears to be developing on a sound footing, as reflected in the Philippines' warm welcome extended to the Chinese Premier Zhao Ziyang during his debut tour of Southeast Asia in July 1981[65] and their shared perception of many regional and international issues, does not necessarily mean that they have no common problems to face. A number of issues, if mishandled or misguided, could still impair their overall relationship, however cordial it now appears.

From the standpoint of the Philippines, the foremost issues on its domestic front are the question of ethnic Chinese and the potential support from China for the Philippine insurgent groups.

At the time of the Philippines' commencement of diplomatic relations with Beijing the total number of ethnic Chinese resident in the Philippines had been estimated very broadly from as few as 100 000 to as many as 800 000, much depending on how the term 'Chinese' is defined. Most sources referred to the figures of 300 000–500 000, although the Overseas Chinese Affairs Commission of the Nationalist Government in Taiwan in 1966 officially quoted 115 501.[66] The figures from Taipei probably referred to those who either held a Chinese passport issued by Taiwan or were actively connected with the Chinese organisations in Manila.

As shown at the beginning of this chapter, the Chinese had maintained trade and social relations with the Filipinos since pre-hispanic times. The relationship between the two communities had been generally peaceful during the early period, and many prominent figures in the Philippines have claimed to be of Chinese descent. However, during the colonial times, the Chinese were occasionally made convenient scapegoats for economic and political ills of the host society and they suffered from persecutions ranging from scandals to outright massacres (two tragic massacres of Chinese residents resulting in 45 000 deaths were reported in the later part of the Ming dynasty). At the beginning of the seventeenth century the Spanish colonial government levied a poll-tax on the Chinese and restricted their commercial activities. With the American occupation of the Philippines in 1898, the Chinese fared better in many ways but they were worse off in terms of entry to the Philippines, as the US immigration law of 1888 prohibited Chinese immigration into the Philippines. During the Japanese occupation of the Philippines 1941–45, the Chinese, like many Filipinos, suffered at the hands of the Japanese militarists. The 1930s witnessed the rise of modern nationalism in China, which found its way to the overseas Chinese communities in Southeast Asia. The episode of the Japanese occupation much heightened the political consciousness of the Chinese in the Philippines, adding a political dimension to the hitherto largely apolitical overseas Chinese community there.[67] The matter was further complicated by the addition of an ideological dimention following the Communist revolution in China in 1949. The politicisation of the Chinese in the Philippines has given ammunition to the anti-Chinese voice in the country, which at the peak of the Cold War raised the spectre of a 'Chinese fifth column', as reflected in a typical statement from a rightwing Philippine Senator:[68]

> When the time of reckoning comes, the communist elements will, for certain, ensure that our 500 000 overseas Chinese will all side with Communist China and their task of completing our destruction will be simple enough because we have permitted by default their inroads in this country.

There were actually only a few cases of Chinese attempting to engage in such 'subversive' activities as supporting the local Communist movement or the Huk.[69] Otherwise, most Chinese chose to be politically inactive. Whatever political activities the energetic few had were organised by the Kuomintang–affiliated bodies and channelled into pro-Taiwan and anti-Communist activities. The Nationalist Chinese maintained a strong representation in the Philippines and operated Manila's second largest embassy. The Kuomintang even had a Party branch in Manila with a membership of 6800.[70] Apart from maintaining close links with such powerful Chinese organisations as the Federation of Chinese Chambers of Commerce and the General Association of Chinese Schools, the Kuomintang was also instrumental in the formation of the Philippine–Chinese Anti-Communist League in 1956. For years, it was believed that, thanks to the political cultivation by the Kuomintang, the Chinese in the Philippines seemed to be the most anti-Communist overseas Chinese community. However, as the Philippines' foreign policy began to shift towards detente with Beijing, the Chinese community began to split and a small pro-Beijing faction began to appear in many Chinese organisations. As Marcos was on the way to Beijing, Chairman Mao's pictures suddenly appeared in Manila's Chinatown, leading the veteran journalist Harvey Stockwin to remark cynically:[71]

> the brisk appearance in Manila of Mao photos in Chinese establishments . . . seems certain to buttress the Southeast Asian myth that many pictures of Chiang Kai-shek [Jiang Jie-shi] owned by Overseas Chinese have all along had Mao on the reverse side.

This dramatic shift of political allegiance not merely shows that the overseas Chinese in the Philippines, as elsewhere in Southeast Asia, are politically flexible, but also points to the lack of deep-rooted commitments to any political ideology. More seriously, as much as showing their political adaptability, the incident actually betrayed the fundamental weakness of the Chinese as an ethnic minority in that they do not really 'constitute a tightly-knit, organised ethnic community, in spite of the presence of ethnic and linguistic homogeneity and formalised social institutions'.[72] If the Chinese are politically and socially fragmented, they are also politically and socially ineffective. In the long run, this no doubt helps to dispel the fear of the ethnic Chinese posing a political threat to the Philippine community. As Benito Lim concluded:[73]

> Our study shows that there is no evidence that a 'fifth column' of any ideological coloration will materialise. What is clear in our study is that the Chinese need the avenues to become part of the Philippine community, and that like all Filipinos, they want a prosperous and peaceful country, and if given a chance, they would give their full allegiance to the Republic of the Philippines.

Viewed in this light the relaxation of the naturalisation procedures under the Letter of Instructions No. 270 in 1975 was a very significant move to bring about legal and political assimilation of the Chinese in the Philippines. Prior to this, the archaic 1939 Naturalisation Law required that the applicant 'own real estate in the Philippines worth not less than five thousand pesos, or must have some known lucrative trade, profession or lawful occupation'. Since the Chinese were legally barred from acquiring land except through inheritance, and from entering most professions, only a handful of wealthy Chinese could have become Philippine citizens.[74]

Initially, the Chinese in the Philippines adopted a 'wait and see' attitude towards becoming Philippine citizens, and only 12 500 applications for citizenship were received. Later the minimum requirements in terms of age and length of residence were further relaxed.[75] Over the years more Chinese have taken up Philippine citizenship, because their options are between two dire alternatives, either sticking to the almost internationally valueless Taiwan citizenship or becoming stateless. It is hard to estimate exactly how many ethnic Chinese in the Philippines still remain 'Chinese citizens', most of whom are likely to be old people.[76]

Along with the legal and political de-naturalisation of the overseas Chinese in the Philippines is the thrust of social and cultural change, which has accelerated the assimilation process since the Philippines' severance of diplomatic links with Taiwan in 1975. The most significant event with long-term consequence on the ethnic Chinese is the official ban on Chinese schools instituted in 1976. Prior to this, there were 138 Chinese schools in the Philippines operating two curricula – one Philippine and one Chinese, set up by Taiwan. Henceforth, all the Chinese schools have been integrated into the Philippine national education system, with Chinese only taught as a language.[77] In the course of time it would be increasingly difficult for the ethnic Chinese to remain Chinese even culturally. Correspondingly, the Philippine Chinese will also be less and less of a 'problem' in the burgeoning Sino–Philippine relationship.

Another well-known sensitive area in the Sino–Philippine relations is the concern of the Philippine leadership over Beijing's potential support for the outlawed Communist Party of the Philippines (CPP). Such fears have been dispelled in recent years, partly due to the practical ineffectiveness of the CPP as a real threat to the authorities and partly because of Beijing's withdrawal of open support for the distant comrades in the Philippines. Ever since the start of the Sino–Philippine rapprochement, China's relations with the CPP have deteriorated. The last time the CPP sent open greetings to China was in September 1973, when Chairman Amado Guerrero of the Central Committee of the CPP congratulated Mao for having cleansed the Chinese Communist Party of 'such traitors and swindlers as Liu Shao-chi [Liu Shaoqi] and Lin Piao [Lin Biao]'.[78] As China established diplomatic ties with the Philippines in 1975, the CPP considered that 'the rug was finally pulled from under them'.[79] In particular, the CPP was bitterly disappointed with the manner in which Beijing seemed to have gone all the way to cultivate close relationships with the United States and the Marcos government. Then in 1977 the CPP's top leadership was almost wiped out when its founder-chairman, Jose Maria Sison, who is its most articulate ideologue, was captured by the Philippine government along with a few high-ranking Party members. Almost equally disastrous to the CPP was the recent de-maoification movement in China, which utterly confused the political and ideological thinking of the CPP. Consequently, the new leadership of the CPP was reported to be shifting its ties with China to other Communist parties in Europe,

Africa and even Cuba.[80] A thorn in the Sino–Philippine relations is thus disappearing.

On the international front, there seem to be very few outstanding issues that could become explosive enough as to bring the Philippines and China into loggerheads with each other. The 'hot' issue now in Southeast Asia is the Kampuchea problem. On this problem, broadly, the Philippines along with other ASEAN countries, has taken a stand quite close to that taken by China. On the whole Manila appears to share with China its anxiety over the potential Vietnamese expansion in Southeast Asia and the potential threat to the security of the region from growing Soviet influence.

Nevertheless, conflict between the Philippines and China could still arise over the disputed islands in the South China Sea, particularly Spratly Island. At present, a few other Southeast Asian countries have also laid claims to these islands. Recent petroleum finds have increased the danger of open conflict among the claimant countries.[81] However, it is quite unlikely that any dispute over those islands could escalate into a direct confrontation between China and the Philippines, because if that situation were allowed to develop, it would no longer be a bilateral problem between the Philippines and China alone, but would turn quickly into an international issue involving other Southeast Asian countries as well the superpowers, including the United States, the Soviet Union and Japan, owing to the strategic importance of those islands.

One can be reasonably optimistic over the future of Sino–Philippine relations. No conceivable issues seem serious enough to jostle the two countries back to their former lop-sided relationship.

6

Thailand's Relations with China

Introduction

A special feature of Thailand's overall relationship with China lies in
their strong historical ties. Thailand among the ASEAN countries –
Singapore with 76 per cent of its population being Chinese is
obviously a special case – has the closest cultural and racial affinities
with China, even though modern Thailand does not share a common
border with China. Yet Sino–Thai relations during the past three
decades have undergone wide fluctuations in terms of sentiments,
mutual perception and actual policy orientation. Historically,
Thailand was well-known for its remarkable flexibility in its conduct
of foreign policy. In order to maintain its territorial integrity,
Thailand used to pursue a policy of accommodation with whoever
was the dominating power in the region. Thus Thailand initially
watched the rising tide of the Communist revolution in China with
disinterest and then with concern, especially after China's entry into
the Korea War. In the circumstances, Thailand decided to adopt a
cautious but passive policy of non-recognition towards the new
government in Beijing.

After the Chinese-supported Vietminh defeated the French in
Dienpienphu, the Thais began to grow increasingly apprehensive of
China as a potential threat to their own security. It was primarily out
of fear of China that Thailand threw in its lot with the United States
by joining the anti-China Southeast Asian Treaty Organization

(SEATO), which set up its headquarters in Bangkok. The military government in Thailand, which came to power after the 1958 coup, further hardened Thailand's policy towards China by banning all forms of contact, including trade. Thailand thus operated its own mini 'cold war' against China, which was kept up at a high level throughout the 1960s, partly due to the escalation of the Vietnam War. Consequently, Thailand's China policy was changed from the pattern of careful avoidance to one of overt and undisguised hostility.[1] In return, China mounted a fierce propaganda attack, decrying Thailand for following 'subservient' foreign policy. At the peak of the Cultural Revolution, Beijing sponsored the formation of the 'Thai Patriotic Front' and openly supported the National Liberation movement in Thailand. As mutual suspicion ran high, Thailand's trade with China, which was already reduced to a trickle in the 1950s, was totally halted.

The Sino–American detente at the start of the 1970s not only removed the Cold War assumptions in Thailand's relations with China, but ushered in a new era of international relations for Southeast Asia. Pragmatic and compliant, the Thais soon perceived the implications of the region's new political and strategic balance caused by the reduction of US military commitments, and decided to join the queue of other Southeast Asian nations to normalise relations with China. The process was hastened by the fall of Indochina in 1975. Thereafter Sino–Thai relations were on the rise, along with the steady deterioration of the situation in Indochina.

After their rapprochement, Thailand and China lost no time in developing a warm relationship unique in the region. Currently, China appears to be sharing more common ground with Thailand than with any other ASEAN country. Their two-way trade is also playing a role, albeit a small one, in strengthening their burgeoning relationship.

The changing pattern of Sino–Thai diplomacy seems to be a clear instance of how relations between countries are more strongly influenced by shifting power balance and national interests than by their outward ideological and social differences. On the other hand, historical forces are no less significant in shaping the pattern of international relations. Viewed in the longer historical perspective, the confrontation between Thailand and China during the 1960s was but one of the many short episodes of friction in their centuries-old relationship.

Historical Background to Sino–Thai Relations

Sino–Thai relations date back to very ancient times. There are historical records to suggest that the Chinese and Thai (or Siamese, before 1939) are cognate races, sharing a common origin long before the dawn of history.[2] But the early contacts were more in the nature of cultural and ethnic interaction than of political or economic significance. Politically, from the beginning of the Ming Dynasty in the twelfth century until the growth of European influence from the mid-nineteenth century, China established a kind of feudal overlordship over Thailand, with the latter sending envoys and tributes fairly regularly to the Imperial Court of China. The tributes from Siam were mainly elephants, ivory, rhinoceros-horns, precious stones, coral, perfumes, and logwood.[3] Such a tributary relationship did not result in the domination of Thailand by China. The tributary system was merely a pragmatic means by which Imperial China managed international relations in a defensive way with the small 'barbarian' states around China. Apart from diplomacy, the regular tributary missions, however, provided the framework for commercial contacts.[4]

It has been documented that during the first 250 years of the Ming dynasty, the Siamese rulers sent 46 tributary missions to China.[5] From the standpoint of the Siamese rulers, the tributary system was not without its political and economic merits. It was often used to legitimise an incumbent Thai king or ruling house while it was also a means of acquiring goods from the Celestial Empire. During the intervals when the tribute missions were not conducted, private traders usually took over, and the trade was an added source of revenue for the royal treasury. Not surprisingly, the Sino–Siamese junk trade thrived in the two centuries preceding the introduction of Western capitalism into East and Southeast Asia, as is clearly illustrated in a recent study by a Thai scholar Sarasin Viraphol.[6] The junk trade became especially active during the reign of the Emperor Qian-lung (1736–1795), with direct involvements from both the members of the Siamese Royal Court and local Chinese mandarins. Accordingly, the trade was considered to be of mutual benefit to both countries, not the least to the courtiers and bureaucrats with vested interests either directly in the trade itself or indirectly in related activities.

Apart from the geographic-specific products Thailand sent to China, the most important commodity for the Sino–Siamese trade in this period was rice, which still figures most prominently in Thailand's overall exports today and also continues to play a crucial role in Thailand's current trade relations with Beijing. Thus Sarasin stated:[7]

> If any one product can be singled out as the main contribution to the Sino–Siamese trade, it is Siamese rice. The rice trade that developed from the second decade of the eighteenth century on was significant for both Siam and China. The serious food shortage (due principally to the phenomenal increase of population coupled with crop failures and natural calamities) in Southeast China generated for the first time an interest by the Chinese government in large quantities of Siamese rice.

Another important 'commodity' of this junk trade by the end of the eighteenth century was the migration of the Chinese into Siam in search of a better economic lot. Apart from its central geographical position, Thailand, as a Buddhist country with rice and fish as the staple foods for its population, was particularly appealing to the potential emigrants from Southern China.[8] Initially, the inflow of Chinese immigrants was connected with the junk trade, the growth of which seemed to be 'directly proportional to the rate of growth of the Chinese minority.'[9] The Chinese, industrious and enterprising, soon came to develop commercial agriculture and dominate internal trade in Thailand as well.

The never-ending stream of Chinese immigrants as a new demographic and social impetus was regarded as 'a very fortunate thing for Thailand which has been underpopulated throughout its history' due to frequent epidemics.[10] Thailand, on the other hand, offered relatively easy opportunity for the Chinese to be fully assimilated into Thai social and cultural fabric, an opportunity largely denied to the immigrant Chinese in other parts of Southeast Asia. As Landon observed:[11]

> The pull into Thai civilisation [for the Chinese] has always been very strong, although little effort was ever exerted by the government. The descendants of the Chinese were merely considered to be Thai and treated as such. Citizenship was granted easily. Under an oriental ruling class with whom the Chinese could feel somewhat akin, the process of assimilation continued naturally. This was in

contrast to Chinese experience in European-dominated colonies, such as British Malaya or the Philippines, where the Chinese were constantly distinguished as Chinese and where racial prejudice made marriage into the ruling class the exception. Nor was citizenship so readily granted.

Such tradition has persisted to this day, and Thailand is one country in Southeast Asia which has put up no artificial political barriers or blatant social discrimination against its Chinese minority, which has in turn created less social friction for the Thai society.

The demise of the Sino–Siamese junk trade coincided with and was actually brought about by the increased Western political and economic penetration into East and Southeast Asia in the nineteenth century. The Europeans wanted to open up both China and Thailand for more free trade. With the signing of the Bowring Treaty in 1855, Thailand immediately severed its tributary links with China and became part of the new international economic system dominated by Western industrialised countries. In this way Western maritime imperialism in the nineteenth century squeezed out the monopolistic, bilaterally-operated junk trade between China and Thailand, even though it did not eradicate the Chinese economic and social influence in Thailand, which had by then taken root.

The brisk Sino–Siamese junk trade over the two centuries prior to the advent of European colonial domination serves to show that historically there were strong economic grounds for Thailand and China to cultivate mutually beneficial trade ties with each other, despite such traditional obstacles as the Chinese official prejudice against overseas trade. Viewed in the context of the past, the close relationship between Thailand and China today is not without its historical base. In the long run, the most significant by-product of early Sino–Siamese trade is the influx of Chinese migrants into Thailand, who have since played a very significant role in the economic development and social evolution of Thai society.

The Pattern of Early Trade

As might be expected, the opening up of Thailand to trade with the West had the immediate effect of diminishing Thailand's trade with

China. From 1868, Thailand's exports to China declined steadily, to almost nothing by 1900, and then suddenly shot up in 1921 by 13 times in one year as a result of the Chinese purchase of Thai rice. Since then, Thailand's exports steadily increased to reach the peak of 39 million Hk. taels in 1932 (cf. 0.6 million in 1868). In 1880, Thailand's share of China's overall foreign trade amounted to only 0.3 per cent but increased to about 3 per cent in 1933, on account of the hugh quantities of Thai rice imported by China. Apart from rice, Thailand also exported fish and sea products as well as bran and other cereals to China. In 1933 foodstuffs constituted 95 per cent of Thailand's exports to China, with tobacco and teak being the main non-food items.[12]

By comparison, Thailand's imports from China showed a markedly different trend. Imports from China increased steadily for the whole period from 1868 to 1933. As China was a bigger economy, the trade naturally figured more significantly from the standpoint of Thailand than from China. In 1932, for instance, the volume of Chinese exports to Thailand, though insignificant in the context of China's total exports, was responsible for 6.4 per cent of Thailand's total imports, thus ranking China as Thailand's sixth largest trade partner. A considerable amount of Chinese goods to Thailand were re-exported as entrepôt trade from Hong Kong. If the entrepôt trade portion were to be duly taken into account, China's position in Thailand's overall trade would become even more important.[13]

Initially, foodstuffs dominated Chinese exports to Thailand, but manufactured items such as paper products, cotton yarn and metal products became increasingly important in the commodity structure of the trade, especially for the 1930s. It should be noted that Sino–Thai trade was conducted throughout this period in the absence of formal diplomatic ties. For over a century since the termination of the tributary relationship, Thailand maintained no official relations with China; formal diplomatic exchange started only in 1946 as part of the postwar settlement. The Thai envoys had barely taken up their posts when the Nationalist government was swept out of the Chinese mainland by the Communist revolution. During the Second World War, Thailand openly sided with Japan. Prime Minister Phibun Songkhram incurred much hostility from the Chinese government in Zhongqing (Chungking) by making open gestures to the Japanese-sponsored Wang Jing-wei (Wang Ching-wei) regime in Nanjing (Nanking).

Non-Recognition Period

The Second World War brought about drastic realignment of political factions in Thailand. The liberals emerged at the end of the war as the dominant political group, as the militarist clique led by Phibun was discredited, albeit temporarily, owing to their wartime association with the Japanese. However, the militarists as a group did not lose their power and prestige. In fact, some of the politically-minded military leaders had developed a strong appetite for political power, establishing a long legacy of military intervention in Thailand's political processes.[14] Most Thai military strong men were royalists and conservatives, lacking broad perceptions of the new political dimensions or social issues that were to affect the postwar Asia, and this has had a profound influence on the overall direction of Thailand's foreign policy in the postwar era, particularly in regard to Communist China. It can thus be seen that apart from the international Cold War politics, Thailand's hard-line policy towards China in the 1950s and the 1960s was also a product of the Thai domestic political situation dominated by conservative militarists.

In the postwar years, as the Communist revolution surged ahead on mainland China, Thailand experienced a brief spell of liberal government under Pridi Phanomyong, a leader of the wartime Free Thai movement. In November 1947, the army staged a coup and ousted Pridi who, after an abortive attempt to stage a comeback to power in February 1949, had to go into exile in Guangzhou. The next coup put Phibun back to power but it also ended Thailand's short-lived constitutional democracy. Such a swing to the right in Thailand's domestic politics, however, coincided with the similar shift of international politics in Southeast Asia. With the Nationalist government in China fast disintegrating under the Communist onslaught and with the Communist guerrilla movement along the Thai–Malayan border starting to stir, both the American and British governments became increasingly apprehensive of the possible spread of Communism in Southeast Asia. The Cold War had thus reached Southeast Asia. Accordingly, the military regime of Phibun received immediate endorsement of support from the West. In a move to bolster his own position within the Thai military-bureaucratic elite, Phibun did much to forge close links with the American government by capitalising on Thailand's strategic position in the new

American policy in Southeast Asia. Thus, 'he promptly voiced the same opinion held by the Americans that the Communists posed a serious threat to Thai national security.'[15] In this way Thailand, under the direction of the highly opportunistic Phibun, completely abandoned its traditionally neutral foreign policy by throwing its whole weight behind the anti-Communist policy of the West.

The Phibun government was in no hurry to recognise the People's Republic of China when it was founded on 1 October 1949. As a matter of fact, Phibun had already made a clear-cut choice in his foreign policy line: Thailand would seek 'security guarantees from the US rather than from the People's Republic of China.'[16] In this connection, Phibun 'further ingratiated himself with the Western powers by recognizing the Bao Dai regime in Vietnam and the French-sponsored governments in Laos and Cambodia.'[17] Even more dramatic was the offer by the Phibun regime to send 4000 troops to South Korea one month after the outbreak of the Korea War in June 1950, making Thailand the first Asian nation openly coming to the aid of the Americans in the Korean conflict. In return for Thailand's pro-Western policy, the United States began to funnel economic and military aid into Thailand after the signing of the Economic and Technical Cooperation Agreement in September 1950. Above all, the Americans operated a Military Advisory Assistance Group (MAAG) in Bangkok.

Following the Korean armistice in 1953, the Indochina crisis flared up, and this further increased the concern of the Thai leaders that the Communists might shift their 'aggression' towards Southeast Asia. In the perspective of the US Secretary of State, John Dulles' Cold War scheme, Thailand would be the next domino to fall after Indochina. Hence Thailand was most eager to join the Southeast Asia Treaty Organisation (SEATO) for a collective defence of Southeast Asia against Communist expansion. Thailand thus 'succeeded in fashioning itself as the bastion of Western defence in Southeast Asia.'[18]

Phibun himself might be too sophisticated to have truly believed in the 'bogey of Communism'; but many powerful military leaders, for example General Sarit Thanarat and Police General Phao Sriyanon, were obviously convinced that Communist China was a real threat to Thailand's security. To these politically unsophisticated generals, China had the military potential to invade Thailand and the two million or so ethnic Chinese in Thailand could be potential fifth column for Beijing. Hence the clear shift of Thai government policy towards the ethnic Chinese in the early 1950s from 'tempered benevolence to harsh containment', with a wave of repressive political and economic measures directed against the Chinese community[19] culminating in the Un-Thai Activities Act. The Thai authorities often made no distinction between or deliberately tried to combine for various political and economic reasons, anti-Communist and anti-Chinese activities. Thus Chinese schools and Chinese newspapers were closed and Chinese establishments in Bangkok constantly raided. No doubt the harassment was done in part out of fear of Communist infiltration, but the mixing of anti-Communism with anti-Sinicism was clearly used to the political advantage of the Thai military leaders, particularly Police General Phao.[20]

Beijing's reaction to the events in Thailand in the early 1950s was quite predictable. At the beginning, Beijing was more preoccupied with Korea and Taiwan, and did not appear to be much concerned over Thailand. As the Thai government kept on persecuting the ethnic Chinese in Bangkok, Beijing was under growing pressure to 'protest' through its mass media against such 'fascist' activites, in order to show that the New China cared for the legitimate rights of the overseas Chinese abroad.[21] As Thailand got itself involved in the Korea War on the American side, and became increasingly committed to the Dullesian policy of 'containing' China, Beijing also became more hostile towards Thailand. This hostility was largely reflected in the more intense propaganda attack on the Thai government for its 'subservience' towards Western imperialism (e.g. 'lackey of Wall Street').[22]

In 1955, the political climate in Southeast Asia was affected by the Bandung spirit of peaceful coexistence and became much more relaxed. Upon his return from a world tour, Phibun announced the introduction of 'popular democracy' in Thailand by permitting Hyde Park style debating centres in Bangkok, similar to the one he himself had seen in London. Meanwhile, anti-China feelings began to wane in Thailand.[23] In fact, some of the government excesses against the Chinese community in Bangkok began to backfire; for example, repression of the Chinese actually delayed the process of their assimilation.[24] Amidst the more liberal atmosphere, a Thai Peace Committee was formed, which advocated the adoption of a more neutral and non-aligned foreign policy, free from excessive dependency on the Cold War policy of the United States. Opposition members and government critics also began to demand more trade with China and some even openly argued for the recognition of Beijing. As Malaya was selling rubber to China in large quantities, the pressure to sell Thai rubber to China rapidly mounted in Bangkok, particularly as the prices for Thai primary products were depressed.

The Thai government's standing arguments against relaxing trade control with China were twofold. Politically, the Thai leaders became the victims of their own rhetoric and believed that trade with Communist China would only open up the avenue for Communist infiltration and carry the political risk of offending Thailand's American ally. Phibun specifically pointed out that American aid and trade far outweighed the advantage of trading with China.[25] Economically, Thai leaders could see no substantial benefits from trading with China, which was still very much an agricultural economy. (It was only after 1956 that Chinese manufactured goods began to flood the Southeast Asia markets.) Such sentiments were vividly expressed in the remark of Thailand's former premier, Khuang Abhaiwong: 'What is Thailand going to get in return for sending rice and timber to Communist China? . . . . will Thailand get sterling or dollars? Or will we get dried vegetables, dried cuttle-fish and thermos flasks?'[26]

Meanwhile, China started a campaign in the form of 'people's diplomacy', to coincide with the convening of the Bandung Conference. To take advantage of the more relaxed domestic politics in Thailand, Beijing moved to increase Sino-Thai contacts at the non-governmental levels. Between early 1956 and the end of 1958, when the spirit of Bandung prevailed, a mixed bag of left-wing party members of the Thai Parliament and journalists, a delegation of trade unionists, a cultural troupe of artists and actors, two delegations of journalists, a basketball team and another delegation of members of parliament were invited to visit China, usually under the sponsorship of the Chinese People's Institute of Foreign Affairs.[27] The first group, carrying the name of the Thai People's Mission for the Promotion of Friendship and headed by Thep Chotinuchit, made the trip to China in January 1956. The group was received by both Mao Zedong and Zhou Enlai. Apart from expounding the Chinese principle of peaceful co-existence and the need for 'Asian solidarity against imperialism', the Chinese leaders expressed their desire eventually to establish diplomatic relations with Thailand. Specifically, Mao drew attention to how Thailand could gain economically from closer relations with China:[28]

> You must depend on yourself . . . . . You cannot find markets for your rice and rubber in South[east] Asia. We want trade with you. If we had diplomatic relations and if you wanted any kind of industry, such as glass, paper or textiles, we would help.

It should be emphasised that the period of Phibun's 'popular democracy' overlapped with similar liberalisation trends in China, the so-called 'Hundred Flowers' period. These were times noted not only for political relaxation in China but also for remarkable economic and social progress when China's First Five-Year Plan was about to be successfully concluded. Not surprisingly, most Thai visitors returned to Bangkok with glowing accounts of China. Some were convinced that Thailand would stand to gain economically from better relations with China, particularly since the Thai economy was not in a good shape in the early part of the 1950s. Rice made up 60–65 per cent of Thailand's total exports, while rubber and tin accounted for another 20–30 per cent. The prices of most primary commodities collapsed after the Korea War. Moreover, Thai rice was out-sold by Burmese or Indochinese rice and Thai rubber and tin by Malayan rubber and tin.[29] Mao had effectively offered the lure of the China market to the Thai visitors.

The official contacts between Thailand and China were made at the Bandung Conference in April 1955, which usefully served 'both to enlighten the Chinese as to the realities of their international environment and to educate leaders of those non-Communist Asian and African states which had little or no contact with Communist China as to the actual attitudes of Beijing's leaders towards both non-Communist Asia and the West'.[30] Zhou Enlai appeared in the Conference to be very moderate and conciliatory, and his personal charm and diplomatic skills made a deep impression on Prince Wan Waithayakon, the head of the Thai delegates, as they did on the Philippines' Romulo. Zhou repeatedly assured the Thai delegates that China had no expansionist intentions in Southeast Asia nor had China given material support to the alleged subversive activities organised by Pridi's Free Thai group. He invited Thailand to send a delegation to visit Yunnan and inspect the situation even before the establishment of diplomatic relations.[31] It was perhaps not so much

Zhou's reasonableness as the highly nationalistic and anti-colonialist sentiments of the Bandung Conference that seemed to embarrass the Thai delegation, which had a hard time in rationalising Thailand's dependent foreign policy such as its adherence to the American-designed SEATO. In short, the most important impact of the Bandung Conference was the way it brought 'the Thai delegation face to face with the majority Asian view of Communist China as a great new Asian power.'[32] The immediate result of the Bandung Conference was a noticeable thaw in Sino–Thai relations during the period of 'popular democracy', 1955–7.

As Sino–Thai tension was reduced, their two-way trade also correspondingly increased. In quantitative terms, Thailand's *direct* trade with China during this period carried no statistical significance, as can be seen from Table 6.1. However, direct trade alone gives a misleading picture, as the bulk of the Sino–Thai trade, particularly before 1955, was carried out via Hong Kong. All along, Hong Kong had been the entrepôt for Sino–Thai trade, and became more so since the Thai government imposed a trade embargo on China following the Chinese entry into the Korea War. In 1953, Thailand's exports to China of 339 million bahts registered a big jump with the sale of a large quantity of tobacco. Since then, Thai exports to China dwindled to almost nothing. The quantum of Thailand's direct imports from China was even smaller. (See Table 6.1). In 1956, Chinese direct exports to Thailand recorded only a meagre 0.3 million bahts, representing only 0.01 per cent of Thailand's total imports. But the shops in Bangkok were full of Chinese-made merchandise: thermos flasks, pens, Chinese wines and canned Chinese food specialities, sewing machines, bicycles, flashlights, textiles, radios, electric fans, and even Chinese books. These goods were mostly trans-shipped through Hong Kong and reached Bangkok on Hong Kong bills of lading. It was conservatively estimated in the middle of 1956 that as much as 4 to 5 per cent of Thailand's imports could be of Chinese origin.[33] It can be seen that Thailand's imports from Hong Kong jumped from 715 million bahts in 1955 to the all-time high of 1174 million bahts in 1956, representing 11.6 per cent of Thailand's total imports for 1956 and making Hong Kong Thailand's second largest source of imports.[34] Clearly, a very large proportion of Hong Kong exports to Thailand must be of Chinese origin.

On 21 June 1956, the Thai government, yielding to increasing pressure, lifted control on trade with China. This led to a doubling of direct trade with China in 1957, but the great bulk of the trade continued to be conducted via Hong Kong. A breakdown of the commodity composition of the Sino–Thai direct trade for 1957 shows that over 70 per cent of Thailand's imports from China were light manufactured goods while Thailand's exports to China were made up of virtually nothing but tobacco (99.9 per cent).[35] Cheap and practical, Chinese goods were widely welcomed by Thais as well as Chinese. 'Some mainland Chinese products have been so popular that in a few cases Chinese Communist trade-marks have been forged on goods made in Thailand'.[36] Little wonder both Thai and Chinese merchants, taking advantage of the more relaxed political climate, pressed hard for closer economic ties with China. They argued that 'China had now solved its economic problems and could assist Thailand by supplying not only cheap goods which would lower the cost of living but also technicians to help build her industry.'[37] Those who argued for more direct trade with China usually also advocated closer political relations or at least a more neutral foreign policy. In August 1957, the Thai Minister of Economic Affairs stated that he would like to see Chinese official trade representatives stationed in Bangkok so as to facilitate more direct Sino–Thai trade as well as to reduce Hong Kong's middle-man role.[38]

Thailand's drift towards neutralism in general and towards rapprochement with China in particular was brought to an abrupt end by the army coup of October 1958, led by Marshal Sarit Thanarat. The Sarit government immediately took strong measures against the leftist political figures, and newspapers as well as the pro-Beijing elements in the Chinese community. Contacts with China at all levels were completely banned by the issue of the famous Revolutionary Decree No. 53, effective from 22 February 1959. Sarit steered Thailand firmly and clearly back to the Western camp, bringing to an immediate halt any pretence of observing the Bandung Spirit. After Sarit's death in December 1963, Marshal Thanom Kittikachorn succeeded to the premiership and he continued Sarit's hard-line policy.

Mutual Antagonism and Avoidance

The return to the military dictatorship marked a distinct retrogression in Sino–Thai relations, putting off their rapprochement process to another decade. Worse still, Sino–Thai relations degenerated into mutual antagonism throughout the 1960s. Whereas the Thai government under Phibun in the 1950s adopted a more or less 'wait and see' attitude towards Beijing and did not completely close all doors of contact, Sarit's group turned the passive attitude of non-recognition into active avoidance. Sarit in fact charged the Phibun government with tolerating 'clandestine contacts with Communist elements', and demanded a clear-cut severance from all Communist elements.

The revival of anti-Communist policy was of course a shrewd manoeuvre on the part of the Thai generals to gain political control of the country, but that policy could not be maintained for long without parallel changes in the international political climate. As Thailand resumed its rigid anti-Communist policy, China was also hardening its overall foreign policy stand. In 1958, Beijing started the Taiwan Straits crisis by shelling the two offshore islands of Quemoy and Matsu, thus evincing a belligerent attitude towards small countries in Southeast Asia. Soon after this, tension in Indochina mounted again, first with the crisis in Laos and then with instabilities in South Vietnam. Deterioration of the political situation in Southeast Asia thus conveniently provided the Thai military leaders with a good excuse for resuming Thailand's former Cold War based foreign policy. Following the Laosian crisis, Thailand entered into a specific agreement with the United States (the 1962 Rusk-Thanat agreement), which placed the United States under obligation to defend Thailand unilaterally regardless of the attitude of other SEATO members. In 1965, Thailand also signed a secret military agreement with the United States, allowing the Americans to build and operate air bases in Thailand for the conduct of the war in Vietnam. As Thailand was a 'willing partner' in the US-designed anti-Communist cause, slowly and inextricably, the Thais 'were drawn into serving US interests and policies, and these increasingly diverged from those of Thailand.'[39]

As the Vietnam War escalated and the Americans got deeper into the quagmire, Thailand also became more involved in the conflict. Just as in the Korea War, Thailand was among the first nations to come to the aid of Saigon, both materially and politically. At the height of the War in Vietnam, Thailand allowed the US Air Force to operate seven bases for direct military action, including the gigantic U Tapao, which was used by the B52s for bombing North Vietnam.[40] But for the undeclared nature of the Vietnam War, Thailand technically came close to being a belligerent nation on the American side. Economically, as its trade gap grew wider, Thailand also came to depend heavily on US economic as well as military aid. From 1951 to 1975, the United States provided some US$650 million for economic development programmes in Thailand, in addition to the total of US$936 million of 'regular military assistance'. Thailand also benefited substantially from direct and indirect US military spending around the various military bases in Thailand.[41]

Thailand's drift towards a more determinedly anti-Communist policy after Sarit took power evoked a predictable denunciation from Beijing. But China did not pursue openly antagonistic policies against Thailand until late 1964 when Thailand began to be actively involved in the Vietnam conflict. In late 1964, China gave open support to the Thai Communist political fronts by sponsoring the formation of two Thai revolutionary movements, the Patriotic Front of Thailand and the Thailand Independence Movement.[42] In the latter half of 1965, China's outspoken Foreign Minister Chen Yi was reported to have remarked: 'We hope to have a guerrilla war going in Thailand before the year is out.'[43] In response to the Thai government's decision to send ground forces to fight in South Vietnam, the Chinese Ministry of Foreign Affairs in January 1967 issue a threatening statement: 'In so doing, are you not afraid that the flames of the war kindled by the United States will spread to yourself?'[44] On 17 August 1967, China's official organ, *The People's Daily*, reported that the armed struggle of the Thai People's Forces had started the spark of 'revolutionary fire'.[45] Meanwhile, China was seized by the convulsive Cultural Revolution. Under the influence of the radicals, Chinese foreign policy became increasingly militant. From late 1967 to early 1968, Beijing repeatedly called on the Communist Party of Thailand to step up its armed struggle to overthrow the rule of 'the reactionary Thanom government.'[46]

In effect, China's belligerence and frequent hostile outbursts during the Cultural Revolution actually operated to the advantage of Thailand's ruling military elite. China's apparent intransigence was often used by the Thai leaders as a convenient *raison d'être* to justify the government's rigid foreign policy stance in Southeast Asia. Internally, it provided the government with an opportunity to magnify the Communist menace so as to create a security scare, which would then be used to curb domestic opposition, particularly the movement for the return of the constitutional democracy. Externally, the alarmist policy of playing up the Chinese communist threat was also an effective means of obtaining more economic and military aid from Washington.[47]

Suffice it to say that Sino–Thai relations towards the end of the 1960s appeared to have come to an impasse. With mutual antagonism running so high, there could be little possibility or incentive for either side to keep up informal contact or even to extend a feeler. It was a rare kind of diplomacy based on 'careful avoidance.' However, Chinese products continued to be available in Bangkok, even though trade with China was totally banned. Some of this merchandise was illegally imported into Thailand through Hong Kong after some minimal processing or a mere change of labels, while others were simply smuggled in through Singapore and Malaysia.

The Road to Normalisation

Foreign policy is a game more suited to major contending powers, with small countries often ending up as pawns in the changing relationship of the large ones. Reflecting on the Philippines' past experience, its veteran Foreign Minister, Carlos Romulo, remarked at the ASEAN's meeting of foreign ministers in Kuala Lumpur in November 1971: 'The continuing tragedy of our time is that our affairs are very much shaped by the ill-considered actions of the superpowers.'[48] This remark aptly high-lights the pathetic aspects of Thailand's Cold War oriented foreign policy at the time when the overall Cold War framework was about to crumble. Having invested so much of its future with the American Vietnam policy, Thailand was caught unprepared when the United States reversed its course on Vietnam in 1968. Worse still, as the Americans later stepped up their withdrawal from Southeast Asia and made a sudden about-turn towards detente with China, 'the Thais were left stranded with a militant anti-Communist commitment, but deprived of the backing to fulfill it'.[49]

It has often been suggested that the Thais traditionally have an enviable national trait in their conduct of foreign policy: they can 'bend with the wind'. But the Thanom regime did not seem to have much of that quality, particularly in regard to its China policy. Thanom continued to operate his 'mini' Cold War against Beijing even though the larger Cold War had ended. That was one reason why the Sino–Thai normalisation process took such a tortuous course. Whether Thailand as a nation easily 'bends with the wind' or not, it is probable that, within Thailand's power elite, it was the technocrats and the civilian politicians who had better perception and greater sense of pragmatism, whereas the military leaders – who wielded real power – were primarily conservative and inflexible, not so easily 'bendable'. Indeed, one finds a parallel experience in Indonesia.

The origin of the Sino–Thai detente is commonly attributed to the thawing of the Cold War in Southeast Asia, sparked off by the new Nixon doctrine which included recognition of China's legitimate interests in the Southeast Asian region and emphasised American willingness to negotiate in order to secure peace. This, apart from the de-ideologising of the American policy in Southeast Asia, virtually amounted to scrapping Dulles' basic policy of containing China. Specifically for the non-Communist states in Southeast Asia, the Nixon doctrine opened the gateways for them to normalise relations with China.[50]

However, credit should not go to President Nixon alone. The Nixon doctrine, particularly the dramatic announcement of his intention to visit Beijing, certainly precipitated changes and set up a new trend for countries in Southeast Asia to review their existing relations with China. But it is also apparent that even without the American initiative, the time had come for many countries in Southeast Asia seriously to tackle their China question. Emerging from the Cultural Revolution, China itself was eager at the time to win new friendships. The Philippines' decision to purchase Chinese rice in 1970 represented an overture on its own, independent of the American move. In Thailand, as early as 17 April 1971, the Deputy Economic Affairs Minister aired the view that the Thai government should repeal the ban on possession and sales of goods from China so as to pave the way for the resumption of trade relations with Beijing.[51] In May 1971, Charoon Sibunruang, President of the Thai Chamber of Commerce and of the Board of Trade, urged the Thai government to permit trade transactions with China through a third country such as Hong Kong.[52] In fact, ever since the turn of 1971, as Beijing was muting its propaganda campaign against Thailand, many prominent Thai industrialists and businessmen were putting pressure on their government to review its decade-old trade ban on China.[53]

Foreign Minister Thanat Khoman was the one person in Bangkok who was least surprised by the so-called 'Nixon shock'. Once a hawkish follower of the American Cold War policy and a strong opponent of neutralisation of Southeast Asia, he had now emerged as the most ardent proponent of normalisation of relations with China.[54] Prior to President Nixon's announcement of his Beijing trip, Thanat began to make bold public statements in regard to Thailand's China policy. In May 1971, he actually referred to China by its correct name, the People's Republic of China, the first time this had ever been done by any high-ranking Thai official. Thanat also openly stated that since Thailand's differences with China had narrowed, it would be high time to consider starting a dialogue with Beijing.[55] Above all, he disclosed that 'through a third country Thailand had let China know that it was interested in developing contacts and that China, through a third country, had also contacted Thailand to show it was interested in Thai opinions'.[56]

As a seasoned diplomat of long service, Thanat had no doubt developed the professional ability to sense early-warning signals and to detect the shift of international political climate. His various manoeuvres in early 1971 clearly represented his last-minute efforts as an astute diplomat to save his country from the embarrassing consequences of a decade-long anti-Communist foreign policy, now in danger of being swept under the carpet by the Americans. Unfortunately, Thanat was too far ahead of the conservative forces in Bangkok, and his conciliatory stance on China evoked strong criticisms from both the Thai press and some of his right-wing cabinet colleagues. In particular, his manoeuvres were misunderstood and often counter-balanced by his superior, Prime Minister Thanom Kittikachorn, who continued to make clumsy anti-Beijing statements even at the time when the US–China 'Ping-Pong Diplomacy' was in full swing.[57] In July 1971, in an attempt to stem the tide of detente with China, Thanom reasserted that he would continue to oppose any commercial or other forms of contact with China until 'Peking [Beijing] stops its sponsorship of the communist insurgency in this country'.[58] Most ironically, when Henry Kissinger made a brief stopover in Bangkok in July 1971, on his first secret mission to meet Premier Zhou Enlai in Beijing, the ill-informed Thanom still urged Kissinger to delay the American withdrawal from South Vietnam for as long as possible, emphasising his long-held position that 'the communists cannot be trusted'.[59] Little wonder, as President Nixon's visit was made official on 15 July 1971, that it came as a real bombshell to many Thai officials who, slow to awake to reality, took the line that the United States had already 'lost face to Peking'.[60] In the wake of the 'Nixon shock', the rather confused Thanom took a defensive line – Thailand's efforts towards any detente with China would have to await the outcome of Nixon's trip to Beijing.

Meanwhile, pressure on the Thai government to open trade relations continued to mount. In late August 1971, 70 Members of Parliament called upon the Prime Minister to repeal the trade ban on China on the ground that it had in any case never been effective in cutting off the flow of Chinese goods into Thailand. Charoon of the Thai Chamber of Commerce further argued that trading with China would be, at least initially, on a government-to-government basis so that it would not entail any serious trade deficit for Thailand.[61] On 4 November 1971, the President of the Chinese Chamber of Commerce, Amphorn Bulapakdi, emphasised that the half-million or so Chinese residents in Thailand would not present any political problem for the government if Thailand opened up trade relations with China, and that most of the second generation Chinese had already considered themselves Thais.[62]

Yielding to increasing public pressure and under Thanat's persistent prodding, the Thai government eventually took some tentative steps towards changing its decade-long Cold War based China policy. On 3 November 1971, in an historic three-hour meeting, the National Executive Council decided to remove the three important barriers to more friendly relations with China – to lift the ban on trade with China, to relax existing anti-Communist laws, and to permit visits to China by sports and non-political missions. At the same time, the Council ruled out diplomatic relations with China in the near future.[63]

The NEC's new decisions on China had hardly been announced before its Chairman, Prime Minister Thanom, unleashed another bloodless coup on 17 November 1971, dissolving the Parliament and suspending the Constitution in a move to cope with increasingly clamorous opposition and spreading insurgent activities. General Prapas Charusathiara, Deputy Chairman of NEC and Minister of the Interior as well as Chief of the Army Staff, emerged from the coup even more influential than before. But Prapas was a real hardliner and was obsessed with internal security matters. Consequently, the question of improving relations with China was for the moment

conveniently shelved, with Foreign Minister Thanat Khoman re-
treating into a monastery, a Thai form of voluntary political
retirement.[64]

In retrospect, President Nixon's China trip had been decisive in
steering Thailand back onto the rapprochement path with China.
The Shanghai Communiqué had produced a strong psychological
impact on the Thai people and thus helped resume pressure on the
government to get its rapprochement machinery rolling again.[65] One
noticeable change in the aftermath of Nixon's visit to China was that
the NEC leaders began to separate the China question from the
internal insurgence issue with the aim of cutting down unnecessary
polemics and rhetoric.[66] The first sign of the Sino–Thai thaw came in
June 1972, when Pote Sarasin, Assistant Chairman of the ruling
NEC, stated: 'Thailand welcomes mutual friendly relations with
China, including exchange of visits by sports teams and trade'.
However, he immediately qualified this otherwise significant state-
ment by stressing that Thailand would continue to recognise
Taiwan.[67]

After the middle of 1972 the diplomatic initiative passed to China,
which let loose its 'Ping-Pong Diplomacy'. The ice was broken in
September 1972, when Thailand accepted China's invitation to send a
ping-pong team to play in Beijing. The event was followed by another
invitation to the Autumn Canton Trade Fair. On both occasions the
Chinese-speaking Prasit Kanchanawat, Deputy Director of
Economic Affairs of the NEC, took a leading role. Prasit also had an
interview with Premier Zhou Enlai on wide-ranging topics, including
trade, diplomatic relations, overseas Chinese, and Thailand's internal security. Prasit returned to Bangkok with Zhou's message, which
was widely discussed among influential personalities. However, the
powerful General Prapas did not react to Prasit's trip enthusiastically, and he even deliberately cooled down public enthusiasm over
the visit by pointing out that Prasit had gone to Beijing purely in his
'individual capacity'.[68]

It had by now become sufficiently clear that as long as rigid military
leaders who lacked political foresight and proper perspectives on
international relations were in charge, the Sino–Thai relationship
was unlikely to achieve any dramatic breakthrough. Being constantly
pre-occupied with internal security matters, the military leaders like
Prapas were still haunted by China's past connection with the local
insurgent activities, real or imagined. Their apprehension was also

reinforced by the fact that the Indochina situation remained unsettled and instabilities there could still easily spill over into Thailand.

Towards the close of 1972, as Thailand was moving gingerly towards political rapprochement with China, those who argued for better relations with China shifted their attention to economic relations, which were also more acceptable to the Thai government. Unlike political relations, which often evoke emotive reactions, economic relations could be tackled in a more hard-headed manner. With the United States accelerating its military withdrawal from Thailand, the Thai economy was faced with the prospects of losing an important source of economic growth in terms of US aid, military procurement and other related expenditures. But as Thailand's trade imbalance had turned chronic over the years, any new trade relations with China (or other socialist countries) would have to avoid aggravating Thailand's trade deficits. Back in December 1968, before the thaw of the Cold War, Thailand's Finance Minister, Serm Vinichayakul, dismissed out of hand any suggestion of trade links with Communist China on the ground that such trade would only 'cause a further trade deficit' for Thailand.[69] What would be the new balance sheet now?

As the Thais began seriously to analyse the various implications of Sino–Thai trade, they soon unearthed problems. First, upgrading Sino–Thai relations could possibly produce the undesirable displacement effect of forcing out Taiwan's sizeable economic interests (mainly in textiles and metal factories), now deeply entrenched in Thailand. At the time, Taiwan was the third biggest investor in Thailand, after Japan and the United States. But Beijing was persistently obdurate on the Taiwan issue, and traders sometimes had to choose between China and Taiwan. Secondly, there was the important question as to what Thailand could offer to sell to China in sufficient bulk so as to keep down Thailand's potential trade deficits with China. It was well-known that China could supply a wide range of manufactured products and industrial raw materials to Thailand, but it would be difficult for China to buy rice from Thailand in exchange as China was also an important rice exporter. Earlier, China had expressed interest in buying tin and rubber, which Thailand produced only in limited amounts.[70] The fact that the resumption of trade relations with China would not promise any immediate substantial benefits to Thailand must have strengthened the hands of those wavering on the issue – like Prapas, who wanted to prolong the status quo.

In the event, the dry spell in Sino–Thai relations did not last long. The 'Ping-Pong Diplomacy', once set in motion, carried its own momentum. In June 1973, a Chinese table tennis team returned a visit to Thailand. The Chinese team was led by a high ranking official from the Chinese Ministry of Foreign Affairs, Chen Rui-sheng, who took the opportunity to confer with Thailand's Deputy Foreign Minister, Chartichai Choonhavan, on issues of mutual interests. At the subsequent press conference, Chen denied that Beijing was directing Communist activities in Thailand.[71] A month later, Thailand's second sports team, a badminton squad, was off to China. The Thai team was led by Police General Chumpol Lochachala, who carried a personal message from Prime Minister Thanom requesting China to help 'restore permanent peace in Southeast Asia'.[72]

Shortly after the visit of the Chinese table tennis team, Prime Minister Thanom announced that the Thai government was taking steps to modify its stringent anti-Communist laws so as to create more conducive grounds for increasing cultural, sports, trade and technical exchanges with China.[73] At the same time, Thanom pointed out that full diplomatic relations with China were still not in sight, as both countries needed time to resolve their differences.[74]

In the long run, exchanges and dialogues fostered the growth of mutual relations on the political level by softening up the hostile conditions, particularly since top government officials were usually assigned to head the various visiting groups. Amidst this flurry of exchanges conducted in the summer of 1973, the Thai cabinet made a positive breakthrough in its relations with China on 15 August 1973 by deciding to amend the Revolutionary Decree No. 53, which forbade any trade dealings with China. The amendment took the form of a legislative Bill which, apart from removing all trade restrictions on China, stipulated that a new state trading corporation should be set up to regulate trade activities with China.[75] The Bill was unanimously approved by Thailand's National Assembly on 21 September 1973. Along with the lifting of the trade ban, the Thai government also undertook other measures to develop a closer relationship with China, for example, the direct communications link-up with China in August 1973.[76]

The new measures had hardly started to take effect when the

Thanom-Prapas government was overthrown by the student revolt of October 1973. The demise of this decade-old military regime removed another stumbling block in Thailand's rapprochement with China. As is by now evident, were it not for the hesitation of Thanom and Prapas the pace of Sino–Thai détente would certainly have been quicker. Prapas, in particular, who had reservations all along on upgrading relations with any Communist country, often dragged his feet over the China issue. China also viewed the departure of these two generals from the Thai political scene as creating a more favourable precondition for Sino–Thai understanding. A few months later, Zhou Enlai told visiting Thai Olympic Chairman, Marshal Dawee Chullasapya, that since Thailand now had a civilian government China would no longer find it necessary to support the local insurgent movement. Further, Zhou admitted that China had in the past done so because 'the former military government had been dictatorial and had curtailed human rights'.[77]

Shortly after the fall of the military regime, Thailand's Deputy Foreign Minister, Chartichai Choonhavan, made the first official visit to China. Chartichai returned to Bangkok to announce that 'Thailand's recognition of China is only a matter of time'.[78] Significantly, Chartichai gave an unusually warm reflection on his China trip: 'We have had relations with China for more than 2000 years. Our meeting this time was a visit to relatives. It is strictly a family affair'.[79] Politically, the most significant aspect of Chartichai's visit to China was Thailand's acceptance, at least in principle, of Beijing's 'one China' policy.[80] This meant that Thailand had to get rid of its 'Taiwan problem' before any move to establish full diplomatic ties with China. Earlier, Thanom had already taken steps to downgrade Thailand's diplomatic relations with Taiwan. In practice, like the Philippines, Thailand found its Taiwan problem difficult to solve on account of Taiwan's strong economic interests as well as the long-standing influence of the Kuomintang on the local Chinese community.

From the economic angle, the downfall of the Thanom regime coincided with the outbreak of the world's first oil crisis, which was accompanied by the food crisis and eventually the world economic recession. Basically unaffected by the world economic crises, China emerged from a strong position and was able to hold considerable leverage *vis-à-vis* the smaller states in Southeast Asia.

As far as Thailand is concerned, the food crisis actually started in the summer of 1973. Owing to the severe drought in 1972, rice production in 1973 fell so sharply that the Thai government had to take emergency measures in June 1973 by prohibiting the export of rice.[81] In the event, countries like Singapore, Malaysia and Indonesia, which regularly imported rice from Thailand, had to make up their shortfalls by increasing rice purchases from their supplementary sources, mainly China. The food crisis served to re-assure the Thais that Chinese rice exports were complementary to rather than competitive with Thailand's own rice exports and could form the basis of a market share arrangement.

Next came the oil crisis, which provided Zhou Enlai an opportunity to play 'petroleum diplomacy'.[82] Towards the end of 1973, as the oil crisis struck the world, several countries in Asia experienced shortages of petroleum fuels. China stepped in to befriend these countries (namely, Japan, the Philippines, Thailand and Hong Kong) by supplying them with considerable quantities. Specifically for Thailand, the oil deal was made during Chartichai's visit to China in December 1973. As a goodwill gesture, China agreed to sell Thailand 50 000 tons of diesel fuels at 'friendship prices', considerably lower than the ruling world prices. This petroleum deal was more than just a political gesture on the part of the Chinese in the sense of conveying the message 'A friend in need is a friend indeed'. But it was going to have a profound impact on the structure of Sino–Thai trade, as can be seen in the next section. Unlike other Chinese exports to Thailand, petroleum is the one commodity considered vitally important for the Thai economy. Thus, the Chinese 'petroleum diplomacy' immediately provided strong economic backup to those who argued in favour of enhancing the overall Sino–Thai relationship. In retrospect, just as the 'ping-pong diplomacy' was employed to 'break the ice' at the initial stages of Sino–Thai relations, the 'petroleum diplomacy' was employed to sustain and upgrade the relationship.

To formalise the import of Chinese petroleum, the caretaker civilian government under Sanya Thammasak followed up the initiative taken by the former military regime to repeal the trade ban by expediting the necessary legal amendments. Since the legislation process in Thailand proceeded very slowly, Sanya issued administrative decrees to allow Chinese goods to be brought directly into Thailand from 1 January 1974. It was not until the end of 1974 that the whole legal process of removing all trade barriers against China was fully completed.[83] The slow legal process also contributed to the sluggish process of normalisation.

In reality, Sino–Thai relations towards the end of 1974 had moved from the stage of exchange of views to the final stage of formal negotiation, with both sides coming to grapple with the concrete issues such as the legal status of 300 000 or so overseas Chinese residing in Thailand, and the American military withdrawal from Thailand.[84]

1975 saw the radical transformation of the political situation in Southeast Asia, and this provided the final impetus for Thailand to establish full diplomatic relations with China. After a series of stunning events, happening to Indochina in quick succession in the spring of 1975, the Thai diplomatic machinery was put into top gear, culminating in the visit to Beijing by the Thai Prime Minister. On 17 April 1975, Phnom Penh fell to Khmer Rouge forces. Two weeks later, South Vietnam fell. In May 1975, a delegation from North Vietnam came to Bangkok to discuss the normalisation of relations with Thailand. Clearly, all these events dwarfed the problems that were still outstanding in the Sino–Thai negotiation. For instance, the new political balance in Southeast Asia had prompted China to change its previous insistence on the American military withdrawal from Thailand. In fact, China dramatically reversed its original position and now wanted the United States to continue its military presence in the region so as to offset any possible rise of Soviet influence.[85]

On 1 July 1975, Thai Prime Minister Kukrit Pramoj and Chinese Prime Minister Zhou Enlai signed a joint communiqué, which formally established diplomatic relations between the two countries. This was four years after their first tentative contacts which started the normalisation process. In recognising China, Thailand had to accept China's stand on the 'one China' policy, which required Thailand to cut off all formal relations with Taiwan. With regard to the role of China in Thailand's domestic insurgence, the Thai government was reconciled to the Chinese view that the government-to-government relations be separated from the party-to-party relations. Specifically, China had pledged to Thailand that China would not interfere with Thailand's domestic affairs, and the Chinese support for the Communist Party of Thailand was confined to the ideological and moral aspects.[86]

Kukrit's party was cordially received in Beijing. The climax to his trip was an audience with Chairman Mao, who allayed considerably Kukrit's fear of the potential Chinese support of the Thai Communists. Mao was reported to have told Kukrit that the Communist Party of Thailand was only a small party whose leaders had never come to see him. More dramatically, Mao even taught Kukrit the 'three principles' for dealing with Communists: 'Don't swear at them because they are thick-skinned; don't fight them because they'll always run away; and don't kill them because you'll only turn them into martyrs. I should know: that's how I fought Chiang Kai-shek.'[87]

Pattern and Structure of Sino–Thai Trade

Sino–Thai trade has been growing at an impressive rate since it was legalised in late 1974, particularly in respect of Thailand's imports from China. In 1980, Thailand imported 8500 million bahts worth of goods (roughly US$440 million) from China, or 4.5 per cent of Thailand's total imports; and exported 2500 million bahts worth of goods to China, or 1.9 per cent of Thailand's total exports in that year. This ranks China as Thailand's fifth largest trade partner in terms of imports into Thailand. In fact, in 1977 or just two years after the resumption of trade, China became one of Thailand's top ten trade partners.[88]

Thailand's exports to China have been expanding less rapidly, and this accounts for Thailand's growing trade imbalance with China. In fact, except for 1975, Thailand's trade has been consistently in favour of China. The trade gap was especially staggering for 1980, with the deficit for Thailand exceeding twice the amount of its exports to China. (Table 6.1).

However, Thailand's trade imbalance with China is part of the structural problem of its overall trade. For years the Thai economy has experienced chronic deficits in its current accounts. In 1980, for example, Thailand's trade deficits amounted to 36 per cent of its total exports. In that year Thailand also incurred a sizeable trade deficit with China. As can be seen in Table 6.2, Thailand suffered from trade deficits with virtually all its major trade partners, but the deficit from its China trade accounted for only 11 per cent of its total trade deficits.

The main explanation for Thailand's unfavourable trade balance with China comes from the peculiar commodity composition of the Sino–Thai trade. As can be seen from Table 6.3, Thailand's exports to China were initially made up almost entirely of rubber and rice, and then rubber and sugar. During the past two years there was some tendency for the commodity concentration to become more diversified, but rice, rubber and sugar combined still accounted for more than half of the trade. Similarly, Thailand's imports from China were also highly concentrated. The single most important commodity in the import structure is petroleum product, which, as discussed earlier, played the crucial role of spearheading the rapprochement between the two countries. In fact, Thailand's direct imports from China started off with petroleum, which have since dominated the import structure. In 1979, the volume of oil imports from China reached the all-time peak of 64 per cent of Thailand's total imports from China as a result of the second world oil crisis, which sharply pushed up the oil prices, and hence the value of oil imports. In 1980, Thailand's oil imports from China still stood at the high level of 58 per cent of the total. This clearly means that Thailand's trade deficit with China is basically on oil bills, which Thailand had to pay in any case. If Thailand were not to buy oil from China, it would have to buy it from the Middle East or other sources, but without the benefit of the preferential prices which accompanied the Chinese crude. This explains why Thailand's existing trade imbalance with China, though uncomfortably large, has not been a real source of irritation to the Thai government.

In March 1979 the Thai government negotiated a five-year oil agreement with China under which China would increase the supply of Shengli crude from 600 000 to 800 000 tons for 1979; 800 000 to 1 000 000 tons for 1980, and one million tons each for 1981, 1982 and 1983.[89] The agreement was meant to be vague so that both sides could meet regularly to adjust price changes. Under the 1980 sales contract, China would sell 700 000 tons of Shengli crude and 250 000 tons of high-speed diesel. The price of Shengli crude was fixed in accordance with the world market price first and then with a special discount of about 2 per cent. For the diesel oil, both sides agreed to a pricing formula under which 80 per cent of the oil was based on the spot market price and the remaining 20 per cent on the Singapore market price.[90]

With the energy crisis now finally spreading to China, there is increasing doubt whether China can afford to continue its petroleum exports in large quantities after the mid–1980s. China has already cut back its petroleum exports to Japan. In the case of Thailand, China would probably continue supplying oil even after the termination of the five-year agreement in 1984, though the quantity is not likely to exceed the ceiling of one million tons, which is just about 1 per cent of China's current petroleum output. China can easily manage to export this relatively small quantity for the sake of maintaining friendship with Thailand. This shows how a large country can have considerable leverage in dealing with a small one. From Thailand's standpoint, the volume of Chinese petroleum imports represents only some 10 per cent of Thailand's total petroleum imports. On account of their high prices, however, even a relatively small quantity of petroleum products can grossly distort the trade structure, as clearly evident in the Sino–Thai trade.

Apart from petroleum products, Chinese exports to Thailand encompass a wide range of manufactured products such as one can find in a typical China emporium in Hong Kong or Singapore. These are mainly consumer-oriented light manufactured goods, but they can provide competition in the Thai market for similar goods from Japan and, more recently, those from South Korea and Taiwan. The case of Chinese silk and transistor radios provides striking example of how the low-cost Chinese goods have made successful inroads into the Thai markets through a 'combination of low price, good quality and patriotism among local Thai Chinese'.[91] The influx of these Chinese products at first sharply reduced the Japanese market share and later brought head-on competition with similar goods from Taiwan and South Korea. So far such competition was not without beneficial effects to Thailand. However, as the Thai economy becomes increasingly industrialised and its own manufactured goods become available, such aggressive sales of Chinese goods would certainly create more trade frictions.

No discussion of Sino–Thai trade is complete without touching upon its organisational aspects. One of the special features of trading with a socialist economy is that the trade is usually of bilateral nature, entailing some complex administrative arrangements. As already mentioned in the previous section, the resumption of Sino–Thai trade was fraught with legal hurdles associated with the prolonged process of revoking the trade ban of the Revolutionary Decree No. 53.

The first step towards the de-regulation of Sino–Thai trade amounted to only a partial lifting of the trade ban. Having negotiated a deal with the Chinese government to import diesel fuels, the Sanya government issued an administrative order in January 1974 to permit the import of eight categories of products from China – machinery and tools, chemicals, iron and steel, raw silk, petroleum products and coal, paper, medicines, and fertilisers.[92] In order to keep the trade under its own control, the Thai government set up a state trading corporation to handle business with China. The government controlled one-third of the shares of the corporation while one-third were sold to various trade associations, and the remaining one-third sold to private business.[93]

On 19 January 1975, the Thai government passed a law 'concerning trade with countries the governments of which conduct trade exclusively' to supersede the previous legal measures on the China trade, as the Revolutionary Decree 53 was by then repealed. In August 1976, the law was also rescinded so as to treat China in the same way as other countries.[94]

At present, the Sino–Thai trade operates on two levels – the government-to-government level, and the level involving China's trading corporation and the Thai private sector. The government level accounts for the bulk of the trade, as all the big deals concerning petroleum, rice and sugar are conducted bilaterally between the Thai and Chinese governments. The participation of the Thai government in the trade is not for the political purpose of over-seeing the trade but rather for steering the trade as far as possible to the advantage of Thailand. It is a means by which Thailand has obtained petroleum from China at concessionary prices as well as exerted pressure on China to increase imports from Thailand (for example, buying rice from Thailand which China does not need) so as to reduce Thailand's unfavourable trade balance with China.

Issues and Problems

If Thailand under Thanom and Prapas had largely failed to apply its traditional 'bend-with-the-wind' tactics in its approach towards détente, it was evidently not the case after Thailand's recognition of

China. Though the fall of Indochina gave Thailand the last push towards recognition of China, it did not restore peace and stability to the region. Instead, it gave rise to fratricidal struggle among the Communist states, which in turn threatened the security of the neighbouring ASEAN countries, especially Thailand. The Indochina conflict was further complicated by Sino–Soviet rivalry in the region, with Beijing backing Kampuchea and Moscow supporting the other contender, Vietnam. Anxious to keep the conflict from spilling over, the ASEAN states were also indirectly involved, especially since China was friendly towards ASEAN while Vietnam was openly hostile to it. In the circumstances Thailand, as a frontline state, became very vulnerable. Thailand's external vulnerability was aggravated by domestic political instability in connection with the frequent change of government in the late 1970's: –from Kukrit Pramoj to Thanin Kravivichien, and then to Kriangsak Chomanan, and now Prem Tinsulanonda.[95]

The fact that Thailand has survived all these turbulent years is due in no small measure to diplomatic manoeuvres drawn from its 'bend-with-the wind' tradition. This is most evident in the pragmatic Kriangsak administration. As Prime Minister, Kriangsak made official visits to Washington, Moscow and Beijing as well as the ASEAN capitals. In 1978 alone, Bangkok played host to high-level state officials from Washington and Moscow as well as to Vietnamese Premier Pham Van Dong and Chinese Vice-Premier Deng Xiaoping.

In November 1978, Deng Xiaoping made a ten-day tour of ASEAN at the time of mounting tension between China, Vietnam and Kampuchea, and Bangkok was his first stop. Deng's visit to Thailand had broader diplomatic objectives, which were to counterbalance or reduce the influence of Vietnam and the Soviet Union on Thailand.[96] In the context of Sino–Thai relations, Deng had managed to win Thailand over by showing that Vietnam might be a bigger threat to Thailand's security in terms of giving material support to the Thai insurgent groups. Deng also defused the overseas Chinese issue by reaffirming Beijing's old policy of urging overseas Chinese to abide by the laws of their adopted countries.[97]

In January 1979, Vietnam invaded Kampuchea. Then came the Chinese 'punitive attack' on Vietnam. This put Thailand in a grave predicament. It had to conduct extremely delicate diplomatic balancing acts by remaining neutral and at the same time prevent the conflict from spreading across its border. Subsequently Thailand, while openly neutral, decided to lean on the Chinese side by unofficially permitting the Chinese arm supplies to the Pol Pot guerrillas to be transferred via Thai territories.[98]

Thus China and Thailand emerged from the Indochina conflict closer together. In January 1980, Chinese leaders told a visiting American congressional delegation in Beijing that China would use force, if necessary, to defend Thailand from any Vietnamese attack.[99] In his first tour to Southeast Asia in January 1981, Chinese Premier Zhao Ziyang reasserted the Chinese pledge to stand by Thailand against any foreign aggression.[100] Zhao's visit was a high water-mark in Sino–Thai friendship. As a result of the visit, China and Thailand were in broad agreement on the strategy to resolve the Kampuchea issue and shared similar views on regional security. Zhao had also done much to allay the fear of the Thai government over the insurgent problem. Zhao re-iterated China's policy of restricting its support to the outlawed Communist parties in Southeast Asia to 'ideological and moral relations'. Further, Zhao emphasised that China would strive not to allow its party-to-party relations to 'affect its friendly relations with the ASEAN countries'.[101] Obviously, Zhao appeared to be even more moderate than Deng on the issue of the Chinese connection with the local Communists. Deng insisted that China had a right to maintain party-to-party relations with the local Communists just as the local authorities had every right to deal with them in any way, with which Beijing would not interfere.[102]

Notwithstanding the cordial relationship which exists now between Thailand and China, there are still some underlying tensions. Economically, Thailand's unfavourable trade balance with China, if further widened, would be a source of great concern for Thailand. But such a structural imbalance would be difficult for Thailand to wipe out as long as it imports a sizeable amount of petroleum from China. Nor has Thailand been able to derive much benefit from the China market so far. At one time, when China was launching its four-modernisation programme with great fanfare, some hope was raised in Bangkok that the Thais could 'cash in' on the China market. With China now scaling down the modernisation drive, such hope for Thailand has largely fizzled out, particularly since China does not seem to have much demand for the kinds of agricultural products which Thailand annually exports. In any case, the base of Sino–Thai economic relations for some time would be too small to have much effect one way or the other on their overall relationship.

The potential sources of their future tensions are likely to come from the large political issues which have shaped the present Sino–Thai relationship. Of greater importance are the Kampuchea problem and the basic structure of the existing Sino–Thai relations.

In response to the Vietnamese invasion of Kampuchea and the subsequent Chinese attack on Vietnam, Thailand's diplomatic line became clearly tilted towards China. Later, Thailand provided indirect aid to the anti-Vietnamese guerrillas in Kampuchea, and also actively supported China's position on retaining UN membership for the deposed Khmer Rouge. During his visit to Beijing in October 1980, Premier Prem sought the assistance of China in forming an anti-Vietnamese Khmer coalition and in calling for an international conference on the Kampuchean problem. In the course of time, ASEAN's support for Democratic Kampuchea has waned, especially after the Khmer Rouge rejected the coalition move. Within ASEAN, Indonesia and Malaysia have softened their stand on Vietnam and become increasingly impatient over the lack of progress in the Kampuchean settlement. In early May 1982, Thai Foreign Minister Siddhi Savetsila went to Beijing specifically to request China to put pressure on the Khmer Rouge to agree to a compromise proposal for the speedy formation of the anti-Vietnamese coalition.[103] Beijing, however, chose to adopt a hands-off attitude, with Vice-Chairman Deng Xiaoping proclaiming: 'We do not want to impose our views on others and do not interfere with their (the Democratic Kampuchea's) internal affairs.'[104] Clearly, without the Chinese backing, the Khmer Rouge would not be so intransigent, and the Khmer Rouge's obstructive policy has greatly embarrassed Thailand, especially in relation to Thailand's ASEAN allies.[105]

Following the ASEAN's Foreign Ministers' Meeting in Singapore in June 1982, the leaders of the three Khmer factions, under strong pressure from ASEAN and the West, finally agreed to go to Kuala Lumpur on 22 June 1982, to sign an agreement to form an anti-Vietnamese coalition. This would by no means reduce the risk of wider conflict in Indochina, although it has given a new lease of life to the Democratic Kampuchea. Prince Norodom Sihanouk had declared that after the coalition he would negotiate with China for military aids in order to boost the resistance movement. In future, the Sino–Soviet rivalry and Sino–Vietnamese hostility would continue, with unpredictable fallout on the Sino–Thai relationship.

This leads to the more fundamental issue related to the basic structure of the present Sino–Thai relationship. The fall of Indochina in 1975 clearly signalled to the Thais the end of the American dominance in the region, and hence the US military umbrella for Thailand. As Vietnam became more aggressive and more hostile, Thailand drifted closer and closer to China. The highly realistic Thais recognised the fact that it was not international diplomacy but Chinese armed intervention that had prevented the Kampuchean crisis from spilling over into Thailand. Furthermore, it was the continuing threat of a renewed Chinese attack (which kept the Vietnamese forces tied down along its northern border) that had successfully deterred Vietnam from further military ventures in the region. But there are costs to be met for 'the Chinese protection'; Thailand could run the risk of over-identifying its interests with those of the Chinese, particularly if Thailand's foreign policy in future becomes more dependent on China.[106] Should Thailand react against such a pattern of relationship, Sino–Thai relations would be in jeopardy.

The 'bend-with-the-wind' diplomacy is essentially a flexible strategy based on shifting allegiance. Currently, Thailand's foreign policy is heavily drawn towards China on the assumption that China is going to sustain a dominant presence in the region. If there is a fundamental change in such a power equation, Thailand would accordingly change its bets and the Sino–Thai relationship, yet to develop strong economic roots, would suffer. The stability of Sino–Thai relationship should not be taken for granted.

Tables

TABLE 1.2 Economic Performance Indicators of China and ASEAN

| | GNP per capita 1980 (US$) | Energy Consumption per capita (kilograms of coal equivalent) | | Average Annual Growth Rate (%) | | | | | | | |
| | | | | GDP | | Agriculture | | Industry | | Services | |
		1960	1979	1960–70	1970–80	1960–70	1970–80	1960–70	1970–80	1960–70	1970–80
China	290*	560	734	5.2	5.8	1.6	3.2	11.2	8.7	3.1	3.7
ASEAN											
Indonesia	430	125	225	3.9	7.6	2.7	3.8	5.2	11.1	4.8	9.2
Malaysia	1620	239	713	6.5	7.8	—	5.1	—	9.7	—	8.2
Philippines	690	147	329	5.1	6.3	4.3	4.9	6.0	8.7	5.2	5.4
Singapore	4430	498	5784	8.8	8.5	5.0	1.8	12.5	8.8	7.7	8.5
Thailand	670	60	353	8.4	7.2	5.6	4.7	11.9	10.0	9.1	7.3

* Chinese per capita GNP as it is presented here is clearly underestimated, and it is not strictly comparable with that of the market economies of ASEAN. The World Bank originally gave a higher figure for China; but it has since been revised downward at the request of Beijing, for unknown reasons. The estimate for China in the 1976 report was already US$ 410.

Source: World Bank, *World Development Report 1982.*

TABLE 1.2 (contd)

	Distribution of GDP (%)			% of GDP for domestic investment		Trade/GDP ratio (%)	Trade Turnover per capita (US$)
	Agriculture 1980	Industry 1980	Service 1980	1960	1980	1980	1980
China	31	47	22	23	31	15	39
ASEAN							
Indonesia	26	42	32	8	22	47	223
Malaysia	24	37	39	14	29	103	1741
Philippines	23	37	40	16	30	39	280
Singapore	1	37	62	11	43	414	18 077
Thailand	25	29	46	16	27	47	334

187

TABLE 1.3 Some Socio-Economic Indicators of China and ASEAN

	Population (million) mid-1980	Average annual population growth (%) 1970–80	Area (1000Km²)	Adult literacy (%) 1977	Infant morality rate, 1980	Life expectancy at birth (years) 1980	Proportion %/labour force in agriculture, 1980	Urban population as % of total population 1980	Population per physician in 1977	Daily per capita calorie supply, as % of requirement, 1977	No. enrolled in secondary school as % of age-group, 1979
China	976.7	1.8	9561	66	56	64	71	13	1100	103	79
ASEAN											
Indonesia	146.6	2.3	1919	62	93	53	58	20	13670	102	22
Malaysia	13.9	2.4	330	—	31	64	50	29	7640	116	52
Philippines	49.0	2.7	300	75	55	64	46	36	2810	107	63
Singapore	2.4	1.5	1	—	12	72	2	100	1250	135	59
Thailand	47.0	2.5	514	84	55	63	76	14	8220	97	29

Source: World Bank: *World Development Report 1982.*

TABLE 1.4 *Commodity Composition of China's Foreign Trade*
(% Distribution)

	1970	1975	1976	1977	1978	1979
IMPORTS						
Capital goods	16.7	30.0	30.6	18.7	19.5	27.0
(machinery)	8.7	17.1	21.6	7.5	9.3	16.9
(Transport equipment)	7.1	12.1	7.8	9.7	9.2	8.7
Consumer durable	0.7	0:5	0.5	0.6	1.0	2.0
Foodstuffs	17.6	12.2	9.4	16.8	13.0	13.0
(grain)	12.5	9.1	5.4	9.9	9.4	10.0
(sugar)	3.6	2.4	3.3	4.5	2.6	2.2
Industrial supplies	65.0	57.6	59.5	63.9	66.5	60.0
(natural textiles fibers)	4.2	3.5	3.2	6.3	6.7	6.9
(rubber)	3.6	2.1	2.6	3.1	1.8	2.2
(fertilizers)	6.2	5.5	3.8	4.8	4.2	4.3
(Iron & Steel)	18.0	21.9	24.1	21.8	27.4	20.0
Total	100	100	100	100	100	100
EXPORTS						
Agricultural Products	46.7	39.8	36.8	32.3	32.7	29.0
Grain	5.3	9.9	6.2	4.9	3.5	2.5
Fruit & vegetables	8.1	5.0	5.3	6.2	5.8	5.3
Minerals & fuels	5.4	15.3	12.0	12.6	13.1	15.0
Coal	—	1.8	1.3	1.0	1.0	1.3
Crude Oil	—	10.6	9.2	9.8	10.1	11.6
Manufacturing	47.9	44.9	51.2	55.1	54.2	56.0
Chemicals	5.0	4.2	4.5	5.1	4.7	5.8
Textile yarn & fabrics	16.2	14.8	16.0	15.3	16.7	16.3
Machinery	4.3	2.9	3.0	3.1	2.7	2.8
Clothing	7.4	4.8	5.8	7.4	7.2	8.2
Total	100	100	100	100	100	100

Source: Various US Government agencies, cited in *The China Business Review* (March–April 1981).

TABLE 1.5 The Pattern of China's World Trade Balance
(US$ Million)

	Total World Trade			With Industrial Countries			With ASEAN			With Hong Kong		
	X	M	B	X	M	B	X	M	B	X	M	B
1955	1375	1660	−285	182	139	+43	85	100	−15	157	32	+125
1959	2205	2060	+145	265	457	−192	207	137	+70	181	20	+161
1965	2085	1770	+315	596	877	−281	279	164	+115	406	13	+384
1970	1674	1896	−222	948	303	+645	212	49	+163	425	12	+413
1975	5694	6551	−857	2428	5050	−2622	618	132	+486	1248	37	+1211
1976	6078	5208	+870	2673	4167	−1494	601	481	+120	1448	33	+1415
1977	6871	6299	+572	2913	4577	−1664	655	515	+140	1578	49	+1529
1978	8731	9893	−1162	3737	7925	−4188	811	700	+111	2045	69	+1976
1979	11807	14112	−2305	5586	11180	−5594	985	865	+120	2746	421	+2325

Sources: in 1955–65, A. Eckstein (ed.), *China Trade Prospects and the US. Policy* (New York: Praeger, 1971); since 1975, IMF, *Direction of Trade Yearbook 1980*.

TABLE 1.6 Direction of Trade of ASEAN
(% distribution)

	Grand Total (US$ Million)	INDUSTRIAL COUNTRIES				Intra-ASEAN	Socialist Countries		Oil-exporting Countries
		Total	USA	Japan	EEC		Total	China	
Exports									
1964	3131	70.5	23.0	21.8	17.0	8.6	—	0.3	—
1975	20 953	60.8	20.1	26.2	13.3	18.0	2.1	0.7	2.1
1976	25 692	63.9	21.3	26.3	15.0	16.7	2.5	1.1	2.1
1977	31 815	64.8	21.5	24.2	14.4	14.4	2.9	1.2	3.2
1978	36 626	63.0	20.6	23.4	14.1	15.3	2.3	0.7	3.6
1979	49 939	72.4	17.7	27.1	14.1	12.0	2.7	0.9	3.6
1980	67 099	61.5	17.2	26.9	12.8	17.9	2.9	1.0	—
1976–80 (Average)	—	65.1	19.7	25.6	14.1	15.3	2.7	1.0	3.1
Imports									
1964	3497	66.2	17.9	25.6	13.0	9.3	—	4.0	—
1975	23 236	59.6	15.7	25.4	15.9	12.3	3.6	2.9	12.8
1976	26 232	55.1	15.4	22.8	14.4	14.9	3.1	2.5	14.1
1977	30 132	59.0	13.6	23.8	14.7	12.5	3.1	2.4	14.0
1978	36 098	60.1	14.2	24.6	14.5	12.4	3.2	2.5	13.1
1979	46 448	58.9	16.1	22.1	13.7	12.5	2.9	2.3	14.7
1980	64 601	57.1	15.3	22.1	12.7	17.8	3.2	2.6	—
1976–80 (Average)	—	58.0	14.9	23.1	14.0	14.0	3.1	2.5	14.0

Source: IMF, *Direction of Trade Statistics Yearbook*, 1981 and the earlier issues.

TABLE 1.7 *Primary-Product Concentration in Sino–ASEAN Trade*
(in percentage)

(1)

Indonesia's Imports from China

	1978	1977	1974
Rice	19.2	41.2	55.0
Sugar & honey	7.1	0.3	40.0

Malaysia's Exports to China

	1978	1975	1971
Rubber	90.6	94.1	98.0

Philippines' Exports to China

	1977	1976
Sugar	65.9	58.6

Thailand's Exports to China

	1979	1976	1975
Rice & maize	29.0	47.7	42.2
Sugar	15.7	33.4	—

(2)

Malaysia's Imports from China

	1978	1975	1971
Food (Rice)	49.7 (27.0)	47.2 (27.6)	39.4 (9.8)

(3)

Philippines' Imports from China

	1977	1976
Petroleum	90.7	89.4

(4)

Singapore's Exports to China

	1980	1976
Rubber	41.6	39.0

(5)

Thailand's Imports from China

	1979	1976	1975
Petroleum	64.2	38.3	33.9

Sources: for Indonesia, Biro Pusat Statistik, *Impor 1976, Impor 1977* and *Impor 1978*; for Malaysia, *Perdagangan Luar*, 1978, 1975 and 1971; for the Philippines, *Foreign Trade Statistics of the Philippines*, 1979, 1977 and 1976; for Singapore, *Singapore Trade Statistics*, 1980, 1976, and for Thailand, *Foreign Trade Statistics of Thailand*, December 1979, 1976 and 1975.

TABLE 1.8   The Balance of Major Primary Commodities in China's Foreign Trade (US$ 1000)

	1975 Imports	1975 Exports	1976 Imports	1976 Exports	1977 Imports	1977 Exports	1978 Imports	1978 Exports	1979 Imports	1979 Exports
A. UNCTAD Ten Core Commodities										
Coffee	318	1700	317	2500	1200	750	1592	4881	1200	4900
Cocoa	8805	—	8805	—	26600	—	2700	—	32000	—
Tea	65	84523	—	84276	—	130332	—	175991	—	195098
Sugar	155000	317241	250000	177500	470000	13332	374000	81400	280000	92580
Cotton	331610	44000	381198	45000	423254	8500	767572	36000	1020199	26500
Rubber	175050	—	192531	—	237093	—	247516	—	337976	—
Jute	8038	95	11300	95	8700	1600	15310	2448	18500	5200
Sisal	7404	934	7400	930	570	9132	1030	8401	820	8610
Copper[1]	9132	—	8752	—	—	—	—	—	8796	—
Tin (metal)[2]	—	97640	—	55086	—	40000	—	68000	—	31000
Sub-total	695422	546133	860263	365387	1168417	203646	1409720	377121	1699491	363888
Balance		−149289		−494876		−964771		−1032599		−1335603
B. Food and Forest Products										
Grain	1035400	940100	805410	477240	1607980	415420	1959820	655510	2632090	575180
(Wheat)	747000	—	442835	—	1275280	—	1436003	—	1766126	—
(Rice)	—	880000	—	450100	—	410294	—	463072	—	559198
Forest Products	221907	201474	256562	191009	430900	336500	519900	444000	519900	444000
Sub-total	1257307	1141574	1061972	668249	2038880	751920	2479720	1099510	3151990	1019180
Balance		−115733		−393723		−1286960		−1380210		−2132810

C. Minerals

Crude oil	—	760 000	—	665 000	—	795 000	—	1 015 000	—	1 580 000
Coal	—	130 000	—	95 000	—	80 000	—	100 000	—	175 000
Crude Minerals	125 000	120 000	125 000	65 000	110 000	85 000	160 000	140 000	140 000	185 000
Sub-total	125 000	1 010 000	125 000	825 000	110 000	960 000	160 000	1 255 000	140 000	1 940 000
Balance		+885 000		+700 000		+850 000		+1 095 000		+1 800 000
Grand Total (A+B+C)	2 077 729	2 697 707	2 047 235	1 858 636	3 317 297	1 915 566	4 049 440	2 731 131	4 991 481	3 323 068
Total balance:		+619 978		−188 599		−1 401 731		−1 317 809		−1 668 413

Notes: 1. Copper from the Philippines only

2. China's exports of tin metal are in tons, and converted into value terms at New York prices.

Sources: FAO, *1979 FAO Trade Yearbook* and earlier issues; *1979 FAO Yearbook of Forest Products* and earlier issues; International Tin Council, *Monthly Statistical Bulletin* (August 1981); *1979 Foreign Trade Statistics of the Philippines*; and *The China Business Review* (March–April 1981).

TABLE 1.9 Exports of Resource-Based Commodities of China and ASEAN
(% of total Exports)

	1964	1965	1966	1967	1968	1969	1970	1971	1972	1973	1974	1975	1976	1977	1978	1979
China	43	46	50	49	49	52	52	52	52	48	49	55	49	45	46	44
ASEAN																
Indonesia	99	98	98	98	97	98	99	99	99	99	99	99	99	98	98	97
Malaysia	94	94	94	95	95	95	91	92	90	89	88	83	84	84	80	79
Philippines	94	95	93	94	94	93	93	93	92	89	92	88	75	75	66	—
Singapore	68	70	72	75	77	77	73	67	59	56	60	58	55	54	53	48
(Singapore)	(50)	(51)	(50)	(49)	(50)	(52)	(50)	(42)	(35)	(36)	(28)	(25)	(26)	(25)	(24)	(24)
Thailand	98	98	98	98	98	96	95	92	88	85	85	79	78	80	75	68
World	49	48	46	49	45	42	47	46	45	47	51	49	50	48	49	—

Note: National resource-based commodities are the items included within SITC Section 0 to 4, plus division 68 (non-ferrous metals) and item 51365 (alumina). For China, no detailed breakdown of trade statistics has been published, and the above is computed on the basis of the US official estimates in accordance with two categories: 'Agricultural' and 'Extractive'.

Sources: for China, US official estimates as contained in the Joint Economic Committee of the United States, *People's Republic of China: An Economic Assessment* (1972); and *Chinese Economy Post-Mao* (November 1978) (Washington DC: US Government Printing Office); after 1976, various US government agencies cited in the *Chinese Business Review* (March–April 1981); for ASEAN, United Nations, *1979 Yearbook of International Trade Statistics*, and previous issues.

TABLE 1.10 *Destination of Manufactured Exports (% of total), 1962 and 1979*

Origin	Industrial Market economies 1962	1979	Developing Countries 1962	1979	Non-Market industrial economies 1962	1979	High-income oil exporters 1962	1979	Value of manufactured exports (US$ Million) 1962	1979
China	—	27	—	70	—	3	—	*	900 (1959)	5311
ASEAN										
Indonesia	52	30	46	65	1	*	1	5	2	488
Malaysia	11	68	89	31	0	*	*	1	58	1966
Philippines	91	80	9	19	*	*	*	1	26	1596
Singapore	5	48	95	48	0	1	*	3	328	7372
Thailand	51	65	49	32	*	*	*	3	21	1327
Korea	83	73	17	20	0	*	*	7	1	13 299
Hong Kong	62	83	37	15	0	*	*	3	642	10 804

* Not significant
Source: World Bank: *World Development Report 1982.*

TABLE 1.11 ASEAN as Markets for China and other Asian Exporters
(%)

Imports from	Indonesia			Malaysia			Philippines			Singapore			Thailand		
	1977	1978	1979	1977	1978	1979	1977	1978	1979	1977	1978	1979	1977	1978	1979
China	2.5	1.8	1.8	3.1	3.7	2.9	1.9	2.4	1.9	2.6	2.6	2.3	1.5	1.7	2.7
Japan	27.1	30.1	29.1	23.4	23.1	23.5	25.1	26.6	22.6	17.5	19.2	16.8	32.4	30.7	26.3
Hong Kong	1.0	2.1	1.4	2.0	1.8	1.7	1.6	2.2	2.4	2.5	2.5	2.5	0.7	1.1	1.3
Korea	0.9	1.5	1.6	0.7	1.0	1.5	1.0	1.1	1.5	1.0	1.1	1.1	1.0	1.5	1.5
Other ASEAN Countries															
Indonesia	—	—	—	1.0	0.7	0.9	3.7	3.0	3.0	*	*	2.3	0.1	0.5	0.7
Malaysia	0.3	0.3	0.5	—	—	—	1.5	1.2	1.4	13.6	12.8	13.2	1.0	1.3	1.9
Philippines	0.3	1.1	0.7	0.6	0.8	0.9	—	—	—	0.6	0.5	0.4	0.1	0.1	0.3
Singapore	8.4	6.6	7.4	8.4	8.5	9.3	0.8	1.0	1.3	—	—	—	2.9	4.1	4.1
Thailand	5.3	1.5	3.0	4.6	4.2	3.6	0.3	0.4	0.2	2.2	2.8	2.7	—	—	—

* Not available
Source: IMF, Direction of Trade Yearbook 1980.

TABLE 1.12   *The Market Shares in the Industrial Countries for China and Other Asian Countries*
(%)

Imports from	USA			Japan			EEC		
	1977	1978	1979	1977	1978	1979	1977	1978	1979
China	0.1	0.2	0.3	2.3	2.6	2.7	0.26	0.26	0.30
Hong Kong	2.0	2.1	2.0	0.5	0.6	0.6	0.59	0.63	0.67
Korea	2.0	2.2	2.0	3.0	3.3	3.0	0.37	0.39	0.38
ASEAN									
Indonesia	2.4	2.0	1.8	7.1	6.6	7.9	0.06	0.24	0.25
Malaysia	0.9	0.9	1.0	2.2	2.4	2.9	0.38	0.37	0.38
Philippines	0.8	0.7	0.8	1.3	1.3	1.4	0.16	0.16	0.17
Singapore	0.6	0.6	0.7	1.0	1.1	1.3	0.20	0.19	0.23
Thailand	0.2	0.3	0.3	1.1	1.1	1.1	0.22	0.26	0.24

Source: IMF, *Direction of Trade Yearbook, 1980*

TABLE 1.13 The Relative Share of Labour-intensive Products in Total Manufactured Exports of some Asian Countries (%)

	1964	1965	1966	1967	1968	1969	1970	1971	1972	1973	1974	1975	1976	1977	1978	1979
East Asia																
China	49	44	44	42	45	52	49	40	43	45	39	44	44	42	44	44
Japan	13	11	10	9	8	8	6	5	4	3	2	2	2	2	2	1
Hong Kong	57	55	54	52	51	49	42	45	44	41	42	46	46	44	42	–
Korea	36	35	35	41	43	42	41	43	38	36	34	36	38	37	37	–
*ASEAN**																
Malaysia	10	10	13	16	17	17	11	13	15	13	11	13	13	14	13	–
Philippines	1	5	9	4	5	5	5	6	8	13	17	17	17	18	17	–
Singapore	17	17	15	15	17	17	15	14	14	12	9	8	9	8	7	–
Thailand	10	10	26	24	42	22	14	24	23	31	22	18	19	21	22	–
World	7	7	7	7	7	7	5	6	6	6	5	5	6	5	6	–

* Indonesia is not listed here as its manufactured exports only started in recent years.

Note: 'Labour-intensive products', commonly taken to mean also 'low value-added products', basically comprise, in the 3-digit SITC classification, textiles (652 and 656) and clothing (84). But they also include leather goods (612), pottery (666) as well as footwear (851). The figures for China are, strictly speaking, not comparable with those for other countries listed above, as the Chinese share refers to 'all textiles and clothing', which includes some higher value-added textiles such as 'textile yarn and thread' (651), 'woven textiles' (653), 'special textiles' (655). On the other hand, the Chinese share excludes leather goods, footwear and pottery, because Chinese official trade statistics do not provide detailed breakdown in accordance with the SITC categorisation.

Sources: for China, estimates from various US government agencies, as contained in the Joint Economic Committee of the US Congress, *People's Republic of China: An Economic Assessment* (1972) and *Chinese Economy Post-Mao* (1978); and the *China Business Review* (March–April 1981), for ASEAN, United Nations, *Yearbook of International Trade Statistics*, 1979, and previous issues.

TABLE 2.1   *Indonesia's Trade with China (US$ million)*

Year	Imports from China Amount	Index	Exports to China Amount	Index	Total China Trade Amount	As % of Indonesia's Total Trade (%)
1938	4.6	46	5.4	83	10.0	1.6
1948	10.3	102	1.6	25	11.9	1.3
1951	2.4	24	0.1	*	2.5	0.1
1952	2.1	21	*	*	2.4	*
1953	2.1	21	*	*	2.1	*
1954	3.5	35	2.8	43	6.3	*
1955	10.1	100	6.5	100	16.6	0.1
1956	30.2	299	11.7	180	41.9	2.4
1957	27.0	267	25.2	288	52.2	2.9
1958	41.8	410	43.4	667	85.2	6.7
1959	61.2	606	53.1	817	114.3	8.6
1960	57.0	564	35.4	544	92.4	6.5
1961	39.9	395	36.4	560	76.3	4.8
1962	34.9	346	34.6	532	96.5	4.2
1963	44.3	438	42.2	649	86.5	8.2
1964	61.0	603	52.2	803	113.2	9.2
1965	98.8	978	40.0	685	138.8	10.8
1966	40.7	403	9.5	146	50.2	3.8
1967	54.2	537	0.7	10	54.9	3.9
1968	38.4	380	*	*	38.4	2.6
1969	43.0	425	*	*	43.0	2.7
1970	30.5	302	—	—	30.5	1.4
1971	31.2	309	*	*	31.2	1.3
1972	38.2	378	—	—	38.2	1.3
1973	45.2	447	—	—	45.2	0.8
1974	113.9	1128	—	—	113.9	1.0
1975	204	2020	—	—	204	1.7
1976	132	1307	—	—	132	0.9
1977	154	1525	—	—	154	0.9
1978	122	1208	—	—	122	0.7
1979	132	1307	—	—	132	0.6
1980	175	1733	—	—	175	0.5

* Statistically insignificant.
Sources: United Nations Yearbook of International Trade Statistics, 1953, 1957 1968, and 1980; IMF and IBRD: *Direction of Trade, Annuals* (1958–62, 1968–72, 1969–73); Biro Pusat Statistik, *Statistik Indonesia 1974–75* (Jakarta).

TABLE 2.2 *The Relative Position of Indonesia's Selected Trade Partners* (%)

	China		Netherlands		Japan		USA		Hong Kong		Soviet Union	
	M	X	M	X	M	X	M	X	M	X	M	X
1938	1.7	1.5	21.1	20.9	15.0	3.3	9.2	14.8	1.4	2.1	—	—
1948	2.4	*	17.7	35.8	16.5	6.7	22.5	17.5	2.3	1.9	—	—
1951	0.3	*	12.1	21.2	18.7	3.2	20.0	13.1	5.4	0.4	—	—
1952	0.2	*	12.8	21.1	13.7	2.6	17.1	25.5	8.4	2.9	—	—
1953	0.3	0.3	11.7	22.5	16.8	4.5	17.9	16.4	7.2	1.3	—	—
1954	0.5	0.3	10.5	19.3	21.7	5.8	14.4	17.1	5.9	4.6	0.1	0.1
1955	1.6	0.6	11.2	15.9	13.7	7.7	15.1	17.6	5.0	0.3	*	*
1956	3.5	1.3	10.7	19.5	15.6	9.4	16.5	16.0	5.5	0.4	*	0.8
1957	3.4	2.6	9.8	16.7	15.1	4.1	16.7	15.2	4.4	1.8	*	1.3
1958	8.1	5.7	6.5	4.1	13.6	3.6	15.9	17.2	4.6	0.9	0.5	1.8
1959	13.4	5.9	3.7	1.1	15.0	3.8	16.0	16.4	2.8	1.3	1.2	3.3
1960	9.9	4.2	3.1	0.3	16.1	4.1	15.5	23.0	3.5	1.1	1.4	4.0
1961	5.0	4.6	0.9	0.3	17.9	7.1	17.2	23.8	5.1	1.3	7.9	4.2
1962	4.7	3.7	0.6	2.1	15.6	9.8	16.2	14.6	2.9	1.6	2.7	5.0
1963	8.1	8.5	1.7	2.8	19.7	18.5	21.8	22.5	3.0	2.0	2.0	3.1
1964	10.8	7.9	2.3	12.9	23.5	17.4	14.3	25.6	8.9	1.7	2.2	3.8
1965	16.5	5.8	6.0	14.5	37.5	19.5	7.6	24.1	6.0	2.1	2.2	3.4
1966	7.3	1.3	1.7	11.6	23.3	21.0	11.8	23.8	15.3	2.8	1.1	2.0
1967	8.1	0.1	7.5	12.0	25.4	23.8	11.2	24.7	18.0	2.2	0.7	2.2
1968	5.4	*	7.1	5.8	22.2	22.9	17.2	14.9	4.6	1.2	0.9	1.7
1970	3.1	—	5.1	3.6	29.6	38.6	18.0	9.5	2.1	0.9	0.6	0.1
1973	1.6	—	2.3	2.2	33.7	57.2	16.4	13.9	4.7	0.6	—	0.3
1977	2.5	—	4.2	3.4	27.1	40.2	12.5	27.7	1.0	0.3	0.2	0.3
1980	1.4	—	2.8	1.3	30.9	48.9	13.0	20.4	4.2	0.2	0.1	0.3

* Statistically insignificant.
M: Imports   X: Exports
Source: Computed from Sources stated in Table 2.1.

TABLE 2.3   *Commodity Structure of Indonesia's Imports from China*
(% distribution)

	1959	1963	1965	1975	1979
Rice	38.2	8.5	20.6	75.2	0
Sugar	*	*	*	4.1	1.4
Textiles	24.8	48.0	50.8	4.3	7.0
Others	37.0	43.5	28.6	16.4	91.6
Total	100	100	100	100	100

Sources: for 1959–65, Biro Pusat Statistik, *Statistical Pocket Book of Indonesia, 1964–1967* (Jakarta); for 1975 and 1979, Biro Pusat Statistik, *Impor 1975* and *Impor 1979* (Jakarta).

TABLE 2.4A   *Imports of Cotton Weaving Yarns into Indonesia (Million Rs)*

Country of Origin	1959	1960	1961	1962	1963	1964	1965
China	82.4	765.5	572.4	601.3	772.4	347.7	547.0
in %	34.2	31.0	22.3	37.2	67.2	25.2	75.5
Japan	41.1	1014.3	1014.3	574.1	134.2	780.5	4.0
Hong Kong	91.0	386.6	503.1	197.6	147.8	80.4	115.8
Others	27.4	298.6	186.1	242.4	94.1	529.6	382.8
Total	242.2	2465.1	2563.0	1615.4	1148.5	1378.2	2049.6

Source: Same as Table 2.3

TABLE 2.4B   *Imports of Cotton Fabrics into Indonesia (Million Rs)*

Country of Origin	1959	1960	1961	1962	1963	1964	1965
China:	90.5	931.0	771.1	999.2	186.3	587.5	711.9
in %	28.4	38.4	17.0	36.3	11.3	23.7	35.1
Japan	96.7	491.7	937.8	599.2	526.6	1320.0	502.4
Hong Kong	39.4	435.5	1173.1	105.9	257.5	224.0	388.3
USSR	10.4	121.4	258.7	160.5	323.4	154.9	208.0
Others	81.3	145.5	1393.3	890.1	350.6	193.5	1810.5
Total	318.3	2425.1	4534.0	2754.9	1644.4	2479.9	2029.6

Source: Same as Table 2.3.

TABLE 3.1 *Pan-Malaya's Trade with China*
(in M$ Million /) †

Year	Imports from China				Exports to China				Trade Balance
	Pan-Malaya	Singapore Component as % of total	As % of Malaysia's total imports	As % of Singapore's total imports	Pan-Malaya	Singapore Component in total (%)	As % of Malaysia's total imports	As % of Singapore's total imports	Total Malaya
1938	23.9	—	4.4	—	3.2	—	0.6	—	−20.7
1947	122.1	—	8.9	—	8.4	—	0.6	—	−133.7
1949	76.1	—	4.1	—	6.9	—	0.4	—	−69.2
1950	95.8	80.3	2.5	3.6	124.0	85.5	1.4	4.3	+28.2
1951	127.1	75.5	2.1	2.8	84.2	99.0	0.8	2.1	−42.9
1952	120.8	77.5	2.8	3.2	*	*	—	—	−120.8
1953	105.2	77.6	2.6	3.5	5.7	71.9	0.2	0.2	−33.3
1954	87.1	78.1	2.4	2.9	19.5	71.3	0.6	0.6	−47.6
1955	115.7	78.8	2.6	3.2	12.8	84.4	0.2	0.4	−102.9
1956	132.0	77.8	2.8	2.6	23.7	64.1	0.6	0.4	−108.3
1957	159.7	77.5	3.3	4.1	74.2	61.6	1.2	1.3	−85.5
1958	195.4	77.0	4.5	4.0	116.4	55.7	4.1	2.1	−79.0
1959	166.5	78.9	2.5	3.4	121.7	95.3	0.3	3.4	−44.8
1960	174.8	80.0	2.7	3.4	86.9	99.9	—	2.5	−87.9
1961	172.2	75.4	3.2	3.3	11.5	99.9	—	0.4	−160.7
1962	201.7	77.4	3.0	3.9	2.5	99.9	*	0.1	−199.2
1963	287.6	73.6	5.0	4.9	16.5	98.8	*	0.5	−271.1
1964	302.5	65.0	6.7	5.6	1.0	99.9	—	0.1	−301.5
1965	325.7	68.9	6.1	5.9	22.5	99.9	*	0.8	−303.2
1966	468.3	58.0	6.6	6.7	139.7	98.2	0.8	4.1	−328.6

* Statistically small.

† One Malayan dollar equalled US$0.58 in 1937; $0.43 in 1949; and 0.33 throughout the 1950s and 1960s.

Sources: Before 1949, UN *International Trade Statistics 1950*, after 1950, for Malaysia, *Malayan Statistics: External Trade*, and *West Malaysia Monthly Statistics of External Trade*, various years; for Singapore, *Singapore External Trade Statistics*, various years.

TABLE 3.2A   *China's Shares in Pan-Malayan Textile Imports, 1953–59 (% of Value)*

Country	1953	1954	1955	1956	1957	1958	1959
China	1.8	2.5	4.3	5.5	7.3	9.3	12.4
Japan	17.4	31.3	42.8	41.5	43.3	47.3	46.0
India	22.7	19.6	14.7	13.9	13.3	16.5	15.6
Hong Kong	10.5	11.0	12.0	9.8	9.7	8.5	3.5
UK	24.2	17.6	12.2	11.5	10.8	6.5	7.6
USA	7.6	9.9	8.0	9.5	6.7	5.3	4.4
Others	15.8	8.1	6.0	8.3	8.9	6.6	
Total	100	100	100	100	100	100	100

TABLE 3.2B   *China's Shares in Pan-Malayan Cement Imports, 1955–59 (% of Value)*

Country	1955	1956	1957	1958	1959
China	1.3	7.0	13.9	6.7	9.0
UK	53.2	41.6	33.6	31.9	20.7
Japan	31.8	42.7	50.2	56.6	63.7
Others	13.7	8.7	2.3	4.8	6.6
Total	100	100	100	100	100

Source: Malayan Statistics: External Trade, various years.

TABLE 4.1 *Malaysia's Trade With China* (Selected Years)
(US $ million)

	Malaysia's imports from China		Malaysia's exports to China		Trade balance for Malaysia
	Amount	As % of Malaysia's total imports	Amount	As % of Malaysia's total exports	
1968	79.4	6.8	25.0	1.9	− 54.4
1970	74.0	5.2	21.6	1.3	− 52.4
1972	69.0	4.3	27.1	1.6	− 41.9.
1974	195.0	4.7	87.0	2.1	− 108.0
1976	134.0	3.5	45.0	0.8	− 89.0
1977	141.0	3.1	120.0	2.0	− 21.0
1978	221.0	3.7	132.0	1.8	− 89.0
1979	223.0	2.8	182.0	1.6	− 41.0
1980	253.0	2.3	216.0	1.7	− 37.0

Source: IMF, *Direction of Trade*, relevant years.

TABLE 4.2   *Commodity Composition of Malaysia's Imports from China*

	1952	1958	1967	1971	1976	1979
Food	64.2	45.3	43.7	39.4	40.1	33.4
Meat	1.4	1.1	2.7	1.4	2.0	2.7
Cereals	12.0	6.3	23.2	12.7	12.1	5.3
(Rice)	—	(4.3)	(20.7)	(9.8)	(9.7)	(4.6)
Fruits & Vegetables	46.0	14.6	14.6	16.0	13.8	13.5
Manufactured goods	27.4	30.1	27.2	27.2	25.5	26.7
Paper	3.5	5.6	2.7	4.8	4.4	3.7
Textiles	3.3	14.7	7.6	9.5	6.4	7.0
Iron & Steel	—	1.5	9.0	2.8	1.4	4.4
Machinery & Transport Equipment	8.6	2.4	2.8	4.3	4.8	5.6
Miscellaneous manufactures	—	7.4	7.8	8.9	7.3	9.4
Clothing	—	1.9	2.3	2.3	1.5	1.8
Others	—	14.8	14.9	20.2	22.3	24.9
Total	100	100	100	100	100	100

Sources: *Malayan Statistics: External Trade*; *West Malaysia Monthly Statistics of External Trade*; and *Peninsula Malaysia External Trade* (relevant issues).

TABLE 4.3 *Singapore's Trade With China (Selected Years)*
(US $ million)

	Singapore's Imports from China		Singapore's Exports to China		Trade Balance for Singapore
	Amount	As % of Singapore's total imports	Amount	As % of Singapore's total exports	
1968	150	11.8	27	1.6	− 123
1970	126	8.1	23	0.9	− 103
1972	142	4.1	20	0.9	− 122
1974	265	3.2	51	0.9	− 214
1976	267	2.9	39	0.6	− 228
1977	275	2.6	59	0.7	− 216
1978	342	2.6	58	0.6	− 284
1979	411	2.3	170	1.2	− 241
1980	629	2.6	307	1.6	− 322

Source: IMF, *Direction of Trade,* relevant years.

TABLE 4.4   *Commodity Composition of Singapore's Imports from China*
(% *distribution*)

	1952*	1962	1970	1975	1980
Food	*64.0*	*39.0*	*21.5*	*22.1*	*22.3*
Meat	1.4	1.4	1,5	2.1	2.3
Cereals	12.0	15.0	5.8	3.1	1.4
(Rice)		(13.3)	(4.7)		
Fruits and vegetables	46.0	11.5	13.5	11.4	11.3
Manufactured goods	*27.4*	*34.7*	*39.1*	*40.8*	*43.0*
Paper	3.5	3.4	2.3	1.8	2.2
Textiles	3.3	19.0	23.3	22.0	18.9
Non-metal mineral		3.3	4.4	5.4	2.8
Iron and Steel		4.0	0.8	1.1	2.6
Nonferrous metal		3.5	1.0	5.0	0.5
Machinery and Transport	—	*2.0*	*5.9*	*5.8*	*6.5*
Miscellaneous manufactures	*8.6*	*11.7*	*12.4*	—	
Clothing		5.2	2.9	3.9	2.0
Others	—	*12.0*	*21.1*	*31.1*	*29.2*
Total	*100*	*100*	*100*	*100*	*100*

* Refers to Pan-Malayan trade, i.e. Malaysia and Singapore.
Sources: for 1952, *Malayan Statistics: External Trade*; for 1962, 1967 and 1970,
Singapore External Trade Statistics (Oct–Dec issues); for 1975 and 1980,
Singapore Trade Statistics: Imports and Exports (December issues of 1975 and
1980).

TABLE 4.5   *Fluctuations in Malaysia's Trade with China, 1950–71*

Period	Imports from China		Exports** to China	Malaysia's Total Imports		Malaysia's Total Exports
	I–I	I–I*	I–I	I–I	I–I*	I–I
1950–57	21.9	19.7	86.1	13.7	13.8	25.0
1958–65	37.1	27.6	194.7	16.4	5.6	13.7
1966–71	10.6	7.6	80.1	12.8	5.9	22.1

I – I: Instability Index, or sometimes referred to as coefficient of variation, is the standard deviation divided by the mean:

$$\sqrt{\frac{\Sigma (Y_i - \overline{Y})^2}{n-1}} \Big/ \overline{Y} = \frac{\sigma}{Y}$$

where Y_i: annual observations
$\overline{Y}$: arithmetic mean of Y_i
N: number of observations
I – I*: Instability index corrected for trend influence:

$$\left[\frac{1}{n-k-1} \sum_{1-1}^{n} (Y_i - Y)^2 \right]^{1/2} \Big/ \overline{Y}$$

where $Y = a + bX$ is a linear trend.
(This index is used by Egon Neuberger in studying exports of primary products by developing countries to the USSR.)
** Only one index is worked out for Malaysia's exports to China because the violent fluctuations plus many 'blanks' in the intermediate years defy meaningful measurement by an instability index incorporating a linear trend.

TABLE 4.6   *Trade Fluctuations of West Malaysia: By Selected Major Trade Partners,*
1965–71

Country	Imports		Exports	
	Instability Index	Rank	Instability Index	Rank
UK	15.5	8	20.2	6
W. Germany	18.1	6	29.2	5
Hong Kong	15.2	9	32.2	4
India	19.3	5	45.6	3
Australia	14.1	10	14.7	10
USA	27.1	4	14.9	9
Japan	33.1	1	96.2	1
Singapore	16.0	7	15.8	8
USSR	29.2	3	16.3	7
Thailand	30.1	2	13.9	11
China	10.0	11	96.0	2
Average	20.7		35.9	
W. Malaysian total	12.6		20.5	

Note: 1965 was the year Singapore separated from Malaysia.

TABLE 4.7 China's Imports of Natural Rubber

Year	From Malaysia & Singapore Tons	% of China's total	From Indonesia Tons	% of China's total	From Ceylon† Tons	% of China's total	Others (Remaining %)	China's Total Rubber Imports (tons)	Index
1947–49	7945	34			1265	5	61	23 562	100
1950	38 568	55			75	0.1	54	70 000	297
1951	22 721	31			5543	7.6	61	73 250	311
1952					29 690	100	0	29 690	126
1953					58 405	97.3	3	60 000	255
1954					56 323	90.5	9	62 250	264
1955					32 349	64.7	35	50 000	212
1956	8707	9.2	1372	1.4	54 686	57.7	32	94 850	394
1957	31 367	26.7	35 852	30.6	50 095	42.7	0	117 314a	498
1958	64 036	38.3	79 250	47.5	23 640	14.2	0	166 926a	709
1959	49 532	32.6	80 344	52.3	23 204	15.1	0	153 070a	650
1960	29 507	24.2	45 375	37.3	38 275	31.4	7	121 750	517
1961	2633	2.9	67 799	75.8	19 023	21.3	0	89 455a	380
1962	766	0.7	55 272	50.1	36 805	33.9	15	108 500	461
1963	9060	7.7	79 206	67.5	29 106	24.9	0	117 372a	498
1964	114	0.1	105 837	73.4	32 533	22.6	4	144 250	612

211

Year									
1965	13475	9.2	87918	60.0	45090	30.8	0	146483a	622
1966	90350	52.3	12312	7.1	59314	34.4	6	172500	732
1967	88525	55.4			58435	36.6	8	159750	678
1968	128431	60.7			81548	38.5	8	211750	899
1969	202145	73.5			71500	26.0	0	275000	1167
1970	101859	54.6			84730	45.4	0	186589a	792
1971	104453	63.2			58471	35.4	1	165250	701
1972	131167	70.0			53668	28.6	1	187500	796
1973	195360	73.6			69288	26.2	0.2	265000	1125
1974	144825	75.9			41843	21.9	0.2	191000	810
1975	140515	58.7			91627	38.2	3.1	239500	1018
1976	150000	67.3		70	84000	37.6	0	222500a	944
1977	167744	68.0		33	64036	25.9	6.1	247000	1048
1978	129402	58.6			62514	28.4	13.0	220000	934
1979	159126	63.6			44648	17.8	18.6	250000	1061
1980	192891	82.1			42212	18.0	0	235000a	997

† Ceylon is officially known as Sri Lanka since 1971.

a The figures are sum totals of China's imports from the three countries, since the source estimates do not tally with the sums. For instance, the independent estimate for China's total rubber imports for 1957 is 115 500 in the source, but the exports of the three countries to China for that year add up to 117 314.

Source: Rubber Statistical Bulletin, International Rubber Study Group, London, various issues.

TABLE 4.8   *Fluctuations in China's Import Demand for Rubber*

	Instability Index[a]
China's Total Rubber Imports	
1950–72	45.98
1950–58	51.04
1961–72	30.39
Imports from Malaysia and Singapore	
1956–65	105.46
(Malaysia's overall rubber exports, 1956–65)	(8.02)
1966–72	32.67
(Malaysia's overall rubber exports, 1966–72)	(19.78)
Imports from Indonesia	
1958–65	25.15
(Indonesia's overall rubber exports, 1958–65)	(9.20)
Imports from Ceylon	
1950–72	18.62
(Sri Lanka's overall rubber exports, 1950–72)	(19.62)

[a] The instability index, sometimes referred to as coefficient of variation, is the standard deviation divided by the mean

$$\sqrt{\frac{\Sigma (Y_i - \bar{Y})^2}{n-1}} \Bigg/ \bar{Y} = \frac{\sigma}{\bar{Y}}$$

where Y_i: annual observations.
where $\bar{Y}$: arithmetic mean of Y_i.
where N: number of observations.
This particular measure is not corrected for trend influence and it could be less effective as an indicator for long time series with rising trends.
Source: John Wong, 'Chinese Demand for Southeast Asia Rubber, 1949–72', *The China Quarterly* (September 1975) p. 514.

TABLE 4.9 *Summary of Singapore's Trade with China since Normalisation*
(Value in S$ Million)

Year	Imports $	% of S'pore's Total Imports	Exports $	% of S'pore's Total Exports	Domestic Exports $	% of S'pore's Total Domestic Exports	Total Trade $	% of S'pore's Total Trade	Balance of Trade
1975	682.0	3.5	98.5	0.8	29.4	0.4	780.5	2.4	−583.5
1976	659.0	2.9	95.4	0.6	53.8	0.5	754.4	2.0	−563.6
1977	670.4	2.6	144.7	0.7	63.9	0.5	815.1	1.8	−525.7
1978	775.5	2.6	130.7	0.6	56.1	0.4	906.2	1.7	−644.8
1979	894.1	2.3	369.6	1.2	176.6	0.9	1263.7	1.8	−524.5
1980	1332.1	2.6	657.9	1.6	301.6	1.1	1990.0	2.1	−674.2
1981	1629.8	2.8	337.3	0.9	121.9	0.4	2007.1	2.0	−1252.5
1981 Jan−May	632.9	2.6	160.4	0.9	58.4	0.5	793.3	1.9	−472.5
1982 Jan−May	790.0	3.1	153.5	0.8	33.9	0.3	943.5	2.1	−636.5
Jan−Jun 1981	759.3	2.6	197.2	0.9	71.1	0.5	956.5	1.9	−562.1
Jan−Jun 1982P	978.3	3.2	205.6	0.9	43.8	0.3	1183.9	2.2	−772.7

P = Provisional
Source: Singapore, Department of Trade.

TABLE 4.10 *Changing Structure of Singapore's Exports to China*
(% distribution)

	1970	1975	1980	1981
Crude rubber	96.4	67.5	41.6	25.7
Fertilisers, manufactured	—	—	1.9	19.1
Ship and aircraft stores	—	—	9.8	16.9
Television receivers	—	—	7.8	8.7
Engineering equipment	—	—	7.9	6.2
Ships and boats (e.g. oil rigs)	—	—	20.4	7.4
Special transactions	—	24.2	—	—
total	96.4	91.7	89.4	84.0

Sources: *Singapore External Trade Statistics* (October–December 1970); *Singapore Trade Statistics Imports and Exports* (December 1975); for 1980 and 1981 Singapore Government Department of Trade.

TABLE 5.1 *Philippines' Trade With China*
(US$ million)

	Exports		Imports		Total balance	Rank in Philippines' total trade
	$ million	% share	$ million	% share	$ million	
A. Republican China						
1938	0.9	0.8	3.1	2.3	−2.2	—
1947	1.4	0.5	14.2	2.8	12.8	—
1948	2.5	0.6	22.9	4.0	−20.4	—
1949	0.8	0.3	10.2	1.8	−9.4	—
B. People's Republic of China						
1971	0.4	*	—	—	0.4	*
1972	0.8	0.1	5.5	0.4	−4.7	28
1973	0.6	0.4	21.3	1.3	−14.7	1.4
1974	13.3	0.49	23.4	2.0	−65.1	16
1975	25.2	1.1	47.0	1.4	21.8	13
1976	39.6	1.5	53.8	1.5	−14.2	12
1977	92.8	2.9	78.4	2.0	14.4	9
1978	47.5	1.4	111.6	2.4	−35.9	13
1979	51.5	1.1	121.0	2.0	−69.5	15

* Insignificant

Sources: For the People's Republic of China period see National Census and Statistics Office, *Foreign Trade Statistics With Philippines* (Manila, various years); for Republican China: UN. *International Trade Statistics 1950*

TABLE 5.2 *Philippines' Trade With China: Commodity Concentration*
%

	Imports from China			Exports to China	
		% of total			% of total
1971	Coconut oil		1971	Coconut oil	100
1972	Rice	100	1972	Coconut oil	100
1973	Rice	99.9	1973	Coconut oil	97.0
1974	Rice and petroleum	88.3	1974	Coconut oil	94.0
1975	Petroleum & rice	92.8	1975	Coffee & coconut oil	65.0
1976	Crude petroleum	48.1	1976	Sugar	23.2
1977	Crude petroleum	71.1	1977	Sugar	71.2
1978	Crude petroleum	90.5	1978	Sugar	72.8
1979	Crude petroleum	80.0	1979	Sugar and coffee	55.5

Source: See Table 5.1.

TABLE 5.3 *The Relative Shares of China and Selected Countries in the Philippines'*
Trade
(average of 1975–8)

	1975–78	Balance of trade in Philippines in these 4 years
	%	
China	1.9	1 in 4 plus
USA	26.3	3 in 4 plus
Japan	26.9	All 4 negative
Germany	3.7	1 in 4 plus
UK	3.3	All 4 negative
Hong Kong	1.6	All 4 negative
Taiwan	1.9	All 4 negative
Indonesia	2.2	All 4 negative
Singapore	1.3	All 4 plus
South Korea	0.9	3 in 4 plus

Source: National Census and Statistics Office (NCSO), *Philippines Yearbook 1979*
(Manila).

TABLE 6.1   Thailand's Trade With China
(million bahts)

	Imports from China		Exports to China		Trade Balance to Thailand
	Amount	As % of total Imports	Amount	As % of total Exports	
1938†	1.2	2.0	5.2	5.9	+4.0
1948†	15.0	–	34.2	–	+25.7
1949†	9.6	–	8.5	–	–1.1
1953	0.239	*	339.121	7.4	+338.882
1954	0.002	*	62.174	1.4	+62.172
1955	1.591	*	0.003	*	–1.588
1956	0.307	*	24.029	0.3	+23.722
1957	0.792	*	68.231	0.9	+67.439
1958 (first quarter)	1.416	*	63.571	–	+62.155
1974	91.9	0.1	2.5	*	–89.4
1975	343.9	0.5	391.4	0.8	+47.5
1976	1462.5	2.0	1265.9	2.0	+196.6
1977	1370.6	1.5	2081.2	2.9	+710.6
1978	1703.7	1.6	1486.2	1.8	–235.5
1979	4939.5	3.4	1567.9	1.5	–3371.6
1980	8535.1	4.5	2527.5	1.9	–6007.6

† Amount in US$ million
* Statistically insignificant.
Source: for 1938, UN Yearbook of International Trade Statistics 1950: for 1948–49, Far Eastern Economic Review (5 Feb 1953); for 1953–8, Thailand's Department of Customs as quoted in the Far Eastern Economic Review (19 Feb 1959); for 1974–80, Thailand's Department of Customs, Foreign Trade Statistics of Thailand (December issues of the relevant years).

TABLE 6.2   *Thailand's Trade Balance With Major Trade Partners, 1980*
(million Bahts)

	Exports	Imports	Balance	% of total
Total	133 197	188 696	− 55 499	100
Japan	20 098	39 984	− 19 886	35.8
U.S.A.	16 834	27 208	− 10 374	18.7
Saudi Arabia	2320	19 103	− 16 783	30.2
W. Germany	5516	8222	− 2706	4.8
Singapore	10 292	12 261	− 1969	3.5
Taiwan	1791	3955	− 2164	3.9
Australia	1431	3549	− 2118	3.8
China	2528	8535	− 6007	10.8

Source: Bank of Thailand, *Quarterly Bulletin*, vol. 21, no. 4 (December 1981).

TABLE 6.3 *Commodity Concentration in Thailand's Trade With China 1975–80*
(%)

	Imports from China			Exports to China			
	Mineral fuel and oil	Machinery	Total	Cereal	Rubber	Sugar	Total
1975	34.1	16.9	51.0	42.2	55.8	–	97.0
1976	38.3	8.7	46.0	47.7	18.8	33.4	99.9
1977	41.8	7.9	49.7	–	87.1	9.8	96.9
1978	46.3	6.5	52.8	10.4	9.8	63.1	83.3
1979	64.2	4.6	68.8	29.0	24.2	15.6	58.8
1980	57.8	8.6	66.4	19.7	18.9	13.9	52.5

Source: Department of Customs, Thailand, *Foreign Trade Statistics of Thailand* (December issues of the relevant years).

Notes and References

Chapter 1

1. Victor Purcell, *The Chinese in Southeast Asia*, 2nd edn (Oxford University Press, 1965) p. 8.
2. John King Fairbank, *Trade and Diplomacy on the China Coast* (Cambridge, Mass: Harvard University Press, 1953) p. 32.
3. Ibid, ch. 2.
4. For a detailed discussion of the 'Chinese world order', see John K. Fairbank (ed.), *The Chinese World Order* (Cambridge, Mass.: Harvard University Press, 1968).
5. Wang Gungwu, 'Early Ming Relations with Southeast Asia: A Background Essay', in Fairbank, *The Chinese World Order*
6. Since Singapore had openly declared that it would be the last country in ASEAN to recognise China, it could not have established full diplomatic relations with China before Indonesia had restored its diplomatic ties with China.
7. Hu Yaobang, *Report to the Twelfth National Congress of the Communist Party of China*, 1 September 1982 (Beijing: Foreign Languages Press, 1982).
8. For a succinct discussion of the main features of the ASEAN economies, see John Wong, *ASEAN Economies in Perspective: A Comparative Study of Indonesia, Malaysia, the Philippines, Singapore and Thailand* (London: Macmillan, 1979).
9. The World Bank's *World Development Report 1981* contains various social indicators for China as well as for ASEAN. For a further discussion of Chinese performance in these areas, see Thomas Rawski, *Economic Growth and Employment in China* (New York: OUP, 1979); Keith Griffin, 'Efficiency, Equality and Accumulation in Rural China: Notes on the Chinese System of Incentives' *World Development*, no. 6 (1978); and A. R. Khan, 'The Distribution of Income in Rural China', ILO World Employment Programme Working Paper (Geneva, July 1976). Also Neville Maxwell (ed.), *China's Road to Development* (Oxford: Pergamon Press, 1975).
10. Dwight Perkins, 'Meeting Basic Needs in the People's Republic of China', *World Development* (May 1978) p. 561.
11. Alexander Eckstein, *China's Economic Revolution* (Cambridge University Press, 1977) p. 233.
12. See John Wong, 'Southeast Asia's Growing Trade Relations with Socialist Economies', *Asian Survey*, vol. 17, no. 4 (1977).

220

13. Zhou Enlai, 'Report on the Work of the Government', *Peking Review* (now called *Beijing Review*), no. 4 (1975) p. 23.
14. Hua Guo-feng, 'Unite and Strive to Build a Modern Powerful Socialist Country', *Peking Review*, no. 10 (1978) pp. 7–10.
15. Some ASEAN governments were worried particularly over the possibility of China and Japan forming some economic bloc. See 'Asia Worried Over Sino–Japan Ties', *S T* (Singapore, 15 December 1978); also 17 November 1978 and 2 December 1978.
16. For a succinct discussion of the 10-Year Plan, see Nicholas R. Lardy, 'Recent Chinese Economic Performance and Prospects for the Ten-Year Plan', in US Congress Joint Economic Committee, *Chinese Economy Post-Mao* (Washington, D. C., 1978).
17. Zhao Ziyang's Report on the Work of the Government at the 4th Session of the 5th National People's Congress, 1 December 1981. *China's Economy and Development Principles: A Report by Premier Zhao Ziyang* (Beijing: Foreign Languages Press, 1982).
18. 'Economic Readjustment: Results since 1979', *Beijing Review*, no. 35 (30 August 1982).
19. 'China's Economic Achievements', *Beijing Review*, no. 40 (1981) pp. 18–23. For 1981 figures, see 'Economic Readjustment: Results since 1979', *Beijing Review*, no. 35 (1982).
20. Zhao Ziyang, 'The Present Economic Situation and the Principles for Future Economic Construction', *Beijing Review*, (no. 51 (1981).
21. Ibid.
22. 'Can China Reach its Economic Targets by 2000?' *Beijing Review* (4 October 1982).
23. Reported in *Asian Wall Street Journal* (17 October 1978).
24. For an analysis of China's wheat imports, see John Wong 'China's Wheat Import Programme', *Food Policy* (May 1980).
25. For a discussion of China's energy relations with ASEAN, see Kim Woodard, *The International Energy Relations of China* (Stanford: Stanford University Press, 1980).
26. For a discussion of China's coming energy problem, see the World Bank's *World Development Report 1981* and *China Business Review* (September–October 1981).
27. See John Wong, 'Rice Exports: A New Dimension in China's Economic Relations with Southeast Asia', *Journal of Southeast Asian Studies*, vol. X, no. 2 (September 1979).
28. International Tin Council, *Tin Statistics 1969–79* (London, 1980).
29 See Zdenek Drabek, 'The Natural Resource Product Absorption in Centrally-planned Economies', University of British Columbia, Department of Economics' Discussion Paper 80–28, (July 1980).
30. *Asian Wall Street Journal* (7 February 1979).
31. *World Development Report 1981*, (World Bank).
32. For further discussion of this subject, see Colin Bradford, Jr, 'ADC's Manufactured Export Growth and OECD Adjustment', in Wontack Hong and Lawrence B. Krause (eds), *Trade and Growth of the Advanced Developing Countries in the Pacific Basin* (Korean Development Institute, Seoul, Korea, 1981).
33. The figures are worked out on the data contained in the *World Development Report 1981*.
34. Ross Garnaut and Kym Anderson, 'ASEAN Export Specialization and the Evolution of Comparative Advantage in the Western Pacific Region', in Ross Garnaut (ed.), *ASEAN in a Changing Pacific and World Economy* (Canberra: Australian National University Press, 1980) p. 403.

35. See Ippei Yamazawa, 'Renewal of Textile Industry in Developed Countries and World Textile Trade', in Hitotsubashi University, Research Unit in Economic and Econometric Working Paper, (No. 82–6) July 1982.
36. For more information on the recent MFA negotiation, see *Asian Wall Street Journal* (5 January 1982); *Business Times* (Kuala Lumpur, 6 January 1982).

Chapter 2

1. Indonesia became a fully independent state on 27 December 1949, just a little over three months after the formation of the People's Republic of China. The Indonesian government under Hatta on 11 January 1950 made a formal request to Beijing via the Dutch government, for Chinese recognition. The message was passed on to Beijing by the Dutch only on 27 February 1950; and it was not till 28 March 1950 that Zhou Enlai formally replied to Hatta, agreeing to establish 'regular diplomatic relations' with Indonesia. And it was only in May 1950 that Zhou sent a cable, suggesting the exchange of envoys. See, David Mozingo, *Chinese Policy Towards Indonesia, 1949–1967* (Ithaca, Cornell University Press, 1976) pp. 89–90.
2. O. W. Wolters, *Early Indonesian Commerce* (Ithaca: Cornell University Press, 1967) p. 27.
3. Victor Purcell, *The Chinese in Southeast Asia*, 2nd edn (Oxford University Press, 1965) p. 390.
4. Mozingo, p. 35.
5. See the recent article of A. R. T. Kemassang, 'The 1740 Massacre of Chinese in Java: A Curain Raiser for the Dutch Plantation Economy', *Bulletin of Concerned Asian Scholars*, vol. 14, no. 1 (1982).
6. Purcell, ch. 43; Also, J. A. C. Mackie (ed.), *The Chinese in Indonesia: Five Essays* (Thomas Nelson, Melbourne, for the Australian Institute of International Affairs, 1976) Introduction.
7. See Charles A. Coppel, 'Patterns of Chinese Political Activity in Indonesia', in Mackie.
8. Mozingo, p. 36.
9. Purcell, ch. 49.
10. Ho Ping-Yin, *The Foreign Trade of China* (Shanghai: Commercial Press, 1935).
11. Mozingo, pp. 98–102.
12. For greater detail, see Donald E. Willmott, *The National Status of the Chinese in Indonesia, 1900–1958* (Ithaca: Cornell Modern Indonesia Project, 1961).
13. See *China and the Asian-African Conference* (Beijing: Foreign Languages Press, 1955).
14. Mozingo, p. 122.
15. See Leo Suryadinata, *Pribumi Indonesians, the Chinese Minority and China* (Kuala Lumpur: Heinemann Educational books, 1978).
16. See Ruth McVey, 'Indonesian Communism and China', in Tang Tsou (ed.), *China in Crisis*, vol. 2 (Chicago: Chicago University Press, 1968).
17. Mozingo, p. 138.
18. Leo Suryadinata.
19. Purcell, p. 147.
20. Leo Suryadinata.
21. For more detail, see J. A. C. Mackie, 'anti-Chinese Outbreaks in Indonesia, 1959–68', in Mackie.

22. Arslan Humbaraci, 'Anti-Chinese Feelings in Indonesia', *FEER* (10 September 1959) p. 389.

23. Mackie, p. 85.

24. Mozingo gives a good analysis of various policy implications for Beijing over this issue, cha. 6.

25. Lea E. Williams, 'Sino–Indonesian Diplomacy: A Study of Revolutionary International Politics', *China Quarterly*, no. 11 (July/September 1962) pp. 184–99.

26. For greater detail of the outbreaks in 1963, see Mackie.

27. For a more detailed discussion of Sino–Indonesian relations in this period, see, Sheldon W. Simon, *The Broken Triangle: Peking, Djakarta, and the PKI* (Baltimore: Johns Hopkins University Press, 1969).

28. Ibid, pp. 50–9.

29. For example, Ide Anak Agung Gde Agung argued that Sukarno's alliance with China brought Indonesia to a position of 'dependency'. *Twenty Years of Indonesian Foreign Policy*, 1945–1965 (The Hague: Mouton, 1973).

30. See Brian May, *The Indonesian Tragedy* (London: Rouledge & Kegan Paul, 1978).

31. For a detailed account of the army's role in the *coup* and its aftermath, as well as of Suharto's patient process of overthrowing Sukarno, see Harold Crouch, *The Army and Politics in Indonesia* (Ithaca: Cornell University Press, 1978).

32. For events following the *coup*, see Justus M. van der Kroef, 'The Sino–Indonesian Rupture', *China Quarterly*, no. 33 (January/March 1968).

33. See P. H. M. Jones, 'Peking's Trade Offensive III – Indonesia', *FEER* (18 June 1959).

34. C. Peter Timmer, 'The Political Economy of Rice in Asia: Indonesia', *Food Research Institute Studies*, no. 3 (1975).

35. In July 1975, Indonesian government representatives for the first time negotiated a direct rice deal with Beijing for the supply of 50 000 tonnes (*Sin Chew Jit Poh*, Singapore, 15 July 1973).

36. John Wong, 'Rice Exports: A New Dimension in China's Economic Relations with Southeast Asia', *Journal of Southeast Asia Studies* (September 1979).

37. For a more detailed discussion of this subject, see John Wong 'Chinese Demand for Southeast Asian Rubber, 1949–72', *China Quarterly*, no. 63 (September 1975).

38. For more details, see Wolfang Bartke, *China's Economic Aid* (London: Hurst and Company, 1975).

39. 'China's Foreign Aid in 1972', *Current Scene* (United States Information Agency, Hong Kong), vol. XI, no. 12 (December 1973).

40. *OECD Development Co-Operation 1974 Review* (Paris, 1974) p. 135.

41. *Current Scene.*

42. For a vivid discussion of the post-coup events, see Brian May; also Harold Crouch.

43. See Jay Taylor, *China and Southeast Asia: Peking's Relations with Revolutionary Movements* (New York: Praeger Publisher, 1974).

44. See John Wong, 'The Economics and Politics of Sino–Indonesian Relations, 1950–1976', *Asian Profile* (August 1977).

45. *ST* (Singapore, 18 November 1975).

46. *ST* (22 November 1975).

47. See Garth Alexander, *Silent Invasion: The Chinese in Southeast Asia* (London: Macdonald, 1973). Also, Adil Rakindo, 'Indonesia: Chinese Scapegoat Politics in Suharto's New Order', *Journal of Contemporary Asia*, vol. 5, no. 3 (1975).

48. *ST* (26 November 1975).

49. 'Malik: China Ties After Polls', *ST* (1 January 1977).

50. 'Decision on China Ties After Polls', *ST* (2 November 1976).

51. 'Peking gets building ready for Indonesian Envoy', *ST* (15 March 1977).

52. 'Indonesian Minister Blames Hua for Hindering Ties', *Sunday Times* (Singapore, 22 May 1977).

53. 'Teng's "No" Setback for Ties', *ST* (14 November 1978). As the *Far Eastern Economic Review* correspondent wrote: 'As far as Indonesian Foreign Minister Mochtar Kusumaatmadja was concerned, Teng's (Deng's) statements were enough to put the issue of Indonesian–China relations back into mothballs'. (Rodney Tasker, 'Indonesia: Old Fears Delay Relationship', *FEER* (15 December 1978) p. 32.)

54. 'Mochtar: China Failed to Convince Them', *ST* (4 September 1981).

55. 'Mochtar: We Are Preparing for China Ties', *ST* (16 October 1978).

56. 'Jakarta-Peking Ties, Mochtar Says "No" Again', *ST* (18 January 1979).

57. 'Mochtar: Position Has Improved: China Ties Fewer Snags', *ST* (16 October 1979).

58. Ingo Hertel, 'Jakarta Prefers to Bide Her Time on China Ties', *ST* (28 January 1980).

59. 'Ties with China in Near Future: Suharto', *ST* (26 February 1980).

60. 'No Reason for Hurry to Make Up with China: Mochtar', *ST* (23 March 1980).

61. 'Jakarta and Peking Start Direct Trade Ties', *ST* (19 February 1980).

62. 'Jakarta to Look into Beijing Ties Next Year', *ST* (3 July 1981).

63. 'Beijing Calls for Normalising Jakarta Ties', *ST* (25 April 1980).

64. 'Indonese–China Trading to Resume After 13 Years', *Asian Wall Street Journal* (20 February 1980).

65. 'Jakarta Revises Foreign Policy', *ST* (25 January 1982).

66. Editorial, *Bangkok Post* (Bangkok, 28 April 1980).

67. Mochtar argued that the Kampuchea problem was not even a problem so far as ASEAN was concerned: 'It's basically a problem between Vietnam and China but with an ASEAN angle to it because Thailand happens to be caught in the middle'. 'The Mochtar Kusumaatadja Interview', *ST* (18 June 1982).

68. *Sin Chew Jit Poh* (Singapore, 25 May 1982).

69. Far Eastern Economic Review's *China Trade Report* (Hong Kong, June 1973).

70. 'No Reason for Hurry to Make Up with China: Mochtar', *ST* (23 March 1980).

71. Editorial, *FEER*, (30 June 1975).

72. Barry Wain, 'China and Indonesia are Moving Closer Towards Establishing Diplomatic Relations', *Asian Wall Street Journal*, (20 December 1979).

73. For example, the editorial of Indonesia's daily *Merdeka*, in supporting General Panggabean's opposition to restoring ties with China, argued that his stance was 'clearly based on combined factors of sensitiveness and sound judgement'. 'China is demonstrating an element which is inconsistent and doubtful. It has become unpredictable and pursued a double-faced policy without guarantee of honesty'. ('No Use in Normal Ties with China', *ST*, 13 March 1981).

74. Many generalisations have been put forward about the anti-Chinese sentiment in Indonesia based on inferences drawn mainly from the overt manifestations of hostility; but as J. A. C. Mackie laments, 'Little or no research in depth into racial attitudes in contemporary Indonesia has been undertaken by social psychologists'. (Mackie, p. 78).

75. See, 'Sudomo Regrets Those Taking Law Into Own Hands', *Indonesian Observer* (Jakarta, 14 April 1980); 'Indonesia Warns Riot Instigators of Stiff Penalty', *Asian Wall Street Journal* (22 June 1980); and, 'Shoot On Sight Order by Sudomo', *ST* (9 December 1980).

76. Even on the domestic social and economic origins of anti-Chinese feelings, there now exist considerable gaps between myths and reality as a result of fast economic development and social change during the past decade. The common notion that Chinese Indonesians dominate the national economy has been challenged by a

recent report published by 'Management Information Foundation' in the daily, *Indonesian Observer*. According to the study, the share of Chinese Indonesians in the economy is virtually negligible compared with that of the state or even foreigners. Nor are the Chinese still money-lenders as 84 per cent of the credits are now provided by state banks (*Business Times*, Kuala Lumpur, 14 December 1981).

77. 'Jakarta Offering Citizenship to Alien Chinese Residents', *Asian Wall Street Journal* (1 March 1980).
78. 'Drive to Register Indonesian Chinese', *ST* (1 April 1980).
79. 'Ties with China: Delay Will Harm Indonesia', *ST* (27 January 1979).
80. 'China to Bar the Holding of Dual Nationality', *ST* (3 September 1980).
81. See, e.g., Roshan Anwar, 'Conflicting Views on Restoring Ties with China', *ST* (14 October 1978).

Chapter 3

1. For a succinct discussion of trade between China and British Malaya before the war, see Ho Ping-Yin, *The Foreign Trade of China* (Shanghai: Commercial Press, 1935), ch. XIV. For the early development of trade of Malaya, see P. P. Courtenay, *A Geography of Trade and Development* (London: G. Bell, 1972), ch. 2.
2. Victor Purcell, *The Chinese in Southeast Asia*, 2nd edn (Oxford University Press, 1965) p. 235.
3. Purcell, ch. 26.
4. P. R. Pearn, *An Introduction to the History of Southeast Asia* (Kuala Lumpur: Longman Malaysia, 1963).
5. Purcell, ch. 30.
6. Ho Ping-Yin.
7. See Shi Yi, 'After the visit of the Malaya–Singapore Trade Delegation to China', *China News Dispatch* (Hong Kong, 16 October 1956) and Nan Xan, 'An Analysis of Sino–Malayan Trade', *Ta Kung Pao* (Hong Kong, 16 August 1950).
8. Ho Ping-Yin.
9. See United Nations, *International Trade Statistics Yearbook, 1950* (New York).
10. See *Rubber Statistical Bulletin*, International Study Group, (London, 1953).
11. *FEER* (9 September 1955).
12. *FEER*, Editorial, (22 March 1956); also issue of 14 June 1956, pp 737–8.
13. *ST* (Singapore, 5 June 66).
14. *FEER* (20 June 1957).
15. 'The prospects of trade development between China and Singapore–Malaysia', *Renmin Ribao*, People's Daily, (Beijing, 30 August 1956) and 'Malaya group signs £3.2 million Peking Deals', *HKS*, (Hong Kong 13 Sept 1956).
16. Tung Shiu Yuen, 'Sino–Malayan Trade', *FEER* (3 Nov. 1960).
17. *ST* (19 September 1958).
18. *FEER* (9 October 1958) p. 476.
19. *FEER* (20 June 1957).
20. Daniel Wolfston, 'Peking's Trade Offensive in Southeast Asia–II: Malaya', *FEER* (14 May 1959) pp. 71–8; and 'Malaya to Stop Dumping of Red Chinese Textiles', *HKS* (2 November 1958).
21. *FEER* (13 November 1958), p. 635; and *ST* (29 October 1958).
22. *ST* (27 November 1958).
23. *ST* (26 November 1958). The China Council also complained of unfriendly acts on

the part of the Malayan authorities: 'Even the construction of a Chinese pagoda in the trade fair in Kuala Lumpur was not allowed'. *HKS* (26 November 1958).

24. *HKS* (4 December 1958).
25. *Sing Tao Daily* (Hong Kong, 28 November 1958).
26. *FEER*, Editorial (20 November 1958).
27. 'Red Export Offensive Said Slowly Fizzling Out to Practically Nil', *HKS* (30 March 1959).
28. 'Singapore Rubber Market Waits for China', *South China Morning Post* (Hong Kong, 24 November 1965).
29. In November, 1965, Dato T. H. Tan led a trade mission to Taiwan and for the next few years he was a strong advocate for banning all trade with China and for establishing stronger economic links with Taiwan. See, *South China Morning Post* (29 Nov 1965 and 11 June 1967).
30. Associated Press dispatch from Seattle, Washington, *HKS* (1 November 1958).
31. Han Suyin, 'Singapore Separation', *FEER* (19 August 1965).
32. Harry G. Johnson, 'Notes on Some Theoretical Problems Posed by the Foreign Trade of Centrally-Planned Economies', in Alan A. Brown and Egon Neuberger, *International Trade and Central Planning* (Berkeley: University of California Press, 1968) p. 395.
33. J. Wilcznyski, *The Economics and Politics of East–West Trade* (London: Macmillan, 1969) p. 23.
34. 'The Threat of Chinese Dumping in Asia', *FEER* (11 November 1958) p. 643.
35. For a detailed discussion of the origin and effects of the US trade embargo against China, see John R. Garson, 'The American Trade Embargo Against China', in Alexander Eckstein, (ed.) *China Trade Prospects and US Policy* (New York: Praeger, 1971).
36. Robert Chabeiron, 'Trade Problems in Southeast Asia', *FEER* (19 July 1956) pp 67–9.
37. For a succinct discussion of the economic importance of rubber and tin to Malaysia in the 1950s, see, David Lim, *Economic Growth and Development in West Malaysia* (Kuala Lumpur: Oxford University Press, 1973).
38. Robert Dernberger, 'Prospects for Trade Between China and the United States', in Eckstein, p. 187.
39. Harry G. Johnson's Foreword to Wilczynski.
40. For a more rational evaluation of the general effects of trade embargoes, see Wilcznyski, ch. 12.
41. *FEER* (16 June 1956) p. 739.
42. *FEER* (23 August 1956) p. 246.
43. Denis Warner, 'China's Bid to Capture Southeast Asian Trade', *ST* (17 December 1958).
44. *The Jetro Survey of 1959* (Tokyo, 1959); see also *HKS* (29 July 1959) and *FEER* (18 June 1959).
45. *Financial Times* (London, 13 January 1959).
46. 'Malaya to Stop Dumping of Red Chinese Textiles', *HKS* (2 November 1958).
47. D. M. Feeney, 'Malaya's Anti-Dumping Law by New Year?', *FEER* (20 November 1958) p. 645 and p. 660.
48. 'China's Dumping in Malaya', *FEER* (1 January 1959) p. 8.
49. Ibid.
50. *HKS* (30 October 1958).
51. *Takung Pao* (Hong Kong, 12 and 15 December 1958).
52. 'Malaya To Stop Dumping of Red Chinese Textiles', *HKS* (2 November 1958).
53. 'Singapore and China Trade', *FEER* (8 January 1958) p. 42.

54. See Jacob Viner, *Dumping: A Problem in International Trade* (New York: Augustus Kelley, reprinted in 1966) ch. 1. The popular definition of dumping from G. Haberler is 'the sale of a good abroad at a price which is lower than the selling price of the same good at the same time in the same circumstance at home', *The Theory of International Trade* (London: Hodge & Co. 1936) p. 296. This would then implicate almost all the dynamic, export-oriented economies in 'dumping'.

55. J. Wilcznyski has assembled and analysed many cases of suspected Soviet and Chinese dumping in various markets, including that of Malaysia. See 'Dumping and Central Planning', *Journal of Political Economy* (June 1966) pp. 25–64; and also Wilcznyski, ch. 9.

56. Peter Wiles took similar view, see P. J. D. Wiles, *Communist International Economics* (Oxford: Basil Blackwell, 1968) pp. 217–18.

57. Ibid.

58. *FEER* (28 September 1961) p. 649; also 13 June 1963.

59. *ST* (21 October 1958).

60. Tan's statement in defence of his government's stand smacked of the classical case of Western timber merchants at one time threatening to boycott Soviet timber exports on the grounds that Soviet wood was cut by forced labour. Both cases relied on political emotionalism for support to disrupt the trade. See Wiles, p. 217.

61. *FEER* (14 January 1960) p. 39. But this is immeasurably better than the clumsy editorial of the *Straits Times* of 27 November 1958, which simply dismissed the Chinese complaint as a 'threat' and in doing so the 'Chinese Government is being very foolish'.

62. The next day after the announcement of the trade ban, the Malayan government conducted a 'fullscale probe into subversion through trade', and officers of the Department of Customs and Industrial Development harassed importers and merchants of Chinese goods by questioning their trade practices and other backgrounds. See *ST* (3 October 1958).

63. 'China's Dumping in Malaya', *FEER* (1 January 1959) p. 8.

64. For a good discussion of this subject, see Stephen Fitzgerald, *China and the Overseas Chinese* (Cambridge University Press, 1972) ch. 7.

65. 'Malaya: One Way Traffic?' *FEER* (9 September 1962).

66. The Japanese have analysed the causes for the immediate success of China's trade advance into Southeast Asian markets. See 'Red China Bid for Southeast Asia Markets', *Oriental Economist* (September 1958) pp. 471–2.

67. For a good discussion of 'Confrontation', see J. A. C. Mackie, *Konfrontasi: Indonesia–Malaysia Dispute, 1963–66* (Kuala Lumpur: Oxford University Press, 1974).

68. The editorial of the *Manila Evening News*, see HKS (8 August 1965).

69. *FEER* (29 September 1969) p. 633.

70. 'Development of Trade Between China and the Asian–African Countries since the Bandung Conference', *China's Foreign Trade*, Beijing Review, no. 1 (1969) p. 17.

71. Anthony Polsky, 'Stakes in Singapore/Malaysia', *FEER* (2 October 1969) p. 53.

72. Harvey Stockwin, 'Malaysia/Singapore; Trouble Up North', *FEER* (29 September 1966) p. 632.

73. Nancy Wong, 'Hong Kong's Communist Banks', *Insight* (Hong Kong, August 1973).

74. Audrey Donnithorne, *China's Economic System* (London: George Allen & Unwin, 1967) ch. 15.

75. *FEER* (20 June 1957) p. 773.

76. *South China Morning Post*, (28 June 1965).

77. Ibid.

78. *ST* (28 June 1965).
79. *South China Morning Post* (29 June 1965).
80. *ST* (29 June 1965).
81. Han Suyin, 'Singapore Separation', *FEER* (19 August 1965).
82. Anthony Polsky, 'Singapore: Compromise?', *FEER* (29 May 1969) p. 482.
83. *Renmin Ribao* (People's Daily) (Beijing, 7 May 1969).
84. For a detailed discussion of the Bank of China Incident up to early 1969, see I Fang, 'The Incident of the Bank of China', *China Monthly* (Hong Kong, no. 63, June 1969).

Chapter 4

1. *Guangming Ribao* (Beijing, 12 December 1967).
2. Harvey Stockwin, 'Malaysia/Singapore: Trouble up north', *FEER*, (29 September 1966) p. 633.
3. Goh Cheng Teik, 'Tearing Down the Curtain of Fear', *FEER*, (10 June 1972) p. 28.
4. See Marvin Rogers, 'Malaysia/Singapore: Problems and Challenges of the Seventies', *Asian Survey*, vol. XI, no. 2 (11 February 1971) pp. 121–9.
5. *China Trade Report* (Hong Kong, September 1971 and January 1972).
6. For more details, see *Natural Rubber News* (Washington D.C., September 1972).
7. Jose Katigbak, 'Sino–Malaysian political ping-pong starts off', *HKS*, (8 June 1973).
8. 'Malaysia: Peaceful Intention', *FEER*, (1 October 1973).
9. 'Malaya Makes the First Move', *South China Morning Post*, (7 July 1973).
10. 'Razak's China Triumph', *Asia Magazine*, (22 September 1974) p. 27.
11. Ibid., p. 31.
12. Ibid.
13. Ibid.
14. 'Where China backs Us: Razak', *ST*, (Singapore, 3 June 1974).
15. 'Malaysia Given Free Hand on Terrorists' *South China Morning Post* (3 June 1974).
16. *Asia Magazine*, p. 27.
17. 'Peking Leaders get Top Billing by Front', *ST* (3 August 1974).
18. *Asia Magazine*, p. 31.
19. The table-tennis match between the Chinese and Singapore teams in Singapore in 1972 marked the last display of 'Chinese chauvinism' in Singapore, when the Chinese Singaporeans actually cheered the Chinese team instead of their national team, much to the anger and bewilderment of Prime Minister Lee Kuan Yew. *ST* (19 July 1972). For a further discussion of the events leading to detente with China, see Lee Lai-To, *China's Changing Attitudes Towards Singapore, 1965–1975* (Department of Political Science, University of Singapore, Seminar Paper No. 22, November 1975).
20. *South China Morning Post* (12 January 1973).
21. 'Singapore in No Hurry for Peking Ties', *HKS* (23 May 1973).
22. 'Raja Off on China Visit', *ST* (12 March 1975).
23. 'The Singapore Identity', *ST* (13 March 1975).
24. 'Chou: We are Willing to Wait', *ST* (18 March 1975).
25. *Business Times* (Singapore, 31 December 1979).
26. *Business Times* (Kuala Lumpur, 9 July 1981) and *ST* (8 July 1981).
27. 'Malaysia: Pernas Man in the Hot Seat', *FEER* (1 August 1972).

28. 'Malaysia: Pernas Apology', *FEER* (3 June 1972).
29. For more detail, see 'Malay–Chinese Frictions', *China Trade Report* (May 1978); also, *ST* (27 December 1974).
30. 'Direct trade links with China soon', *Business Times*, (Kuala Lumpur, 24 March 1981).
31. 'Scrapped: Service Charge on Goods', *ST* (11 May 1976).
32. See also Lum Weng Leen, *Singapore's Changing Economic Relations With China*, Academic Exercise of the Department of Economics, University of Singapore, 1980/81 academic session; written under the supervision of the author.
33. Harvey Stockwin, 'Into the Red', *FEER* (15 April 1965) p. 111.
34. Anthony Polsky, 'Stakes in Singapore/Malaysia', *FEER* (2 October 1969) p. 54.
35. The survey was conducted by Mr Zhuan Zue-lian, with a grant from Singapore's Institute for Southeast Asian Studies; 2300 questionnaires in both English and Chinese were administered, with a 35 per cent response rate. The findings were published in *Sin Chew Jit Poh* in three series (21 December and 27 December 1971 and 3 January 1972).
36. It is generally recognised that primary commodities are subject to greater price fluctuations so that specialisation in their exports would therefore bring about greater export instability. However, empirical studies by Massell, Michaely, and MacBean on specific groups of countries, give a low correlation between the degree of commodity concentration and export instability. It is explained that differences in the degree of export instability among countries may be due to differences in the commodity composition rather than to commodity concentration in their exports, e.g. some primary products are inherently more susceptibly to price fluctuations. See B. F. Massell, 'Export Concentration and Fluctuations in Export Earnings: A Cross-Section Analysis', *American Economic Review* (March 1974); M. Michaely, *Concentration in International Trade* (Amsterdam: North-Holland, 1962); and A. I. MacBean, *Export Instability and Economic Development* (London: Allen & Unwin, 1966). For Malaysia, see David Lim, 'Export Instability and Economic Development in West Malaysia, 1947–1968', *Malayan Economic Review* (October 1972).
37. K. M. Mohamed Ariff's study shows that the Soviet Union's imports from Malaysia for 1947–65 give an instability index of 578 as against 31 for the average of all countries. See *Export Trade and West Malaysia: An Enquiry into the Economic Implications of Export Instability*, Monograph Series on Malaysian Economic Affairs, (Kuala Lumpur, University of Malaya, 1972) p. 21. S. J. Khoo's study of Malaysia's exports for the period 1947–64 also gives China and the Soviet Union the highest average annual percentage rate of change of imports from Malaysia. See 'Malayan Exports: Instability and Prospects', Ph.D thesis, (Cornell University, 1967) pp. 59–64.
38. J. Wilcznyski, *The Economics and Politics of East-West Trade* (London: Macmillan, 1969) p. 206. The study by E. Neuberger also shows that the Soviet imports for the period 1955–61 were not significantly more stable than those of the western countries.' 'Is the USSR Superior to the West as a Market for Primary Products?' *Review of Economics and Statistics* (August 1964) pp. 287–93.
39. See Cheng Siok-Hwa, *The Rice Trade of Malaya* (Singapore: University Education Press, 1973).
40. See John Wong, 'Rice Exports: A New Dimension in China's Economic Relations with Southeast Asia', *Journal of Southeast Asian Studies*, vol. X, no. 2 (September 1979).
41. International Rubber Study Group, *Rubber Statistical Bulletin* (January/February 1982).
42. 'Blazing in the Peking Trail', *FEER* (10 June 1974).

43. 'Malaysia: Quiet Backlash', *FEER* (4 Oct. 1974).
44. Harvey Stockwin, 'A Back-Burner Problem', *FEER* (1 October 1976).
45. 'Ghazali on Differing Styles of Dong, Deng', *ST* (30 November 1978).
46. 'No China Pledge to Stop Backing CPM, Says PM', *ST* (13 November 1978).
47. 'Teng's Statements in Kuala Lumpur points Up China-Malaysia Differences' *Asian Wall Street Journal*, (November 14, 1978).
48. 'No China Pledge to Stop Backing CPM, Says PM', *ST* (13 November 1978).
49. 'Don't Take Advantage of Teng's Visit: Senu', *ST* (7 November 1978).
50. 'Malaysian Chinese Indifferent to Deng's KL Visit', *ST* (5 December 1978).
51. 'D. Bonavia and K. Das: All Alone and Far From Home', *FEER* (24 November 1978).
52. 'K. Das: A Tough Guy Takes Over', *FEER* (30 October 1981).
53. 'Defection of Musa: A Big Blow to CPM, Say Officials', *ST* (8 January 1981). In September 1982 it was reported that the MCP leader, Chin Peng had passed away two years ago. This was neither denied nor confirmed by the Malaysian security authorities: *Sin Chew Jit Poh* (26 September 1982).
54. 'Editorial', *New Straits Times* (Kuala Lumpur, 11 August 1981); also 'Zhao Failed to Reach Total Accord on Four', *ST* (17 August 1981).
55. 'Chinese Teams Urged to Look into Product Prices', *Business Times* (Singapore, 3 August 1982).
56. 'Singapore Drives Home A Point', *ST* (14 November 1978).
57. Peter Weintraub, 'Laying on an Official Yawn', *FEER* (24 November 1978).
58. 'Zhao and His Delegates Leave for Bangkok', *ST* (14 August 1981).
59. *Mirror* (Ministry of Culture, Singapore, 1 September 1981); also, John Drysdale, 'Another Look at Questions Left Over from History', *ST* (15 August 1981).
60. See Prime Minister Lee Kuan Yew's Interview with the Editor of the *US News and World Report*, on 7 December 1981. See *ST* (2 February 1982).
61. During the first quarter of 1982, Singapore imported 1.5 million barrels of Chinese crude oil for its refineries. Currently, Singapore is the world's third largest oil refining centre and is actively seeking to diversify its crude oil sources. 'Refiners now importing Chinese crude oil', *ST* (15 September 1982).
62. Estimates made by the Hong Kong-based *China Economic News*. See *Asian Wall Street Journal* (26 May 1982).
63. For further discussion of the financing of the China trade, see Lin Chi-Hsin, 'Financing China Trade', and Ahmet Arsan, 'Financing Business in China', in Hong Hai and Roy Mackie (ed.). *Trade with China* (Singapore: Times Book International, 1980).
64. 'Studies Soon on Joint Singapore-China Scheme', *ST* (3 December 1980).
65. *ST* (20 June 1981).
66. For a further discussion of Singapore's capacity to benefit from the China trade, see 'Ho Kwon Ping: Singapore Takes Up Peking's Challenge', *FEER* (7 September 1979); also *The China Trade Report* (October 1979).

Chapter 5

1. A remark by Manuel Collantes, the Philippines' Undersecretary of Foreign Affairs, 'President Marcos' Visit to the People's Republic of China: Its Significance', *Fookein Times Philippines Yearbook 1975*, (Manila, 1976).
2. Ibid.
3. Chou Ju-Kua, A Sung superintendent of Customs in Chuan Zhou Fu and a noted

historian wrote in his *Chu-fan-zhi* (Records of Foreign Lands) a vivid account of the barter trade between the Chinese merchants and the 'natives'. Liu Ti Chen, 'An Approach to the Study of Early Sino–Philippines Relations' in Alfonso Felix, Jr, (ed.) *The Chinese in the Philippines, 1570–1770*, 2 vols (Manila: Solidaridad Publishing House, 1966) vol. I, p. 266. Also, in a recent work edited by Zhong-shan University's Institute of Southeast Asian Historical Studies, *Compendium of Chinese Materials Concerning the Philippines* (Beijing, 1980).

4. See Antonio Tan, *The Chinese in the Philippines, 1898–1935: A Study of Their National Awakening* (Quezon City, Philippines: Garcia Publishing Co., 1972).
5. See Ho Ping-Yin, *The Foreign Trade of China* (Shanghai: Commercial Press Ltd, 1935) ch. XVI.
6. Cornelio Balmaceda, 'The Changing Pattern of Philippines Foreign Trade', *Far Eastern Economic Review* (6 March 1958).
7. Ho Ping-Yin.
8. Garel A Grunder and William E Livezey, *The Philippines and the United States* (Norman, University of Okhlahoma Press, 1951) p. 71 and p. 281. Also, see William J. Pomeroy, *American Neo-Colonialism: Its Emergence in the Philippines and Asia* (New York: International Publishers, 1970).
9. Ho Ping-Yin.
10. Man Mohini Kaul, *The Philippines and Southeast Asia* (New Delhi: Radiant Publisher, 1978) p. 48. In January 1950, Quirino also told the US press in San Francisco that the Philippines' recognition of China was 'inevitable'.
11. For a good discussion of the Philippines' relations with Nationalist China in Taiwan, see Hsiao Shi-Ching, *Chinese–Philippine Diplomatic Relations, 1946–1975* (Quezon City: Bookman Printing House, 1975).
12. See Evelyn Colbert, *Southeast Asia in International Politics 1941–1956* (Ithaca and London: Cornell University Press, 1977).
13. Man Mohini Kaul, p. 42.
14. The reasons for the wholesale commitment to the American policy on the part of the Philippine ruling elite are well-known and have been frankly explained by Kaul: '. . . there was the feeling of gratitude that the political *elite* or at least a majority of its members felt towards the United States for delivering their country from the ruthless Japanese Occupation and for offering generous post-war reconstruction assistance. It may also be noted that most members of the Philippine ruling *elite* had a personal interest in the Philippine economy; and various sectors of the economy were susceptible to pressure from the United States. Thus, the efforts to promote and maintain a special relationship with the United States were actuated as much by the enlightened self-interest of the Philippine *elite* as by "gratitude" or "shared ideals"' (Man Mohini Kaul, p. 180).
15. *FEER* (12 June 1971) p. 24.
16. See Hsiao Shi-Ching, ch. IV.
17. See *China Yearbook 1959–1960* (Taipei: China Publishing Co., 1959) p. 227.
18. Michael Leifer, *The Foreign Relations of the New States*, Studies in Contemporary Southeast Asia (Victoria, Australia: Longman, 1974) p. 83.
19. J. L. Vellut, *The Asian Policy of the Philippines, 1954–1961* (Canberra: Australian National University Press, 1965) p. 26.
20. Hsiao Shi-Ching, p. 120.
21. Later, when the Philippine Trade Mission visited China in 1973, Zhou Enlai asked the leader Dr Wigberto Clavecilla, 'How is my friend Romulo, my Bandung friend since 1955?', *Wen Hui Pao* (Hong Kong, 1 June 1973) p. 1.
22. UP Dispatch, *HKS*, (Hong Kong, 18 January 1958).
23. For a good discussion of the undercurrent of opposition to the official foreign policy line in the Philippines, see Man Mohini Kaul, especially pp. 166–7. The

outspoken Senator Jovito Salonga also stated: 'For the moment we identify ourselves closely with the United States, we become suspect in the eyes of our Asian neighbours. The term "puppet" has an immediate attraction for those who do not see eye to eye with us'. See Jose Veloso Abueva and Raul P. de Guzman (ed.), *Foundations and Dynamics of Filipino Government and Politics* (Manila: Bookmark, 1969) p. 500.

24. Kaul, p. 140.
25. See, for example, 'Sober Nationalism' *FEER* (8 June 1967).
26. *HKS* (30 March 1966).
27. *Sing Tao Daily*, Hong Kong, (14 May and 10 July 1966).
28. *HKS*, HK, (17 July 1966).
29. *HKS* (4 March 1967) and *South Ching Morning Post* HK, (31 March 1967).
30. Kaul, p. 169.
31. Ibid.
32. Carlos Romulo, 'Point of Departure', *The Ambassador*, vol. 11, no. 2 (November 1971).
33. *NEDA Development Digest*, Manila, vol. III, no. 3, (15 June 1975) p. 2.
34. Hsiao Shi-Ching, pp. 79–81.
35. *FEER* (12 June and 30 October 1971).
36. *FEER* (18 March 1972).
37. For details, see *FEER* (3 March 1972).
38. *FEER* (12 August 1972).
39. See Hsiao Shi-Ching, pp. 81–6; pp. 113–20.
40. *FEER* (18 March 1972).
41. For more detail, see *South China Morning Post*, Hong Kong, (18 January 1973).
42. *FEER* (1 October 1973).
43. *HKS* (12 May 1973).
44. *HKS* (3 December 1973).
45. *ST*, Singapore (1 June 1974).
46. *South China Morning Post* (2 November 1973).
47. *ST* (23 and 24 September 1974).
48. *ST* (15 October 1974).
49. *ST* (8 October 1974).
50. See Santiago Medrana and Horacio Buno, *People's Republic of China–Philippine Relations and the Local Chinese Community* (Manila: Advocate Book Supply Co., 1976).
51. *Government Report*, Manila (13 May 1974) quoted from Hsiao Shi-Ching p. 134.
52. *NEDA Development Digest*, Manila, vol. III, no. 3 (15 June 1975).
53. *Daily Express*, Manila (6 October 1974).
54. *Sin Chew Jit Poh*, Singapore (6 May 1975).
55. Harvey Stockwin's 'Marcos' New Friends', *FEER* (20 June 1975).
56. See NEDA Development Digest.
57. Manuel Collantes, p. 24.
58. Ibid, p. 26.
59. Ibid, p. 26.
60. *Sing Tao Daily* (1 October 1954).
61. For a further discussion of the illegal entry of Chinese products into the Philippines in the 1950s and 1960s, see *HKS*, (8 March 1955, 21 June 1958); *FEER* (9 August 1956, p. 193); *South Ching Morning Post* (2 May 1966); and *Hong Kong Times* (11 October 1964).
62. *Philippines Yearbook 1979* (Manila) p. 59.
63. *Petroleum News* (August 1979) p. 8. Also *New Straits Times* (Kuala Lumpur, 9 September 1978).

64. *Philippine Yearbook 1979* (Manila) p. 694.
65. See *Beijing Review*, no. 33 (1981) p. 5.
66. See Chun-hsi Wu, 'Overseas Chinese' in Yuan-li Wu (ed.) *China: A Handbook* (New York: Praeger, 1972) p. 416.
67. Quite a huge volume of literature on the overseas Chinese in the Philippines is available. See, e.g., Antonio S. Tan, and Victor Purcell, *The Chinese in Southeast Asia* (Oxford Univ. Press: 1965) Part VIII.
68. Senator Rodolfo T. Ganzon, privileged speech before the Philippine Senate, on 19 March 1965. Quoted in James Ronald Blaker, 'The Chinese in the Philippines: A Study of Power and Change', Ph.D dissertation, (Ohio State University, 1979) p. 2.
69. For example, a wealthy Chinese merchant, Co Pak, was charged with financing the Huk elements. See Mel Andrew B. Molnar, *et al., Undergrounds in Insurgent, Revolutionary and Resistance Warfare* (Washington, DC: American University Press, 1963); also, Eufronio Alip, *Ten Centuries of Philippine–Chinese Relations* (Manila: Alip & Sons, 1959).
70. See Hsiao Shi-Ching, p. 103.
71. *FEER* (20 June 1975) p. 15.
72. Benito Lim, 'The Silent Minority', in the special ethnicity issue on the Overseas Chinese by the *Philippine Sociological Review*, vol. 24, nos. 1–4 (January–October 1976) p. 17.
73. Ibid, p. 24.
74. Frank Golay, *et al, Underdevelopment and Economic Nationalism in Southeast Asia* (New York: Cornell University Press, 1969) p. 50.
75. *FEER* (16 June 1978).
76. No official figures are available. The latest *Philippine Yearbook 1979* states: 'As of 1975 the Philippines admitted 108 860 aliens from various countries reflecting a decrease of 11.09 percent from the preceding figure of 122 435 persons. A substantial portion of the decrease may be attributed to the more liberalised naturalisation law passed on the first half of 1975 which was benefited mostly by the Chinese', p. 128.
77. *ST* (4 April 1976).
78. *Peking Review*, no. 46, (18 November 1973).
79. Abby Tan's dispatch, *ST* (22 April 1980).
80. *ST* (26 March 1981).
81. See, 'Trouble over Oil and Waters', *FEER* (7 August 1981). During his visit to Manila in 1978, Vice-Premier Li Xian-nien said that conflicting claims over Spratly Island should be settled by negotiation and other diplomatic means, and not by force. *ST* (14 March 1978).

Chapter 6

1. George Modelski, 'Thailand and China: From Avoidance to Hostility' in A. M. Halpern (ed.), *Policies Toward China: Views from Six Continents* (New York: McGraw-Hill, 1965) p. 365.
2. Kenneth Perry Landon, *The Chinese in Thailand* (New York: Russell & Russell, 1941, reissued, 1973) part I.
3. Ho Ping-Yin, *The Foreign Trade of China: Shanghai* (The Commercial Press: 1935) ch. 8.
4. John K. Fairbank, *Trade and Diplomacy on the China Coast* (Cambridge, Mass.: Harvard University Press, 1953) ch. 2.

5. G. William Skinner, *Chinese Society in Thailand* (Ithaca: Cornell University Press, 1957) pp. 5–6.
6. Sarasin Viraphol, *Tribute and Profit: Sino–Siamese Trade, 1652–1853* (Cambridge, Mass.: Harvard University Press, 1977).
7. Ibid, pp. 247–8.
8. Skinner, p. 29.
9. Sarasin, p. 211.
10. Landon, p. 16.
11. Ibid, pp. 16–17.
12. Ho.
13. Ibid.
14. See Walter F. Vella, *The Impact of the West on Government in Thailand* (Berkeley: University of California Press, 1955).
15. Frank C. Darling, *Thailand and the United States* (Washington, D.C.: Public Affairs Press, 1965) p. 70.
16. Daniel D. Lovelace, *China and 'People's War' in Thailand, 1964–1969* (Berkeley: University of California Press, 1971) p. 28.
17. Darling, p. 78.
18. George Modelski (ed.), *SEATO: Six Studies* (Vancouver, University of British Columbia for Australian National University, 1962).
19. Skinner, ch. 9.
20. Ibid.
21. David A. Wilson, 'China, Thailand and the Spirit of Bandung' *China Quarterly*, nos 31 and 32 (April–June and July–September, 1967, 2 parts).
22. Ibid.
23. See Benjavan Charoenratha, 'A Comparison of Thailand's Relations with the United States and China: 1965–1975', M. A. thesis (North Texas State University, Denton, Texas, August 1978).
24. Skinner, p. 380.
25. Darling, p. 151.
26. *FEER Review* (25 October 1956) p. 259.
27. Wilson.
28. Ibid, pp. 119–20.
29. See S. Y. Lee, 'A Critical Review of Thailand's Foreign Trade after the War', *FEER* (31 March 1955).
30. George McT. Kahin, *The Afro-Asian Conference* (Ithaca: Cornell University Press, 1956) pp. 6–7.
31. Wilson.
32. Skinner, pp. 380–1.
33. *FEER* (26 June 1957).
34. *FEER* (14 August 1958).
35. Daniel Wolfstone, 'Peking's Trade Drive in SE Asia–1. Thailand and Her Ban', FEER (19 February 1959).
36. *FEER* (26 June 1957).
37. Skinner, p. 342.
38. *Ta-kung Pao*, Hong Kong (24 August 1957).
39. John L. S. Girling, *Thailand: Society and Politics* (Ithaca: Cornell University Press, 1981) ch. 6.
40. 'Unbreakable Thais?' *FEER* (18 April 1968).
41. Girling, pp. 235–6.
42. See Melvin Gurtov, *China and Southeast Asia* – The Politics of Survival (Lexington, Mass.: Heath Lexington, 1971) ch. 2.
43. Gurtov, p. 25; Also, 'A Land at Peace?' *FEER* (10 February 1966).

44. *Peking Review* (now *Beijing Review*) (27 January 1967) p. 29.
45. *Renmin Ribao* (The People's Daily) (17 August 1967).
46. See e.g. 'Resolute Support for Armed Struggle led by Communist Party of Thailand', *Peking Review* (8 December 1967); and 'Thai People's Victorious Road to National Liberation', *Peking Review* (20 October 1967); and 'Holding High the Great Banner of Mao Tse-tung's Thought the Thai People's Armed Forces Advance Courageously', *Peking Review* (8 December 1967).
47. See 'Thailand's Border Alarms', *FEER* (27 May 1965).
48. 'The Neutralization Stakes', *FEER* (11 December 1971).
49. Girling, p. 239.
50. See Walter F Hahn, 'The Nixon Doctrine: Design and Dilemma', *Orbis* (Summer, 1972).
51. FEER, *China Trade Report*, Hong Kong (April 1971) p. 4.
52. *Bangkok Post*, Bangkok (8 May 1971).
53. *The Nation*, Bangkok (2 July 1971).
54. Interviewed by *FEER*'s Harold Munthe-Kaas, Thanat said: 'No self-respecting nation in the world would accept one-sided neutralisation of non-Communist Asia', *FEER* (19 May 1966). Also, 'Neutrals? Never', *FEER* (11 April 1968).
55. 'An Independent Line', *FEER* (10 July 1971).
56. 'Bangkok, First and Last', *FEER* (30 October 1972).
57. 'Bangkok Nudges Peking', *FEER* (7 August 1971).
58. *Bangkok Post* (5 July 1971).
59. 'Thailand, Un-person Thanat', *FEER* (17 July 1971).
60. 'Thailand's Hopes and Fears', *FEER* (14 August 1971).
61. *Bangkok Post* (5 November 1971).
62. Ibid.
63. *Bangkok Post* (4 November 1971).
64. 'Thailand: Gathering Storm', *FEER* (15 January 1972).
65. 'Thailand: Cold War Shadows', *FEER* (21 August 1972).
66. 'Thanom's Middle Course', *FEER* (18 March 1972).
67. *China Trade Report* (June 1972) p. 13.
68. 'Report from Peking', *FEER* (14 October 1972).
69. *Bangkok Post* (28 December 1968).
70. 'Thailand: The China Market', *FEER* (18 November 1972).
71. *South China Morning Post*, Hong Kong (22 June 1973) and *ST*, Singapore (21 June 1973).
72. 'Sports Diplomacy', *FEER* (1 October 1973).
73. *HKS*, Hong Kong (31 July 1973).
74. *ST* (21 June 1973).
75. *South China Morning Post* (16 August 1973).
76. *HKS* (26 August 1973).
77. 'Thailand and the Superpowers', *Bangkok Bank Monthly Review* (August 1975) p. 465.
78. *The Nation* (30 December 1973).
79. *ST* (30 December 1973).
80. *South China Morning Post* (31 December 1973).
81. *Ta-kung Pao* (2 July 1973).
82. *Tien-tien Daily*, Hong Kong (30 December 1973).
83. 'Trade: Dismantling the China Barrier', FEER (20 December 1974) and *Sin Chew Jit Poh*, Singapore (4 January 1974).
84. 'Gaining Momentum', *FEER* (4 October 1974).
85. *ST* (16 January 1975).

86. 'Interview with Anand Panyarachun', *Bangkok Bank Monthly Review* (August 1975).
87. 'Thailand: Formal Ties at Last', *FEER* (3 October 1975) p. 34.
88. Department of Customs, *Foreign Trade Statistics of Thailand*, (Bangkok, December 1980).
89. *Business Times*, Kuala Lumpur (3 March 1980).
90. *Asian Wall Street Journal*, Hong Kong (11 January 1980).
91. 'Thais Tune in to China', *FEER* (4 April 1980).
92. 'Trade Relations between Thailand and the People's Republic of China', *Bangkok Bank Monthly Review* (December 1978).
93. *ST* (11 June 1974).
94. *Bangkok Bank Monthly Review* (December 1978).
95. For a good discussion of events, see Girling.
96. *Asian Wall Street Journal* (7 November 1978).
97. *ST* (10 November 1978).
98. *ST* (8 and 13 February 1979).
99. *Sunday Nation*, Singapore (20 January 1980).
100. *Beijing Review* (9 February 1981); and *Sunday Times*, Singapore (1 February 1981).
101. *ST* (2 February 1981).
102. The Thai Deputy Army Chief-of-staff announced in September 1982 that the government forces had destroyed all camps and strongholds of the banned Communist Party of Thailand, which would no longer be in a position to take up arms against the government. It was also noted that China had also scaled down support to the CPT as part of its wider effort to improve state-to-state relations with Southeast Asian countries. 'Thai Reds broken beyond repair', *ST* (9 September 1982).
103. *ST* (12 May 1982).
104. Editorial of the *ST*; 'There is a limit to everything' (21 May 1982).
105. *ST* (10 June 1982).
106. 'Thailand's Unequal Relationship with China', *Asian Wall Street Journal* (7 June 1982).

Index